AF717248

ADVANCES IN PACIFIC BASIN BUSINESS, ECONOMICS AND FINANCE

ADVANCES IN PACIFIC BASIN BUSINESS, ECONOMICS AND FINANCE

Series Editors: Cheng Few Lee and Min-Teh Yu

ADVANCES IN PACIFIC BASIN BUSINESS, ECONOMICS AND FINANCE VOLUME 5

ADVANCES IN PACIFIC BASIN BUSINESS, ECONOMICS AND FINANCE

EDITED BY

CHENG FEW LEE

Rutgers University, New Brunswick, NJ, USA

MIN-TEH YU

China University of Technology, Taipei City, Taiwan

emerald PUBLISHING

United Kingdom – North America – Japan
India – Malaysia – China

Emerald Publishing Limited
Howard House, Wagon Lane, Bingley BD16 1WA, UK

First edition 2017

Copyright © 2017 Emerald Publishing Limited

Reprints and permissions service
Contact: permissions@emeraldinsight.com

No part of this book may be reproduced, stored in a retrieval system, transmitted in any form or by any means electronic, mechanical, photocopying, recording or otherwise without either the prior written permission of the publisher or a licence permitting restricted copying issued in the UK by The Copyright Licensing Agency and in the USA by The Copyright Clearance Center. Any opinions expressed in the chapters are those of the authors. Whilst Emerald makes every effort to ensure the quality and accuracy of its content, Emerald makes no representation implied or otherwise, as to the chapters' suitability and application and disclaims any warranties, express or implied, to their use.

British Library Cataloguing in Publication Data
A catalogue record for this book is available from the British Library

ISBN: 978-1-78743-410-3 (Print)
ISBN: 978-1-78743-409-7 (Online)
ISBN: 978-1-78743-463-9 (Epub)

ISSN: 2514-4650 (Series)

Printed and bound by CPI Group (UK) Ltd, Croydon, CR0 4YY

ISOQAR
REGISTERED
Certificate Number 1985
ISO 14001

ISOQAR certified Management System, awarded to Emerald for adherence to Environmental standard ISO 14001:2004.

FSC
www.fsc.org
MIX
Paper from responsible sources
FSC® C013604

INVESTOR IN PEOPLE

CONTENTS

LIST OF CONTRIBUTORS

Ghulam Ali Bhatti	University of Gujrat, Pakistan
Xiaoyu Chen	Shanghai Stock Exchange, PR China
Thomas C. Chiang	Drexel University, USA
Hwei-Lin Chuang	National Tsing Hua University, Taiwan
Wei-Chiao Huang	Western Michigan University, USA
Yu-Ping Huang	National Dong Hwa University, Taiwan
Edward J. Kane	Boston College, USA
Lie-Jane Kao	KaiNan University, Taiwan
Cheng Few Lee	Rutgers University, USA
Jin-Ping Lee	Feng Chia University, Taiwan
Edward M.H. Lin	Providence University, Taiwan
Eric S. Lin	National Tsing Hua University, Taiwan
Tyrone T. Lin	National Dong Hwa University, Taiwan
J. Huston McCulloch	Ohio State University, USA
Hao-Chang Sung	Jinan University, Guangzhou, China
Chiung-Min Tsai	Central Bank of the Republic of China, Taiwan
Chia-Jung Tu	Kainan University, Taiwan
Jingjing Yang	Guangdong University of Foreign Studies, Guangzhou, China

Xiaojun Yang	Zhongnan University of Economics and Law, China
Min-Teh Yu	China University of Technology, Taiwan
Yang Zhao	National Chiao Tung University, Taiwan
Sayyed Mahdi Ziaei	Xiamen University Malaysia, Malaysia

EDITORIAL BOARD

Mike J. Alderson
University of St. Louis, USA

James S. Ang
Florida State University, USA

Hong-Yi Chen
National Chengchi University, Taiwan

Sheng-Syan Chen
National Chengchi University, Taiwan

Anna Chernobai
Syracuse University, USA

Thomas C. Chiang
Drexel University, USA

Thomas J. Frecka
University of Notre Dame, USA

Robert R. Grauer
Simon Fraser University, Canada

Puneet Handa
University of Iowa, USA

Cheng Hsiao
University of Southern California, USA

Der-An Hsu
University of Wisconsin, Milwaukee, USA

Prem C. Jain
Georgetown University, USA

Sung S. Kwon
York University, USA

Jevons C. Lee
Tulane University, USA

Wayne Y. Lee
University of Arkansas, USA

Scott C. Linn
University of Oklahoma, USA

Yaw Mensah
Rutgers University, USA

Thomas H. Noe
University of Oxford, UK

Thomas Noland
University of Houston, USA

Michael Pagano
Villanova University, USA

Oded Palmon
Rutgers University, USA

Kwangwoo Park
KAIST, Korea

Fotios Pasiouras
University of Bath, UK

Andrew J. Senchak
University of Texas, Austin, USA

David Smith
University of Nebraska–Lincoln, USA

K. C. John Wei
Hong Kong Polytechnic University, Hong Kong

William W. S. Wei
Temple University, USA

James P. Winder
Rutgers University, USA

Tong Yu
University of Cincinnati, USA

David A. Ziebart
University of Kentucky, USA

INSURANCE CONTRACTS AND DERIVATIVES THAT SUBSTITUTE FOR THEM: HOW AND WHERE SHOULD THEIR SYSTEMIC AND NONPERFORMANCE RISKS BE REGULATED?

Edward J. Kane

ABSTRACT

Traditionally, individual states have shared responsibility for regulating the US insurance industry. The Dodd–Frank Act changes this by tasking the Federal Reserve with regulating the systemic risks that particularly large insurance organizations might pose and assigning the regulation of swap-based substitutes for insurance and reinsurance products to the SEC and CFTC. This paper argues that prudential regulation of large insurance firms and weaknesses in federal swaps regulation could reduce the effectiveness of state-based systems in protecting policyholders and taxpayers from nonperformance in the insurance industry. Swap-based substitutes for traditional insurance and reinsurance contracts offer protection sellers a way to transfer responsibility for guarding against nonperformance into potentially less-effective hands. The CFTC and SEC lack the focus, expertise, experience, and resources to adequately manage the ways that swap transactions can affect US taxpayers' equity position in global safety nets, while regulators at the Fed refuse to recognize that conscientiously monitoring accounting

Advances in Pacific Basin Business, Economics and Finance, Volume 5, 1–17
Copyright © 2017 by Emerald Publishing Limited
All rights of reproduction in any form reserved
ISSN: 2514-4650/doi:10.1108/S2514-465020170000001001

capital at financial holding companies will not adequately protect taxpayers and policyholders until and unless it is accompanied by severe penalties for managers that willfully hide their firm's exposure to destructive tail risks.

Keywords: Dodd–Frank Act; systemic risk; nonperformance risk; regulatory culture; financial reform

JEL Classification: E61; G21; G22; G28

For federal regulators, the Dodd–Frank Act (DFA) of 2010 resembles an earthquake so massive that its aftershocks threaten to go on forever. The overarching purpose of this legislation is to end the perception that very large financial organizations can and do make themselves economically, politically, and administratively so difficult to fail and unwind that their liabilities implicitly enjoy near-perfect government guarantees. To create at least the appearance of progress on this herculean task, US and foreign regulators are simultaneously trying to reforge national systems of balance-sheet requirements, activity constraints, and information flows and to reconcile the new systems with still-evolving cross-border agreements for monitoring and unwinding the affairs of globally important firms.

This paper ties a difficult-to-unwind (DTU) firm's systemic risk to its ability to command safety-net support by means of a politically coerced "taxpayer put." This ability varies across firms, but the value of any DTU institution's taxpayer put grows with the size of the risk of ruin its management can live with. As a firm makes itself more and more DTU, the taxpayer becomes more firmly an *equity investor* of last resort. For DTU firms, the value of safety-net access comes from managers' dual capacity to under-reserve for ruinous losses and to persuade government officials in difficult circumstances to make taxpayers cover obligations that their institution's asset value can no longer meet (Kane, 2010).

National regulatory systems are shaped by endless adaptation and negotiation between government officials and representatives of the industries being regulated (see, e.g., Kaiser, 2013). This paper stresses that in and across countries regulatory deal-making is conditioned by: (1) inherited differences in the norms of contract-based national regulatory cultures, and (2) expanding opportunities to fashion swap contracts that substitute for instruments (such as bank deposits) whose signature purposes define the boundaries of existing regulatory jurisdiction.

The discussion highlights the dominant role accorded to states in regulating the US insurance industry (an industry to which the DFA offers little love) and the need to integrate federal regulation of swap-based substitutes for traditional insurance and reinsurance contracts into this state-based system. Whatever advantages swap-based substitutes offer protection buyers, for protection sellers they serve as a form of regulatory arbitrage that circumvents pre-existing forms of supervisory discipline and transfers responsibility for guarding against seller nonperformance to less-experienced and usually under-budgeted hands. My concern is to underscore the tendency for authorities to "under-supervise" such regulatory arbitrage and to clarify how reframing insurance, reinsurance, and annuity commitments as swaps simultaneously generates performance risk and extends the institutional and geographic boundaries of the financial safety net.

I believe that US taxpayers would be better served if safety-net abuse were prosecuted as a felony and innovative financial instruments were routinely screened for their abusive potential. The screening could be assigned to a reconstituted and repurposed Office of Financial Research (OFR) whose task would be to identify the ways in which such innovations promise to reallocate supervisory responsibility, to conceal their issuer's nonperformance risk and risk of ruin, and to expand the taxpayer loss exposures these risks imply. Regulators and firms could be required to prepare and publish estimates of the incremental value of tail risks and to refocus examination and accounting activity to surface data needed to inform the estimation process, so that confidence intervals on the estimates developed become tight enough to encourage the Department of Justice to prosecute abusers.

As illustrated by the messy rescue of the American International Group (AIG) in 2008, when regulatory arbitrage opens gaps in information access and supervisory focus, authorities are apt to learn too late that safety-net arbitrageurs operating under their purview have taken ruinous risks. AIG rang up crippling losses in products that substituted for traditional forms of banking business, but the responsibility for supervising AIG on a consolidated basis lay with a clueless Office of Thrift Supervision (OTS) rather than falling within the jurisdiction of the Federal Reserve which would have been better-equipped for the task.

To minimize incentive conflict, the OFR ought to focus on the detection of systemic risk and be kept free of specific regulatory responsibilities. To reduce bureaucratic recognition lags, each and every issuer of instruments that reallocate supervisory authority should be required to alert the OFR to investigate the risks we have enumerated as soon as its volume of trading in a jurisdiction-altering contract surpasses a *de minimis* level of activity. Authority to disallow or adjust the parameters of contracts that the OFR finds to be dangerous to counterparties or taxpayers could be assigned individually or collectively to various existing federal and state agencies, based on each agency's ability to demonstrate to the OFR its capacity to design and enforce a reliable system for monitoring and reserving for the risks and loss exposures the OFR calculates. An ancillary goal of the analysis is to warn that safety-net subsidies generated by swaps that substitute for insurance and reinsurance contracts must be monitored closely, but in ways that do not compromise traditional programs for minimizing nonperformance risk that customers face in insurance policies in New York and other states. It is imperative that systemic-risk regulators help state agencies to supervise the pass-through of nonperformance risk to insurance contracts from insurance-firm swap and securities lending programs.

1. DIFFERENCES IN REGULATORY CULTURES FOR DIFFERENT CONTRACTUAL FORMS OF PROTECTION SELLING

Anthropologists study how and why people living in different places develop idiosyncratic cultures. One aspect in which cultures differ from one another is in the languages and tools that residents employ. Conceiving of a region's laws as regulatory languages and government institutions as tools used to regulate the behavior of financial institutions leads to the narrower concept of a "regulatory culture." As traditional boundaries between institutions and markets melt away, differences in the tools and languages of sectoral and national regulatory cultures become more consequential (Kane, 2005).

Although banks and other financial institutions offer their customers similar wealth-management services, their corporate and regulatory cultures are very different. The principal tools of US bank regulation are on-site examinations, administrative orders, and agency-enforced balance-sheet restrictions. The principal tools for regulating activity in securities and derivatives contracts differ from this. In these sectors, regulators' main activities are to set fair-play standards of market conduct and information disclosure. Efforts to impose new standards or to correct violations are often delayed by having to weather industry-initiated challenges in state and federal courts.

Financial products typically offer customers some degree of protection against losses from adverse events. In the United States, individuals and corporations can buy specific protection in diverse ways. Protections can be crafted in at least three different contractual forms: as an insurance contract, as a swap contract, or as a contingent guarantee. Although each of these contracts is bilateral in form, third-party regulation plays an indispensable role in generating trust and enforcing fair and timely contract performance. But in the United States and elsewhere, the tools, expertise, and traditions that have developed in each contract's regulatory culture differ in important ways.

Like most other corporations, protection sellers routinely seek to conceal unfavorable or embarrassing information from outsiders. Customers and counterparties cannot easily surface negative information without the help of trusted and trustworthy third parties. Although private watchdogs can and do help in the process, some form of government chartering and supervision of protection sellers inevitably develops. A principal goal is to protect society from the consequences of aggressive risk-taking, capital shortages, loss concealment, and customer abuse at protection-selling firms. In practice if not in theory, an often unspoken goal is to protect the protection sellers as well.

An over-riding task of financial regulation is to resolve incentive conflicts in financial transactions at minimum net cost to society. The boundaries of an industry's or nation's regulatory system co-evolve with popular perceptions of what financial transactions engender unwelcome social problems. This is what makes crises so impactful. When citizens believe a sector's incentive-control system is working adequately, it is hard to cobble together politically a coalition strong enough to win marked changes in the strategies and tactics used to regulate that sector. This status-quo bias is why changes in regulatory culture are apt to occur only in the wake of large-scale crises. In noncrisis times, lobbying activity can seldom achieve more than marginal adjustments either in the objectives that officials pursue or in the character of the policy instruments that officials manipulate within the limits of inherited regulatory norms.

How particular policy strategies actually work in practice is co-determined by the structure of rules that officials promulgate and by regulatees' ability to find and exploit circumventive loopholes in the enforcement of these rules. Exploiting loopholes often entails moving activities from the jurisdiction of traditional overseers who might be equipped and staffed to regulate these activities effectively into the jurisdiction of an agency whose regulatory tools and staff experience render it less qualified to confront the risks and social problems that the innovative products create. To develop cross-agency responses to regulatory arbitrage, the Dodd–Frank Act of 2010 created a multimember interagency Financial Stability Oversight Council (FSOC). But FSOC has yet to frame the issues of jurisdictional migration, regulatory culture, and performance risk that concern us here.

2. LINKS BETWEEN REGULATORY NORMS AND REGULATORY MACHINERY

A culture may be defined as customs, ideas, and attitudes that members of a group share and transmit from generation to generation by systems of subtle and unsubtle rewards and punishments. A regulatory culture is more than a system of rules and enforcement. It incorporates higher-order norms about how officials should comport themselves. These norms limit the ways in which uncooperative or even unscrupulous players can be monitored and disciplined. It includes a matrix of attitudes and beliefs that define what it means for a regulator to use its investigative and disciplinary authority honorably. In effect, these attitudes and beliefs set standards for the fair and efficient use of government power.

The higher-order social norms that underlie formal regulatory structures penetrate and shape the policy-making process and the political and legal environments within which intersectoral bargaining takes place. Various checks and balances restrain each agency's authority and limit its exercise. Such limits express a distrust of government power that often traces back to abuses observed in a distant past when the country was occupied, colonized, or run by a one-party government. These underlying standards, taboos, and traditions are normative in two senses. They simultaneously define which behaviors are "normal" and what behaviors regulators should follow to avoid criticism or shame.

In the United States, the tools of financial regulation are imbedded in bureaucratic machinery that has four interacting sets of moving parts. Each set is administered respectively by industry, state regulatory bodies, federal agencies, and the courts. The precise machinery, the behavior it controls, and linkages across which different operators interact are organized differently in different financial sectors (e.g., in insurance, banking, securities, and derivatives product lines). Regulatory tools include: chartering, licensing, and registration procedures; disclosure, capital, and liquidity requirements; margin and collateral restrictions; business-conduct rules; stress tests; and administrative orders. Although regulatory toolkits vary within and across the sectors over time, efforts to effect regulatory capture are always and everywhere a potent force.

Prudential regulation imposes on financial regulators a duty to identify and curb excessive risk-taking within their client base and to find and resolve individual-firm insolvencies in a timely fashion. Within any industry or product line, the regulatory culture within which this duty is discharged is spanned by six specific components:

- Legal authority and reporting obligations.
- Formulation and promulgation of specific rules.
- Burdens of proof regarding the projected benefits and costs of rule changes. (These burdens entail duties of consultation and accountability that guarantee that regulated parties will be treated fairly: i.e., accorded rights of participation and due process).
- Technology for monitoring violation and compliance.
- Penalties for material violations.
- Regulatees' rights to judicial review of regulatory findings and actions (so that intervened parties have access to appeals procedures that serve to bond the fairness guarantee).

As a practical matter, any system of controls generates imbalances in the costs and benefits that accrue to different citizens. Year in and year out, financial industry spokespersons complain about the costs of regulatory compliance and consumer advocates complain about the cost of financial-institution bailouts and instances of abusive activities such as predatory lending or mistreatment of delinquent borrowers.

Social norms subject an agency's disciplinary tactics to intragovernmental checks and balances and require its staff to treat firms that violate its rules or procedures as innocent until proven guilty. These norms also make sure that punishments meted out do not exceed the importance of the behavior being disciplined. As insurance firms such as AIG and Prudential are subjected to bank-like systemic-risk regulation, it is important for federal banking, swaps, and securities regulators to distinguish between efforts to manage an insurance or brokerage firm's risk of contract nonperformance and efforts to control the systemic risks that reflect taxpayers' equity stake in the US safety net. Given the traditional shortsightedness of federal efforts at crisis management, it would be a mistake to assume that efforts to manage the value of the government's side of the financial sector's aggregate taxpayer put might not make it harder for retail customers of insurance and brokerage firms to collect funds when they are due.

For both classes of risk management, administrative burdens of proof tend to delay the exercise of regulatory discipline more for undeserving thieves, fraudsters, and bumblers than for those whose grievances are legitimate ones. This is because undeserving plaintiffs typically have more at stake. They raise due-process issues to extend the lives and endgame risk-taking of what is apt to be a deeply insolvent firm. Buttressed by the industry's direct and indirect exercise of political clout, regulators' obligation to justify punitive action makes it impossible to impose strong penalties promptly enough to squeeze scams and safety-net subsidies completely out of the system.

Having to establish the fairness and reasonableness of disciplinary actions increases the bureaucratic difficulties of determining that a firm is insolvent and slows the process of resolving insolvencies. Deeply insolvent institutions maliciously delay and short circuit disciplinary actions in three ways:

- By delaying write-downs of impaired assets.
- By restructuring their operations to move troublesome issues into the jurisdiction of a more-sympathetic or less-wary regulator.
- By accumulating political clout and using it to generate (not always proper) interference in disciplinary processes.

3. THE ROOTS OF AIG'S INSOLVENCY

AIG can serve as the poster child for such behavior. Two things made AIG's problems different from other insurance insolvencies. First, at the time of its implosion it had $1.06 trillion in assets. This made it by far the largest insurance firm in the country. Second, although its traditional life, casualty, and retirement business was supervised by state officials in traditional ways, various "insurance-related activities" morphed out of the jurisdiction of state regulatory regimes. These activities were conducted in opaque subsidiary corporations that transacted with a large number of foreign counterparties. To clarify the regulatory arbitrage this entails, consider the advantages of using a swap to guarantee payments due on a bond. A bond insurance contract would have had to be written by a state-regulated entity. This underwriter would explicitly have to estimate and reserve for the loss exposures generated by its guarantee, establish the existence of an insurable interest on the part of the counterparty (i.e., a long position in the bond), and counterparty claims would be settled over time by assuming the string of future payments specified by the bond contract. Although Dodd–Frank rulemaking might change this, credit default swaps (CDS) dispensed with these restrictions. Over-the-counter CDS market makers like AIG could write contracts with counterparties that had no insurable interest, did not have to document how they reserved for losses, and at settlement would usually be required to come up with a large lump-sum payment.

The highly concentrated risks taken in swap and securities-lending activities would have been hard for state commissioners to reconcile with their traditional concern for policyholder interests had they thought themselves responsible for overseeing them. They took some comfort in the fact that AIG subsidiaries and the firm as a whole were supervised at the consolidated level as a thrift-institution holding company by the OTS. Unfortunately, this regulator lacked both the expertise and the incentives to monitor and control the leverage and volatility inherent in AIG's, burgeoning derivatives, and securities-lending businesses.

AIG illustrates the maxim that firms – like people – are born simple, but die of complications. Corporate complications are both structural and contractual. Table 1, which is taken from Sjostrum (2009), shows how AIG partitioned its activities and that the profitability of AIG's financial-services subsidiaries declined steeply in 2007 and 2008. These losses triggered cash flows and collateral calls in CDS and securities lending programs that AIG proved unable to sustain.

One alleged benefit of segregating different product lines within a holding-company structure is to erect constructive firewalls intended to stop losses in one unit from spreading to other units of the firm. Another is that this arrangement can facilitate the restructuring of the firm if and when it falls into distress. However, neither of these benefits was realized in the AIG debacle. Having made sure that aggressive top management decisions could not be closely monitored, AIG officials could use cross-guarantees from the traditional insurance units to lessen the collateral requirements imposed or increase the fees collected on other subsidiaries' deals with swap and securities-lending counterparties. In the absence of interaffiliate guarantees and in states where such guarantees might prove unenforceable, the profits of the insurance units would have stayed

Table 1. Sources of AIG Profit and Loss, 2005 through September 30, 2008.

(In Millions)	Nine Months Ended 9/30/08	2007	2006	2005
Revenues				
General Insurance	$35,854	$51,708	$49,206	$45,174
Life Insurance & Retirement	14,271	53,570	50,878	48,020
Financial Services	(16,016)	(1,309)	(7,777)	(10,677)
Asset Management	658	5,625	4,543	4,582
Other	531	457	483	344
Consolidation & Eliminations	(436)	13	500	(16)
Total	*$34,862*	*$110,064*	*$113,387*	*$108,781*
Operating Income (Loss)				
General Insurance	$ (393)	$10,562	$10,412	$2,315
Life Insurance & Retirement	(19,561)	8,186	10,121	8,965
Financial Services	(22,880)	(9,515)	383	4,424
Asset Management	(2,709)	1,164	1,538	1,963
Other	(2,899)	(2,140)	(1,435)	(2,765)
Consolidation & Eliminations	237	722	668	311
Total	*$(48,205)*	*$8,943*	*$21,687*	*$15,213*

Source: Sjostrum (2009), p. 947.

positive because counterparties could not have reliably forced the parent to honor claims written against loss-making affiliates. At least arguably, the doctrine of corporate separateness would have allowed the claims of derivatives counterparties to be separated from the insurance units in a prepackaged bankruptcy and given appropriate haircuts.

Both at the Treasury and the Fed, the initial justification for rescuing AIG and keeping its many counterparties whole was not protecting the firm's policyholders and pension-plan participants from nonperformance, but "unusual and exigent circumstances" (i.e., systemic issues) in banking, commercial-paper, and derivatives markets. It was asserted that "a disorderly failure of AIG could add to already significant levels of financial market fragility and lead to substantially higher borrowing costs, reduced household wealth, and materially weaker economic performance" (9/16/08 Federal Reserve Press Release cited by Sjostrum, p. 977). The irony is that the system-wide events envisioned were bound to occur whether or not AIG's counterparties were forced to take their lumps in bankruptcy. Because blanket guarantees typically finance negative-value gambles for resurrection, Kane (2009) argues that keeping zombie institutions like AIG in play without eliminating shareholders and subjecting creditors to some level of triage prolongs and intensifies – rather than mitigates – the adverse effects that these firms exert over time on the real economy. The behavior of indices of consumer and business confidence makes it likely that Presidential fear-mongering designed to win passage of the Emergency Economic Stabilization Act and curious differences in the extravagance of Treasury and Federal Reserve assistance across the chain of 2008 GSE and investment-firm bailouts created doubts about the competence and sectoral priorities of the nation's top economic officials. Unlike Santa Claus, the Fed and Treasury seemed determined to give their gifts only to firms that had behaved badly.

An authoritative account has yet to emerge of which officials knew what and when they knew it. But as a minimum, state and federal regulators should have noticed that profitability of AIG's financial-services units had been declining for several years at a rate that, thanks to implicit and explicit intracorporate cross-guarantees, threatened its ability to cover in full policyholder and pension claims in its traditional and retirement insurance businesses. The breakdown in supervision was not just that state and OTS personnel failed to observe and curb AIG's growing losses and loss exposures, but that the Fed and counterpart agencies in Europe turned a blind eye to the nonperformance risk that was building up in banking and securities firms that held the other side of AIG's deals. The depth and breadth of the global regulatory failure suggest that an unspoken reason for rescuing AIG's creditors and counterparties was bureaucratic blame avoidance. In the United States in particular, top officials of a highly unpopular Bush administration could not reasonably expect to hold office beyond January 20, 2009. The rescue's generous treatment of AIG creditors and counterparties converted what would have been immediate industry criticism for being asleep at the wheel into applause for the Treasury's fast action and political bravery and shifted the unpopular task of explicitly financing the rescue forward onto the Fed and succeeding administrations.

4. REGULATION OF INSURANCE PRODUCTS

In regulating the insurance industry in the United States, federal authorities have remained at the periphery. The McCarran–Ferguson Act of 1945 exempts insurance companies from federal antitrust legislation in ordinary (i.e., noncoercive) circumstances and allows US insurance firms to be chartered and their behavior overseen by agencies of individual states for good (if not sufficient) reasons. In fact, a Federal Insurance Office (FIO) did not even exist until July, 2010 when it was established as part of the Treasury Department by the Dodd–Frank Act. The Dodd–Frank Act also empowers the multiagency FSOC to classify insurers as "systematically important financial institutions" subject to prudential regulation for their systemic risk by the Federal Reserve.

A strong case can be made for eventually making the FIO into a regulator of reinsurance contracts. But currently it is tasked only with collecting information on the industry and providing advice to other federal bodies on domestic and international insurance matters. Domestically, it will search for gaps and inconsistencies in state regulation and is likely to serve as a channel for touting the advantages of a federal insurance charter to win the expanded jurisdiction a federal chartering option would entail. But even if it never gains licensing and supervisory authority, by being able to influence the shape of binding international agreements that promote financial stability, the FIO could eventually force substantial changes in state and industry regulatory machinery.

Among other things, the antitrust exemption is meant to allow firms to share actuarial data and projections as well as to help state insurance commissioners to fix prices and control entry. In practice, industry executives conceive of state insurance regulators as if they were their partners in designing, pricing, and enforcing contract coverages and performance that earn rents (Randall, 1999). The desire to protect these rents may explain why in many circumstances insurance firms allocate capital above and beyond the minimum levels that the state commissioners set.

Recognizing the usefulness of a centralizing authority, state commissioners voluntarily formed a National Association of Insurance Commissioners (NAIC) in 1871. The goals of the NAIC are to assure the solvency of insurers, to protect policyholders, and to create a nationwide regulatory system that preserves state-by-state regulation.

Although the NAIC carefully characterizes itself as a trade association composed of government regulators from different states, Randall (1999) describes it as performing "centralized duties that mirror those of federal regulators in other industries, including the prescription of standard forms for insurance company annual financial statements; the coordination of regional financial examinations of insurance companies; the creation and maintenance of an extensive system of national databases to facilitate state monitoring of insurers and insurance agents; the rating of non-US insurers for the states; the periodic review and accreditation of state insurance departments; the drafting of model laws and regulations, many of which have been adopted by state legislatures; the valuation of insurance company investments; training of state insurance regulators; the preparation of statistical reports for state regulators; the assistance to state regulators with technical financial analysis and the assistance to US officials negotiating international trade agreements that concern insurance issues" (Randall, pp. 636–638).

The NAIC is not accountable to voters or subject to direct federal oversight. But its members live in fear of a federal takeover of its centralizing functions. Fanning the flames of this fear is the principal way that federal officials can influence NAIC's decision making. Surges in this fear undercut regulatory capture when industry scandal arises. For example, in the late 1980s when a spate of insurance-company insolvencies generated pressure for federal insurance regulation, the NAIC developed and promulgated new standards, information systems, and procedures and tried to impose them on state insurance departments.

Of course, the NAIC is inherently weaker than a federal regulator, in that it lacks the coercive powers of a governmental enterprise. The coercive powers that accrue to the NAIC's commissioner-members do not include the right to compel one another to adopt common laws, standards, or procedures. The result was that the 1980s effort to force state commissioners to submit to an enhanced NAIC accreditation process did not get very far. The efficacy of this effort was undermined by the absence of further crisis, by industry resistance, and by state legislatures' insistence on preserving their sovereignty from NAIC incursion (Randall, 1999).

Even though state-based supervision of market conduct has proved weak in practice, it has one great advantage. State insurance officials cannot easily supplement the resources of their state guaranty schemes to shift industry losses at state-chartered institutions to state or federal taxpayers. Lacking the power to issue currency, state officials cannot credibly guarantee or otherwise support the liabilities of deeply insolvent firms without explicitly budgeting for them by enacting transparent tax increases, raising new debt, or raiding assets set aside as reserves for future expenditures (such as pension obligations). In a crisis, the difficulty of generating state funding keeps expectations of an insurance-industry rescue low unless the Federal Reserve or Treasury can be incentivized to open the spigot of federal support. Except for the bailout of the AIG in September 2008, defaulting obligations of insolvent US insurance firms have in fact been paid from the reserves held in state guaranty funds.

5. REGULATION OF SWAPS

Constructively, a swap agreement is a multiperiod forward contract between two counterparties. In a swap, the parties agree to exchange cash flows from one hypothetical or "notional" instrument at specified settlement dates for the cash flows from a second designated instrument. Either or both of the instruments may, but need not, have a precise cash-market counterpart. The specified life of the contract is called its "tenor." The two sides of each swap may be regarded as a synthetic incremental balance sheet that renders each counterparty long a series of claims (known as the "receive half") and short a series of obligations (the "pay half"). As a balance sheet, the two halves have a net worth. Because the net worths "derive" from the referenced instruments, swaps are financial derivatives.

But the statutory definition of the term "swap" embraces a broader set of deals than this. It includes, in part, any agreement, contract, or transaction "that provides for any purchase, sale, payment, or delivery (other than a dividend on an equity security) that is dependent on the occurrence, nonoccurrence, or the extent of the occurrence of an event or contingency associated with a potential financial, economic, or commercial consequence."[1]

Historically, most swaps have been arranged with a third-party dealer or market-maker. This trader collects a fee for lessening the due-diligence and search costs that its customers might otherwise face. The fee may be expressed as a spread between the terms offered for taking up one side or the other of a particular swap. As compared with a brokered market, the customer receives immediate execution and the dealer becomes the counterparty for both sides.

Swaps are financially engineered substitutes for any other intermediated form of indirect finance, forms that themselves serve as substitutes for arrangements that offer direct funding from savers to investors. Whether an individual is a saver or an investor, the opportunity costs encountered in undertaking a swap parallel those met in comparing the benefits and costs of transacting directly with a borrower or saver against using (say) a bank to intermediate the deal. Prudent savers and investors have to assess the differences in the benefits of contracting indirectly and weigh these benefits against the differences in transaction costs. Most households, lack the expertise needed to make direct lending or borrowing the better alternative. Efficient deal-making generates two types of transactions costs: precontract shopping, negotiating, and due-diligence expense and postcontract enforcement and unwinding expense.

The dollar value of the cash flows due at each settlement date is calibrated by applying contract terms to a notional principal amount. The contract will also indicate whether differences in the values due at each date are to be settled in cash or in kind.

When the two halves are equally valuable, the swap is said to be "at" or "on" the market. Usually, however, the incremental balance sheet of one counterparty will show positive net worth. That party faces a risk that the party with negative net worth will renege on some or all of its obligation. If it were not for this nonperformance risk, one could construct combinations of swap contracts that would reproduce synthetically the exact cash flows generated by any cash market portfolio or government-chartered financial intermediary. This means that differences in the dangers of nonperformance (known in the trade as "counterparty risk") are along with systemic risk an essential part of the regulatory problems that swaps and other derivatives pose for society.

Because banking, securities and insurance products have existed for hundreds of years, the dimensions of their regulatory environments have been nailed down in important ways. But because swap contracts are less than a half-century old, their regulatory environment is much more fluid. The volume of interagency rule-making to be completed under the Dodd–Frank Act of 2010 makes the toolkits and language of swaps regulation particularly swampy today.

Prior to the crisis, data on the size of actual and potential imbalances in dealer positions were not readily available. A crisis-engendered G20 agreement seeks to change this by requiring swaps to be centrally cleared and the terms reported to so-called swaps data repositories. In line with this agreement, the Dodd–Frank Act required the Securities and Exchange Commission (SEC) and the Commodities Futures Trading Commission (CFTC) to set rules whose intent is to force swap trading as far as possible onto securities execution facilities (SEFs) and organized exchanges where it would be reported to swap data repositories (SDRs) and might be monitored and supervised more effectively by government officials.[2]

On an exchange, deals are undertaken jointly by brokers who transmit customer bids and offers to the exchange and by the exchange. As a central clearing party (CCP) the exchange margins and novates[3] the trades and accepts the risk that out-of-the-money counterparties may default on the execution date.

Contract performance is supported by broker and exchange due diligence, financial resources, collateral evaluation, and margining procedures. At both the exchange and broker levels, margin and net-worth requirements are set relative to the perceived volume and character of a counterparty's trading activity. Brokers protect themselves by screening customers and margining the value of short sales and pending trades. Exchanges support contract performance further by screening brokers for reputation, competence, and net worth and by holding margin accounts posted by brokers. If, on the execution date, both a customer and its broker fail to complete their half of the trade, the exchange's clearing corporation or partnership must complete the transaction. Efforts to recover the cost of doing this begin with liquidating the assets the defaulting parties have previously posted in margin accounts with them. Shortfalls in a defaulting party's margin account have traditionally been covered from the exchange's guaranty fund, equity, and (where necessary) from special assessments on clearing members.

Across the globe in recent memory, this fail-safe structure has broken down at least three times: in France (1974), in Malaysia (1983), and in Hong Kong (1987). Authorities must recognize that expanding the role of CCPs in derivatives trading increases their systemic importance at the expense of banks and enhances the ability of large CCPs to extract safety-net subsidies from their home government and global hegemons. The rest of the paper builds on my belief that the US agencies the DFA makes responsible for overseeing CCPs (the SEC and CFTC) lack the focus, expertise, experience, and resources to manage adequately the way that swaps transactions affect US taxpayers' equity position in global safety nets and that banking regulators are fooling themselves in thinking that conscientiously monitoring accounting capital at banks and financial holding companies will accomplish this task.

6. RETHINKING EFFORTS TO CONTROL SYSTEMIC RISK

The existence of safety-net guarantees creates a loss-absorbing contra-liability for complex megainstitutions that economists describe as a "taxpayer put." Even in quiet times, the put makes private equity and debt funding available to entities that are perceived to be DTU at lower cost and in larger amounts than would otherwise be available. During the recent crisis, guarantees were pushed farther beyond statutory and national limits than ever before. Moreover, the Fed's right to extend loans to firms headquartered in other countries when unstable market conditions exist has been made explicit by the Dodd–Frank Act.

Around the world, governments are finally acknowledging that complex megainstitutions receive near-perfect guarantees, but the existence and value of the corresponding contraliability are not currently recognized in law or accounting practice, nor are its effects clearly understood by the taxpayers who provide it. This lack of recognition facilitates amoral and felonious profiteering at firms who have access to the put.

Government officials are encouraging megainstitutions to simplify their organizations (Adler, 2014). But they seem unwilling to punish these firms and their managers commensurately for willfully expanding the value of safety-net guarantees in ways that unjustly enrich themselves at taxpayer expense. Because modern legal theory characterizes corporations as persons, giant holding companies could be prosecuted and convicted for engaging willfully either in securities fraud or even in what I call "theft by safety net" (Kane, 2014). Achieving a few such convictions would dramatically change the costs and benefits of safety-net abuse and lessen competitive inequities by reversing regulation-induced increases in the size and complexity of the country's largest financial holding companies. This is because convicted felons cannot own insured commercial banks or be licensed to function as broker-dealers or future commission merchants.

The failure to characterize the nature and consequences of safety-net support correctly in law and in public discussion leaves the door open to shady and hard-to-monitor behaviors that increase the value of the put. These behaviors should be monitored more directly in the future and their legal boundaries deserve to be carefully remapped. These activities include but are not limited to:

- Regulatory capture (deliberately sewing loopholes into statutes, rules, and enforcement procedures);
- Influencing the funding and staffing of regulatory agencies;
- Exploiting jurisdictional gaps and ambiguities;
- Persuading politicians and regulators to favor domestic institutions unfairly over foreign ones;
- Using innovative financial institutions and contract forms to bypass or reduce reporting and other supervisory burdens.

Legal categories and definitions will always lag financial realities because the regulated are more adept at taming and gaming changes in regulators' rules than the regulators are at understanding and adapting to financial innovation. Long time lags exist between the first occurrence of activities that exploit the put and adequate legislative and regulatory responses to them. In recent years, megainstitutions have been generating urgent new problems even before old ones are fully addressed. Many of these new problems cross international boundaries in ways that serve to multiply loophole opportunities and regulatory conflicts of interest.

The DFA sets out more than a dozen characteristics that FSOC must use in determining whether nonbank firms are deemed systemically important financial institutions (SIFIs). Listing so many characteristics creates unnecessary discretion that invites political manipulation. Measuring systemic risk by the value of a firm's taxpayer put provides a more concrete and accountable way for FSOC to determine who is and is not a SIFI.

The DFA and Basel III treat the symptoms of supervisory breakdown, but not the conditions that bring the symptoms about. These alleged regulatory remedies measure risk exposures a tad more accurately, but falsely suppose that instability can be cured by adjustments in formal structures of regulation and supervision without also enhancing procedures for monitoring and punishing safety-net abuse. A nice first step would be to classify corporate and personal safety-net abuse as criminal behavior per se and require the Department of Justice to prosecute this crime.

NOTES

1. CEA Section 1a(47)(A)(ii), 7 U.S.C. 1a(47)(A)(ii).
2. However, although information on swaps is now flowing to the SEC and CFTC, the SDR submissions are incomplete and the resulting data are impossible to aggregate in a timely and meaningful fashion. The SDRs claim that it is not their job to police the submissions, while the SEC and CFTC cannot remedy the situation without new rounds of rulemaking.
3. A contract is "novated" when the original two-party contract is torn up and replaced by two new contracts in which responsibility for the separate contractual obligations and rights of each party is transferred in whole to the novator.

ACKNOWLEDGMENT

The author wishes to thank the Networks Financial Institute for financial support and Robert Dickler, Thomas Ferguson, and Jack Tatom for valuable comments on an earlier draft.

REFERENCES

Adler, J. (2014). OCC pushing to simplify big banks. *American Banker* (March 1), 1 and 3.

Kaiser, R. G. (2013). *Act of congress: How America's essential institution works and how it doesn't*. New York, NY: Vintage Books.

Kane, E. J. (2005). Confronting divergent interests in cross-country regulatory arrangements. *Reserve Bank of New Zealand Bulletin*, *69*(3), 5–17.

Kane, E. J. (2009). Incentive roots of the securitization crisis and its early mismanagement. *Yale Journal on Regulation*, *26*, 405–416.

Kane, E. J. (2010). Redefining and containing systemic risk. *Atlantic Economic Journal*, *38*, 251–264.

Kane, E. J. (2014). Shadowy banking: Theft by safety net. *Yale Journal on Regulation*, *31*, 773–797.

Randall, S. (1999). Insurance regulation in the United States: Regulatory federalism and the National Association of Insurance Commissioners. *Florida State University Law Review*, *26*, 625–699.

Sjostrum, W. K., Jr. (2009). The AIG bailout. *Washington and Lee Law Review*, *66*, 943–991.

A FURTHER EQUITY PREMIUM PUZZLE

J. Huston McCulloch

ABSTRACT

Mehra and Prescott (1985) point out that it is difficult to reconcile certain empirical facts about equity and debt returns and the process of consumption growth with reasonable assumptions about the relative rate of risk aversion and the pure rate of time preference, in a conventional infinite-horizon model with an additively separable, constant relative rate of risk aversion (CRRA) utility function. The present note adds the further puzzle that if the mean rate of growth of consumption is not known with perfect certainty in such a model, both stocks and real perpetuities have an infinite price in terms of consumption goods. When maturity-specific claims on real output are introduced, the equity premium is seen to increase without bound at the most distant horizons. These in turn dominate asset pricing, so that the equity premium on claims on all future output is indeed infinite.

Keywords: Equity premium; consumption growth; relative rate of risk aversion

1. INTRODUCTION

Mehra and Prescott (1985) point out that it is difficult to reconcile certain empirical facts about equity and debt returns and the process of consumption

Advances in Pacific Basin Business, Economics and Finance, Volume 5, 19–26
Copyright © 2017 by Emerald Publishing Limited
All rights of reproduction in any form reserved
ISSN: 2514-4650/doi:10.1108/S2514-465020170000001002

growth with reasonable assumptions about the relative rate of risk aversion and the pure rate of time preference, in a conventional infinite-horizon model with an additively separable, constant relative rate of risk aversion (CRRA) utility function. The present note adds the further puzzle that if the mean rate of growth of consumption is not known with perfect certainty in such a model, both stocks and real perpetuities have an infinite price in terms of consumption goods. When maturity-specific claims on real output are introduced, the equity premium is seen to increase without bound at the most distant horizons. These in turn dominate asset pricing, so that the equity premium on claims on all future output is in fact infinite.

2. A CONVENTIONAL ASSET PRICING MODEL

Consider the following simplified infinite-horizon, continuous-time asset pricing model, that abstracts from the small negative first-order serial correlation of consumption growth found by Mehra and Prescott: The log of real per capita consumption C_t follows a Brownian diffusion with constant drift rate μ:

$$d \log C_t = \mu dt + \sigma dz(t) \tag{1}$$

so that

$$\log C_t = \log C_0 + \mu t + \sigma z(t) \tag{2}$$

where the cumulative diffusion error $z(t)$ is a zero-mean normal random variable with variance t. The utility of the representative agent is assumed to be CRRA in consumption and to be additively separable across time, so that

$$U = \int_0^\infty u(C_t) e^{-\delta t} dt \tag{3}$$

where

$$u'(C) = C^{-\eta} \tag{4}$$

$\eta > 0$ is the relative rate of risk aversion, and $\delta > 0$ is the pure rate of time preference, assumed to be a constant.

It is customarily assumed that agents know the growth rate μ with perfect certainty. In this case,

$$\begin{aligned}\log u'(C_t) &= -\eta \log(C_t) \\ &= \log u'(C_0) - \eta\mu t - \eta\sigma z(t)\end{aligned} \tag{5}$$

The risk-free real interest rate $R^f(t)$ at time 0 on zero-coupon, price-level-indexed bonds maturing at time t will be determined by the first-order condition

$$\exp(-tR^f(t)) = \frac{Eu'(C_t)e^{-\delta t}}{u'(C_0)} \tag{6}$$

where the expectation operator E is conditional on C_0 and the representative agent's knowledge of the parameters. Applying the elementary formula for the expectation of a log-normal random variable to Eq. (5),[1]

$$Eu'(C_t) = u'(C_0)\exp\left(-\eta\mu t + \frac{1}{2}\eta^2\sigma^2 t\right) \tag{7}$$

Therefore, the real yield curve is flat at a risk-free real interest rate R^f somewhat below the value $\delta + \eta\mu$ that would prevail with zero variance:

$$R^f(t) = R^f = \delta + \eta\mu - \frac{1}{2}\eta^2\sigma^2 \tag{8}$$

As long as μ is positive and the volatility of consumption is not too large, R^f will be positive and consols will have a finite market value of $1/R^f$.

Mehra and Prescott model equity as shares in all the resources that produce output in the economy. The time 0 price S of a per capita share in these resources will be

$$S = \frac{\int_0^\infty E\left[C_t u'(C_t)e^{-\delta t}\right]dt}{u'(C_0)} \tag{9}$$

We have

$$C_t u'(C_t) = C_0 u'(C_0)\exp[(1-\eta)\mu t + (1-\eta)\sigma z(t)] \tag{10}$$

whence

$$\frac{E\left[C_t u'(C_t)e^{-\delta t}\right]}{u'(C_0)} = C_0\exp\left[\left((1-\eta)\mu - \delta + \frac{1}{2}(1-\eta)^2\sigma^2\right)t\right] \tag{11}$$

The price of a per capita share in output, as given by Eq. (9), is then

$$S = C_0/d \tag{12}$$

where

$$d = \delta + (\eta - 1)\mu - \frac{1}{2}(\eta - 1)^2\sigma^2$$

so long as

$$\delta + (\eta - 1)\mu > (\eta - 1)^2\sigma^2$$

so that the integral in Eq. (9) converges.

The time 0 arithmetic real rate of return on equity implied by Eq. (12) is

$$\begin{aligned} r^e &= dS/(Sdt) + C_0/S \\ &= dC_0/(C_0dt) + d \\ &= \mu + d + \frac{1}{2}\sigma^2 + \sigma dz/dt \end{aligned}$$

since by Itô's Lemma,

$$\begin{aligned} dC_t/C_t &= d\log C_t + \frac{1}{2}\sigma^2 dt \\ &= (\mu + \frac{1}{2}\sigma^2)dt + \sigma dz(t) \end{aligned}$$

The expected real return on equity is therefore

$$\begin{aligned} R^e &= Er^e \\ &= \mu + d + \frac{1}{2}\sigma^2 \\ &= \delta + \eta\mu - \frac{1}{2}\eta^2\sigma^2 + \eta\sigma^2 \\ &= R^f + \eta\sigma^2 \end{aligned}$$

and the equity premium is $p := R^e - R^f = \eta\sigma^2$. As we would expect, this premium is always positive, and increases with both the relative rate of risk aversion and the uncertainty of future consumption.[2] Abstracting from the moderately negative first-order serial correlation of consumption growth, the equity premium and variance of consumption growth found by Mehra and Prescott[3] would imply $\eta = 48.5$, which is indeed a perplexingly high figure.[4]

3. UNCERTAIN MEAN GROWTH RATE

In practice, however, the representative agent would not know the mean growth rate μ with perfect certainty, but would only have some estimate $\hat{\mu}$ of it, with some standard error of estimation s. Thus, Mehra and Prescott estimate that per capita real consumption grows at 1.83 %/yr., but admit that this has a standard error of 0.38%/yr.[5] It will be shown that such parameter uncertainty, no matter how small, leads to an infinite price for both perpetuities and stocks.

For simplicity, it is assumed that the distribution of the estimation error is Gaussian rather than Student t, and that s itself has no measurement error, so that

$$\mu = \hat{\mu} + sZ_m \tag{13}$$

where Z_m is a zero-mean, unit-variance normal measurement error, that is independent of the diffusion error $z(t)$. Then Eq. (2) becomes

$$\log C_t = \log C_0 + \hat{\mu}t + \sigma z(t) + stZ_m \tag{14}$$

Equations (5), (7), and (8) become

$$\begin{aligned} \log u'(C_t) &= -\eta \log(C_t) \\ &= \log u'(C_0) - \eta\hat{\mu}t - \eta\sigma z(t) - \eta stZ_m \end{aligned} \tag{15}$$

$$Eu'(C_t) = u'(C_0)\exp\left(-\eta\hat{\mu}t + \frac{1}{2}\eta^2\sigma^2 t + \frac{1}{2}\eta^2 s^2 t^2\right) \tag{16}$$

$$R^f(t) = \delta + \eta\hat{\mu} - \frac{1}{2}\eta^2(\sigma^2 + s^2 t) \tag{17}$$

In this case, the growth rate uncertainty, whose variance grows in proportion to t^2, eventually dominates the Brownian diffusion uncertainty, whose variance only grows in proportion to t. As a result, the real interest rate declines linearly with maturity, ultimately going permanently and increasingly negative. This implies that the value of a consol with growth rate uncertainty is actually *infinite*, no matter how small the measurement standard error s is, so long as it is nonzero.

Furthermore, Equations (10) and (11) become

$$C_t u'(C_t) = C_0 u'(C_0) \exp((1-\eta)\hat{\mu}t + (1-\eta)\sigma z(t) + (1-\eta)stZ_m) \tag{18}$$

$$\frac{E\left[C_t u'(C_t)e^{-\delta t}\right]}{u'(C_0)} = C_0 \exp\left((1-\eta)\hat{\mu}t - \delta t + \frac{1}{2}(1-\eta)^2(\sigma^2 t + s^2 t^2)\right) \tag{19}$$

Except in the unlikely case that η exactly equals unity, the integral of Eq. (19) is infinite, so that stock prices, as given by Eq. (9), are infinite as well as perpetuity prices. The rate of return on equity cannot be computed from this expression, since it includes the difference of two infinities, divided by infinity.

4. MATURITY-SPECIFIC EQUITY

The indeterminacy in the premium on a share in all future output can be eliminated by considering maturity-specific claims on future output – in effect "equity strips" – with value

$$s_t = \frac{E\left[C_t u'(C_t)e^{-\delta t}\right]}{u'(C_0)}$$

as given in Eq. (19). Then C_t/s_t equals the time t payoff of 1 unit invested at time 0 in t-specific shares. We have

$$EC_t = C_0 \exp\left(\hat{\mu}t + \frac{1}{2}(\sigma^2 t + s^2 t^2)\right)$$

so that the expected gross return to t-specific shares is

$$\begin{aligned}\exp(R^e(t)t) &= EC_t/s_t \\ &= \exp\left(\eta\hat{\mu}t + \delta t + \eta(1-\eta/2)(\sigma^2 t + s^2 t^2)\right)\end{aligned}$$

whence the rate of return embodied in the expected gross return to equity is

$$R^e(t) = \eta\hat{\mu} + \delta + \eta(1-\eta/2)(\sigma^2 + s^2 t)$$

It follows that the equity premium (specific to maturity t) is

$$\begin{aligned}p(t) &= R^f(t) - R^e(t) \\ &= \eta(\sigma^2 + s^2 t)\end{aligned}$$

This is finite for any finite horizon, but clearly grows without bound as t rises to infinity. Under the assumptions of the model, distant future output constitutes 100% of the intertemporal budget, and therefore dominates current asset pricing.[6] The equity premium on claims on all future output is therefore indeed infinite.

5. CONCLUDING REMARKS

In the presence of diminishing marginal utility, expected utility maximization gives higher weight to the worst-case scenarios than it does to the best- or even median-case scenarios. If the variance of the uncertainty of log consumption merely accumulates in proportion to the horizon t, the real interest rate is just depressed somewhat, relative to the expected log growth rate, below which it would be under perfect certainty. However, when the variance of this uncertainty accumulates in proportion to t^2, as it does when the growth rate is only known with measurement error, the worst-case scenarios take over and make claims on very-distant-future output actually more valuable than claims on near-future output. The equity premium on maturity-specific claims increases without bound with maturity, so that the premium on claims on all future output is infinite.

Default risk would tend to keep the value of real-world perpetuities finite, since they could be expected to default in the problematic worst-case scenarios. However, the prices of such bonds would then depend critically on the very distant future prospects for the leverage ratios of the firms that issued them. Furthermore, the value of the implicit reserved put option would only increase the market value of the issuing firms. Hence, the consideration of default risk would do nothing for the infinite price of equity, nor for the infinite equity premium.

It may well be that real-world stocks represent claims on physical assets with finite productive lives, rather than on all future output, so that their values and equity premia are finite. Furthermore, bonds may be priced by individuals who face a rising hazard function of death, and who therefore do not price bonds with the assumed constant pure rate of time preference, making the price of perpetuities constant.[7] In these cases, however, asset pricing and the equity premium will depend sensitively on the relevant effective horizon.

NOTES

1. If $X \sim N(\mu, \sigma^2)$, $E\exp(X) = \exp(\mu + \sigma^2/2)$.
2. It can be shown, again using Itô's Lemma, that the log equity premium, computed in terms of the expectation of $d(\log S)/dt + C/S$, is $(\eta - 1/2)\sigma^2$. Since this can be negative,

it seems appropriate in the present context to focus on the arithmetic equity premium, as in the text.

3. The Mehra and Prescott stylized empirical facts are that per capita real consumption grows at 1.83 %/yr (S.E. = 0.38) with an annual standard deviation of 3.57% and first-order serial correlation coefficient of −0.14, real returns on a relatively riskless security average 0.80%/yr (S.E. = 0.60), and real returns on the S&P 500 average 6.98%/yr (S.E. = 1.74). Their estimated average equity premium is 6.18%/yr (S.E. = 1.76%).

4. A 95% confidence interval for the Mehra–Prescott equity premium would extend down to about 6.18−2(1.76) = 2.66%, which would still imply a perplexingly high $\eta = 20.9$. However, the US Treasury's new indexed bonds have typically yielded more than 3.50% = 6.98−2(1.74), the lower bound of a 95% confidence interval for the Mehra–Prescott real rate of return on equity (see McCulloch & Kochin, 1998). Unless the expected real return on equity has increased substantially, there may be no statistically significant equity premium at all at present.

5. Investors would in fact have had even less information about the future rate of consumption growth ex ante, than Mehra and Prescott did ex post.

6. Using the Mehra and Prescott estimates $\sigma = 3.57\%$ and $s = 0.38\%$, the ratio σ^2/s^2 equals 88.3, so it would take at least 88.3 years for the parameter uncertainty s^2t to exceed the future shock uncertainty σ^2. However, the figure 88.3 is not an intrinsic property of the economy, but rather merely reflects the fact that the Mehra and Prescott time series ran from 1889 to 1978, so that $s^2 = \sigma^2/n$, where $n = 88.3$ to within rounding error.

7. The author is grateful to Jim Peck for this insight.

ACKNOWLEDGMENTS

The author is grateful to participants in the Ohio State University Macroeconomics Seminar and the Econometrics Society Meetings in Boston, Massachusetts for helpful comments and suggestions.

REFERENCES

McCulloch, J. H., & Kochin, L. A. (1998) *The inflation premium implicit in the US real and nominal term structures of interest rates*. Ohio State University Economics Working Paper # 98-12 (August 1998). Downloadable, with data archive, from http://economics.sbs.ohio-state.edu/jhm/ts/ts.html

Mehra, R., & Prescott, E. C. (March 1985). The equity premium: A puzzle. *Journal of Monetary Economics*, *15*, 145–161.

CREDIT CRUNCH AND SAVING GLUT IN TAIWAN: EMPIRICAL EVIDENCES☆

Cheng Few Lee, Chiung-Min Tsai and Lie-Jane Kao

ABSTRACT

The main purpose of this paper is to identify the developments for bank credit allocation in Taiwan since 1994. Using a disequilibrium model, we evaluate whether there is a situation of excess demand, that is a credit crunch, or excess supply, that is a saving glut, during these periods. We find a considerable excess demand, or credit crunch, particularly during the Asian financial crisis. The main cause of this credit crunch can be attributed to the tightening in the money market because of capital outflow. On the contrary, the empirical result also shows that there were some periods experiencing an excess supply from 2001 to 2004, or a situation of saving glut as mentioned by Bernanke (2005). Furthermore, the saving glut was still prevailing during the periods of global financial crisis. This is probably due to the aggressive and pre-empt policy actions taken by the financial and monetary authorities to avoid a possible meltdown in the credit market.

Key words: Credit crunch; saving glut; bank credit allocation; Asian financial crisis

☆Any views or opinions presented in this publication are solely those of the author and do not necessarily reflect those of the Bank.

Advances in Pacific Basin Business, Economics and Finance, Volume 5, 27–38
Copyright © 2017 by Emerald Publishing Limited
All rights of reproduction in any form reserved
ISSN: 2514-4650/doi:10.1108/S2514-465020170000001015

1. INTRODUCTION

There are two types of disequilibrium in the credit market: credit crunch and saving glut. A credit crunch is a "significant reduction (increase) in the supply (demand) of credit available to commercial borrowers in a temporarily market disequilibrium due to exogenous shock" (Berger & Udell, 1994). On the other hand, a saving glut refers to the excess of gross saving over borrowing (Bernanke, 2005). The disequilibrium of credit demand and supply is consistent with the theory of credit rationing, which occurs either because of some friction in the market or some government policy that prevents supply and demand from being equalized (De Meza & Webb, 1987, 1992; Jaffee, 1971; Stiglitz & Weiss, 1981).

Although the recent deregulation and liberalization in the financial market has reduced the magnitude of market disequilibrium by improving the credit rationing, the risk of credit crunch and saving glut cannot still be ruled out in the real world. Especially, the global imbalance and financial crisis in 2008 had proved that sometimes the government has to step in and play a role in the market. Taiwan, due to its market structure and cross-strait economic ties with China, is very sensitive to the riskiness of China's banking system. The opening up of RMB business also facilitates the credit demand in Taiwan as cross-strait remittances, businesses, and investments accelerate. There were increasing concerns that the massive over-the-counter shadow banking in China, including hedge fund, private financing, trust loans, private funds and other nonbank financial institutions could lead to costly defaults (Bloomerg News, 2016). This development has evoked concerns that whether there is an excess demand of credit volume in Taiwan, which might have aggravated the banking sector in the long run.

Usually, the disequilibrium outcomes are considered as temporary adjustments to economy shocks, and thus can be alleviated through changes in policy or simply through time (Jaffee, 1971; Jaffee & Modigliani, 1969). For this reason, the disequilibrium does not reflect chronic or structural features of the credit market, as compared to the long run equilibrium that will be attained over some indeterminate amount of time in the absence of more external shocks.

In the credit rationing theory, the supply and demand of the loan market are determined by the interest rate and riskiness of the loans: a rising interest rate increases the default probability of commercial loans and reduces banks' return rates. Accordingly, as the interest rate rises, banks restrict lending to firms so that credit demand exceeds credit supply. This rational behavior of banks, nevertheless, is immoral and might have negative effects on the economy as a whole (Mueller & Reize, 2010). On the other hand, because of asymmetric information, persistent excess credit supply equilibria exist (Stiglitz & Weiss, 1981). This can happen if banks attract only customers with high creditworthiness but will not accept to reduce their interest rates. This results in an excess credit supply in the banking sector, without a fall in the interest rate to clear the loan market.

After the global financial crisis in 2008 and the European debt crisis in 2010, credit crunch problem in banking industry, again, catches the eyes of some researchers. For example, Wehinger (2014) discussed the issues related to SMEs' (small- and medium-sized enterprises) financing difficulties and the importance of large injections of liquidity by central banks during the crisis. Korab and Pomenkova (2017) found that the financial crisis revealed the vulnerability of the Eurozone's banking sector to adverse macroeconomic shocks. Their empirical evidence exhibited a credit crunch and credit rationing in Greece between 2008 Q4 and 2012 Q4.

This paper aims to study Taiwan's credit market via that of equilibrium credit rationing: if the long run market equilibrium is the result of structural features of the credit market. The paper is structured as follows. In the section "A Disequilibrium Model of the Bank Loan Market," a generalized disequilibrium model is introduced and the alternative methods of estimating this disequilibrium model are also discussed. The section "Data and Testing the Existence of Price Adjustment Process in Taiwan's Commercial Loan Market" describes the data used to perform empirical studies of the model. The empirical findings for the hypotheses and tests constructed earlier in the paper are also presented in this section. Our summary and concluding remarks are presented in the section "Summary."

2. A DISEQUILIBRIUM MODEL OF THE BANK LOAN MARKET

Disequilibrium models, or partial adjustment models, on the commercial loan market have a very long history. Early studies of the disequilibrium model of commercial loan markets include those by Jaffee (1971), Fair and Jaffee (1972), Maddala and Nelson (1974), Amemiya (1974), Laffont and Garcia (1977), Sealey (1979), Kugler (1987), Sealey (1979), Quandt (1988), Nehls and Schmidt (2003) and Baek (2005). Sealey (1979) argued that models fail to include the effects of market disequilibrium and are likely to yield inconsistent parameter estimates, and developed a generalized disequilibrium model to examine whether there is an excess demand in the commercial loan market. In the work by Nehls and Schmidt (2003), a disequilibrium methodology similar to Sealey (1979) was adopted to examine whether the Germany economy was affected by a credit crunch in the early years of 2000. Their empirical results indicate a credit crunch in the second half of 2002 and suggest that restrictions on the loan supplies are not in line with market interest rates and profitability of investment projects.

Usually, the disequilibrium models are formulated in terms of a special case of simultaneous equation models. All disequilibrium models share the feature that prices do not fully adjust to the market clearing level. This has been discussed in more detail in Lee, Tsai, and Lee (2013). The model used throughout this section was first proposed by Fair and Jaffee (1972) and Amemiya (1974), and later modified as model C by Quandt (1988). This generalized model consists of the following equations:[1]

$$Q_t^D = \alpha_1 P_t + \boldsymbol{\beta}'_1 X_{D,t} + \mu_t \tag{1}$$

$$Q_t^S = \alpha_2 P_t + \boldsymbol{\beta}'_2 X_{S,t} + \upsilon_t \tag{2}$$

$$Q_t = \min(Q_t^D, Q_t^S) \tag{3}$$

$$\Delta P_t = P_t - P_{t-1} = \gamma(Q_t^D - Q_t^S), \quad 0 < \gamma < \infty : \text{price adjustment factor} \tag{4}$$

where Q_t^D and Q_t^S are the quantities of ~~securities~~ loans demanded and supplied, respectively; Q_t is the observed quantity of ~~securities~~ loans in the market; P_t is the observed price of the ~~securities~~ loans; $\boldsymbol{X}_{D,t}$ and $\boldsymbol{X}_{S,t}$ are vectors of exogenous variables; α_1 and α_2 are unknown parameters for P_t; $\boldsymbol{\beta}_1$ and $\boldsymbol{\beta}_2$ are vectors of unknown parameters for exogenous variables; γ is an unknown positive scalar parameter; the disturbances μ_t and ν_t are assumed to be jointly normally distributed as $N(0, \sigma_\mu^2)$ and $N(0, \sigma_\upsilon^2)$, respectively. Note the disturbances μ_t and ν_t are independent over time.

Equation (3) indicates that when the demand Q_t^D exceeds the supply Q_t^S, that is, the market is in the condition of excess demand, the observed quantity Q_t lies on the supply schedule in that borrowers can be provided with loans supplied. Similarly, in the presence of excess credit supply, borrowers will not borrow more than they need. Equation (4) specifies the price adjustment process, which is proportional to the excess demand $Q_t^D - Q_t^S$. Models (1)–(4) should be identified by different sets of exogenous variables $\boldsymbol{X}_{D,t}$ and $\boldsymbol{X}_{S,t}$.

Clearly, the equation system, Eqs. (1)–(4), is a special case of simultaneous equation models. Equations (1) and (2) represent an identified equation system; therefore, from these two equations we can consistently estimate α_1, α_2, $\boldsymbol{\beta}_1$, $\boldsymbol{\beta}_2$, γ, σ_μ^2, and σ_υ^2 by using methodologies of simultaneous equations. Since we have Equation (3) we, therefore, need to introduce Equation (4) into the system for estimation of α_1, α_2, $\boldsymbol{\beta}_1$, $\boldsymbol{\beta}_2$, γ, σ_μ^2, and σ_υ^2. However, one primary problem exists in this disequilibrium model, which is that Q_t^D and Q_t^S are not observable variables in the absence of the market clearing condition.

In this paper, we are also interested in the market adjustment parameter, γ, in Equation (4). Comparing with the equilibrium model in which the existence of supply effect is the core issue, the parameter of most interest in the disequilibrium model is the market adjustment parameter, γ. In the case of continuous time, the limiting values of γ are zero and infinity. If $\gamma = 0$, then there is no price adjustment in response to an excess demand, and if γ is infinity, it indicates instantaneous adjustment. In other words, if one assumes there is price rigidity in response to an excess demand, then the value of γ should be equal to zero. That is, the most important test of the disequilibrium model is to examine whether the price adjustment parameter is zero. This will be examined in the following section.

In this section, we discuss and develop a disequilibrium model and methodology similar to those issues regarding commercial loan markets.

The goal is to estimate the parameters α_1, α_2, β_1, β_2, γ, σ^2_μ, and σ^2_υ with the observations $X_{D,t}$, $X_{S,t}$, Q_t and P_t for $t = 1, 2, ..., T$.

2.1. Estimation Methods

In this section, we first reformulate the disequilibrium asset pricing model required for empirical study. Then we discuss the alternative methods of estimating and testing for the price adjustment process in capital asset pricing.

To estimate α_1, α_2, β_1, β_2, γ, σ^2_μ, and σ^2_υ with observations of $X_{D,t}$, $X_{S,t}$, Q_t and P_t for $t = 1, 2, ..., T$ in Equations (1), (2), (3), and (4), it is quite clear that ordinary least squares will produce inconsistent estimators. Following Fair and Jaffee (1972), Amemiya (1974), and Quandt (1988), we discuss two estimation methods to obtain consistent estimators. The first method is the two-stage least square (2SLS) estimator, and the other is the maximum likelihood estimator (MLE).

One can reformulate the above model by considering periods of rising prices $\Delta P_t > 0$ and periods of falling prices $\Delta P_t < 0$. As a result, in the period with rising prices, the supply function (2) can be estimated using the observed quantity, Q_t, as the dependent variable since there will be excess demand and thus Q_t will equal to Q_t^S. Thus, the disequilibrium system described as equations (1) to (4) can be reformulated and summarized as the following equations:

$$\begin{aligned} &\text{(a)} \quad Q_t = \alpha_1 P_t + \beta_1' X_{D,t} - \frac{1}{\gamma}\Delta P_t^+ + \mu_t \\ &\text{(b)} \quad Q_t = \alpha_2 P_t + \beta_2' X_{S,t} - \frac{1}{\gamma}\Delta P_t^- + \upsilon_t \end{aligned} \tag{5}$$

where $\Delta P_t^+ = \begin{cases} \Delta P_t & \textit{if } \Delta P_t > 0 \\ 0 & \textit{otherwise} \end{cases}$,

$$\Delta P_t^- = \begin{cases} -\Delta P_t & \textit{if } \Delta P_t < 0 \\ 0 & \textit{otherwise} \end{cases}$$

Two alternative methods (2SLS and MLE) for estimating the above disequilibrium model are now proposed in the following paragraphs.

2.1.1. 2SLS Estimator

The equations system shown in Eq. (5) contains the jointly dependent variables Q_t, P_t, ΔP_t^+, and ΔP_t^-. The parameters in the modified model can be consistently estimated by the conventional two-stage least squares (2SLS) method. This can be briefly described as the following two stages. In the first stage, regress ΔP_t^+ and ΔP_t^- on all of the exogenous variables, $X_{D,t}$ and $X_{S,t}$ to obtain the estimations of $\hat{\Delta P}_t^+$ and $\hat{\Delta P}_t^-$; then, in the second stage, regress Q_t on X_{1t} and $\hat{\Delta P}_t^+$ in equation (5a), and regress Q_t on X_{2t} and $\hat{\Delta P}_t^-$ in equation (5b). However, the estimators of $\hat{\alpha}_1$, $\hat{\alpha}_2$, $\hat{\beta}_1$ and $\hat{\beta}_2$ are not asymptotically efficient in this model, though they could be consistent if the predictions of the endogenous variables are used for all observations.[2] The reasons are, first, there is no imposed restriction to force the same γ to appear in both equations and, second, ΔP_t^+ and ΔP_t^- are not, strictly speaking, linear functions of the $X_{D,t}$ and $X_{S,t}$.

2.1.2. Maximum Likelihood Estimator

Quandt (1988) employs an appropriately formulated full-information maximum likelihood technique. He suggests one can use the log likelihood function represented as equation (6) to find the ML estimator.

$$L = T\log|\alpha_2 - \alpha_1 + \frac{1}{\gamma}| - T\log 2\pi - \frac{T}{2}\log|\Omega| - \frac{1}{2}\sum_t u_t'\Omega^{-1}u_t \tag{6}$$

where $u_t' = \left(Q_t - \alpha_1 P_t - \beta_1' \mathbf{X}_{D,t} + \frac{1}{\gamma}\Delta P_t^+,\ Q_t - \alpha_2 P_t - \beta_2' \mathbf{X}_{S,t} + \frac{1}{\gamma}\Delta P_t^-\right)$.

On the other hand, Amemiya (1974) shows that the following iterative method can be used to obtain MLEs. He suggests that the MLEs can be obtained by solving the following equations simultaneously:

$$\alpha_{1,\text{MLE}} = \alpha_{1,\text{LS}} \quad \boldsymbol{\beta}_{1,\text{MLE}} = \boldsymbol{\beta}_{1,\text{LS}} \tag{7a}$$

$$\alpha_{2,\text{MLE}} = \alpha_{2,\text{LS}} \quad \boldsymbol{\beta}_{2,\text{MLE}} = \boldsymbol{\beta}_{2,\text{LS}} \tag{7b}$$

$$\sigma_\mu^2 = \frac{1}{T}\left[\sum_A (Q_t - \alpha_1 P_t - \boldsymbol{\beta}_1' \mathbf{X}_{D,t})^2 + \sum_B \left(Q_t + \frac{1}{\gamma}\Delta P_t - \alpha_1 P_t - \boldsymbol{\beta}_1' \mathbf{X}_{D,t}\right)^2\right] \tag{7c}$$

$$\sigma_\upsilon^2 = \frac{1}{T}\left[\sum_B (Q_t - \alpha_2 P_t - \boldsymbol{\beta}_2' \mathbf{X}_{S,t})^2 + \sum_A \left(Q_t - \frac{1}{\gamma}\Delta P_t - \alpha_2 P_t - \boldsymbol{\beta}_2' \mathbf{X}_{S,t}\right)^2\right] \tag{7d}$$

$$T\gamma+\frac{1}{\sigma_{\upsilon}^{2}}\sum_{A}\left(Q_t-\frac{1}{\gamma}\Delta P_t-\alpha_2 P_t-\boldsymbol{\beta}_2'\mathbf{X}_{S,t}\right)\Delta P_t-\frac{1}{\sigma_{\mu}^{2}}\sum_{B}\left(Q_t+\frac{1}{\gamma}\Delta P_t-\alpha_1 P_t-\boldsymbol{\beta}_1'\mathbf{X}_{D,t}\right)\Delta P_t=0 \tag{7e}$$

That is, the ML estimators of α and $\boldsymbol{\beta}$ are the same as the LS estimators given γ applied to Eq. (5). The equations for σ^2_{μ} and σ^2_{υ} (equations 7c and 7d) are the residual sums of squares of Eqs. (5a) and (5b), given γ, divided by T as for the usual ML estimators. Equation (7d) is a quadratic function in γ. Following Amemiya's suggestion, one can solve the above parameters by using the following iterative procedures:

Step 1: Use 2LSL estimates of α, $\boldsymbol{\beta}$, σ^2_{μ}, and σ^2_{υ} as the initial estimates.

Step 2: Substitute $\hat{\alpha}$, $\hat{\beta}$, $\hat{\sigma}^2_{\mu}$, and $\hat{\sigma}^2_{\upsilon}$ into (7e) and solve for the positive root of γ, $\hat{\gamma}$.

Step 3: Use $\hat{\gamma}$ in Eq. (5) to obtain least squares estimates of α, $\boldsymbol{\beta}$, σ^2_{μ}, and σ^2_{υ}.

Step 4: Repeats step 2 and 3 until the solutions converge.

3. DATA AND TESTING THE EXISTENCE OF PRICE ADJUSTMENT PROCESS IN TAIWAN'S COMMERCIAL LOAN MARKET

3.1. Model Specification

In order to examine the commercial loan market in Taiwan, one needs to explicitly specify the demand and supply equations for the commercial loan market. Empirically or theoretically, the exogenous variables in the model should have their economical implications. The exogenous variables in the supply function are those related to the capacity of the banking industry, to the most important items in the balance sheet or income statement of a bank, and to the monetary policy direction. The most used proxy of the capacity of the banking sector or the available fund/resources of the bank is the amount of total bank deposits. The second potential variable is the rate difference between loan and deposit or bond yield, since a larger difference encourages a bank to allocate more of its funds to loan. We can see a similar model specification in the works of Sealey (1979), Nehls and Schmidt (2003), and Baek (2005). One other candidate is the required ratio of reserve, such as in Baek's (2005) specification. This variable can capture the cost of the fund resource as well as the monetary policy signal, which will affect the willingness of a bank to lend.

For the demand function, the exogenous variables are the ones connecting to the real economic activities. The most used proxy for this reason is the index of industry production. We can see this model specification in the work of Sealey (1979) and Baek (2005). Some use the real GDP instead of industry production to determine the loan demand behavior, such as Nehls and Schmidt (2003), since the concept is almost the same. Other variables are those related to the spread between cost and return for firm's investment, the capital market rate, and so on.

We use a similar model specification in this paper to examine the commercial loan market in Taiwan. The demand for commercial loans is as follows:

Demand function: $Q_t^D = \alpha_1 r_t + \beta_{11} IP_t + \beta_{12} X_t + \mu_{1t}$ where ${Q^D}_t$ is the demand for commercial loan, which is unobservable; r_t is the rate of commercial loans that is observable, IP_t is the industrial production index, collected in a monthly base, that measures firms' expectations about future economic activity, and X_t is the growth rate of export, which affects the demand for commercial loans as the export sector plays a very important role in the economic performance of Taiwan.

For the supply function, the specification is as follows:

Supply function: $Q_t^S = \alpha_2 r_t + \beta_{21} TD_t + \beta_{22} OR_t + \mu_{2t}$ where Q_t^S denotes the supply of commercial loan, TD_t is the amount of total deposits, and OR_t is the interbank overnight interest rate. The TD_t is used to capture the capacity of the banking sector to lend, which is the major variable to the supply function. The third variable, OR_t, is used for two reasons. In Taiwan, this rate can be seemed as an indicator of monetary policy direction and is also related to the banks' profit margin indirectly as well.

Intuitionally, the expected signs of the coefficients in the above functions should be as follows. The sign of α_1 and α_2 should be negative and positive respectively since a higher price (i.e., loan rate) means a decline in demand but encourages banks to lend more. β_{11} and β_{12} are expected to be positive since proper economic activities boost the demand for a loan. And finally, β_{21} and β_{22} should be positive and negative respectively. For the former, an increase in total deposits gives the banking industry more ability to lend. For the latter, a lower interbank overnight rate will increase one bank's profit margin and it also means an easing in monetary policy. Both of the reasons will encourage banks to lend more.

3.1.1. Empirical Results

Analyzing the commercial loan market by using a disequilibrium model, most of the empirical studies focus on the following topics: to make sure the existence of market disequilibrium, to identify the period in a situation of credit crunch, and to understand the characteristics of these credit crunches if they exist. Some results thus need to be examined. One is to examine the estimation of $\hat{\gamma}$ since it captures the market adjustment character. The second one is to calculate the excess demand in each period so as to find the existence of credit crunch. For example, Nehls and Schmidt (2003) use the difference between the calculated credit demand and supply at a ratio of estimated supply, as an indicator of excess demand and excess supply respectively. They identify those periods with a ratio larger than two standard deviations as the periods in a situation of credit crunch.

In this paper, we use the financial and economic data from the third quarter of 1994 to the end of 2009. This is because though the banking industry was deregulated in 1989, the number of institutions and branches peaked around 1994. The business of the banking industry then becomes more stable and reliable.

Table 1 summarizes the maximum likelihood estimates of the presented disequilibrium model. From the table, the signs of the estimated parameters are all in the correct direction and at a significance level of 5%. For example, α_1 and α_2 are negative and positive respectively, which means that a higher loan rate will curb the demand for a loan but will give the bank more incentive to lend. Both β_{11} and β_{12} are positive reflecting that a better economic situation will boost the loan demand. On the other hand, β_{21} is positive since it measures the capacity to lend while β_{22} is negative since a decrease in the overnight rate increases banks' motivation to lend.

The parameter of most interest in the model, the market adjustment parameter γ, is slightly larger than zero and significant. Both extreme values, zero and infinity, are excluded in a confidence interval (even 15 times of the standard error). This reflects the partial adjustment mechanism, the most special character of a disequilibrium model.

As we obtain the estimates of the parameters, we can then trace back to find out the real or the desired supply and demand for commercial loan. And then, using the difference between the desired demand and supply, divided by supply, we can calculate the excess demand ratio as mentioned previously (Fig. 1). According to the calculation, there are three periods of time in a situation of credit crunch. They are 1996Q1, 1997Q1 to 1998Q1, and 2007Q2. The first one can be related to the Taiwan Strait tension in 1996. The second credit crunch is coincident with the Asian financial crisis. The third one is related to a near-bank-run event and tension in the money market in early 2007.

Table 1. MLE of Commercial Loan Market.

Parameter	Estimates	Std. Error	z-Statistic	p-Value
α_1	−0.6720	0.2236	−3.00	(0.0027)
β_{11}	0.3443	0.0703	4.90	(0.0000)
β_{12}	1.3562	0.3796	3.57	(0.0004)
α_2	2.9898	1.4670	2.04	(0.0415)
β_{21}	2.2138	0.0838	26.42	(0.0000)
β_{22}	3.9260	1.8813	−2.09	(0.0369)
γ	0.0135	0.0009	15.55	(0.0000)

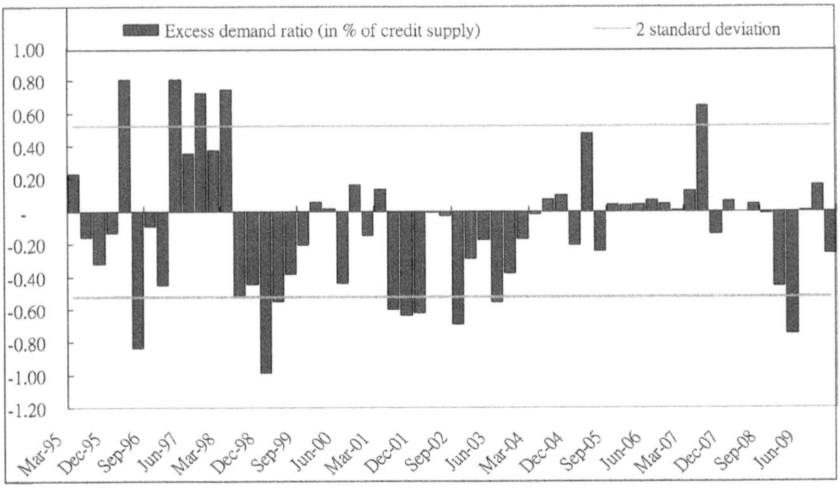

Fig. 1. Excess Demand for Bank Loan.

The figure also shows that there exists excess supply in some periods, especially during the periods from 2001 to 2004. This may be reflecting the so-called saving glut as Bernanke (2005) mentioned.

4. SUMMARY

The main purpose of this paper is to identify the developments for bank credit allocation in Taiwan since 1994. In order to evaluate whether there is a situation of a credit crunch or an excess saving, we derive a simultaneous function for credit allocation in terms of the disequilibrium model developed by Fair and Jaffee (1972), Amemiya (1974), Quandt (1988), and others. MLE and 2SLS are our two methods for estimating the loan market with disequilibrium price adjustment effect.

Using bank loan data from five major commercial banks in Taiwan, the loan rates and other related data, we find that a disequilibrium price adjustment process does in fact exist, and thus, the loan market has been sometimes in a situation of excess demand or excess supply. These empirical results show that there was one major credit crunch and there were also some periods of experiencing so-called saving gluts in Taiwan's credit market from 1994 to 2009. The major credit crunch occurred in the periods of the Asian financial crisis. However, after the Asian financial crisis and up to the year of 2004, there were evidences showing the existence of excess supply of bank loan, or the saving gluts as Bernanke (2005) has mentioned.

Furthermore, the phenomenon of saving gluts was still prevailing during the periods of global financial crisis, or, from the second half of 2008 to the beginning of 2009. This is probably due to the pre-empt policy actions of the financial and monetary authorities to avoid a possible meltdown in the credit market. According to our specification of supply function, the overnight interest and bank deposits are two major exogenous variables. The authorities lowered the interest rate fast enough and adopted the policy of blanket guarantee on deposits in time that had supported the banking sector to resist the crisis.

Though existing debates in the model specification, for example, lack some variables such as the return on equity or the profit margin of the banking industry, all the coefficients estimated in both functions are in the expected directions and are significant. Besides, the periods of excess demand/supply for bank loan are coincident with those periods of some specific economic events. We believe these evidences have showed the disequilibrium character in Taiwan's bank loan market successfully and are helpful in policy discussion.

NOTES

1. There are four major models and some alternative specifications in constructing disequilibrium issues (see Quandt, 1988, though the time period notation is slightly different from the models here).
2. Amemiya show that the 2SLS estimators proposed by Fair and Jaffee are not consistent since the expected value of error in first equation, $E\mu_t$ given t belonging to period B, is not zero, or, according to Quandt, the plim X_a' μ_a/T is not zero (see Amemiya (1974) and Quandt (1988)).

REFERENCES

Alloway, T. (2016). Four fresh worries about China's shadow banking system. *Bloomberg News*, 7 September 2016.

Amemiya, T. (1974). A note on a fair and Jaffee model. *Econometrica*, *42*, 759–762.

Berger, A. N., & Udell, G. F. (1994). Did risk-based capital allocate bank credit risk and cause a "Credit Crunch" in the United States? *Journal of Money, Credit and Banking*, *26*(3), 585–628.

Bernanke, B. S. (2005). The global saving glut and the U.S. current account deficit. Speech delivered for the Sandridge Lecture at the Virginia Association of Economists, Richmond, March 10.

De Meza, D., & Webb, D. C. (1987). Too much investment: A problem of asymmetric information. *Quarterly Journal of Economics*, *102*, 281–292.

De Meza, D., & Webb, D. C. (1992). Efficient credit rationing. *European Economic Review*, *102*, 1290.

Ehung Ggi Baek. (2005). A disequilibrium model of the Korean credit crunch. *The Journal of the Korean Economy*, *6* (2005 Fall), 313–336.

Fair, R. C., & Jaffee, D. M. (1972). Methods of estimation of market in disequilibrium. *Econometrica*, *40*, 497–514.

Jaffee, D. M. (1971). *Credit rationing and the commercial loan market*. New York, NY: Wiley.

Jaffee, D. M., & Modigliani, F. (1969). A theory and test of credit rationing. *American Economic Review*, *59*, 850–872.

Korab, P., & Pomenkova, J. (2017). Credit rationing in Greece during and after the financial crisis. *Czech Journal of Economics and Finance*, *67*, 2017, no. 2.

Kugler, P. (1987). Credit rationing and the adjustment of the loan rate: An empirical investigation. *Journal of Macroeconomics*, *9*(4), 505–525.

Laffont, J. J., & Garcia, R. (1977). Disequilibrium econometrics for business loans. *Econometrica*, *45*(5), 1187–1204.

Lee, C.-F., Tsai, C.-M., & Lee, A. C. (2013). Asset pricing with disequilibrium price adjustment: Theory and empirical evidence. *Quantitative Finance*, *13*(2), 227–239.

Maddala, G. S., & Nelson, F. D. (1974). Maximum likelihood methods for models of market in disequilibrium. *Econometrica*, *42*, 1013–1030.

Mueller, E., & Reize, F. (2010). *Loan availability and investment: Can innovative companies better cope with loan denials?* ZEW Discussion Papers, No. 10-025.

Nehls, H., & Schmidt, T. (2003). Credit Crunch in Germany? Discussion Papers No.6, Rheinisch-Westfalisches Institute.

Quandt, R. E. (1988). *The econometrics of disequilibrium*. New York, NY: Basil Blackwell Inc.

Sealey, C. W., Jr. (1979). Credit rationing in the commercial loan market: Estimates of a structural model under conditions of disequilibrium. *Journal of Finance*, *34*, 689–702.

Stiglitz, J., & Weiss, A. (1981). Credit rationing in markets with imperfect information. *The American Economic Review*, *71*(3), 393–410.

Wehinger, G. (2014). SMEs and the credit crunch: Current financing difficulties, policy measures and a review of literature. *OECD Journal: Financial Market Trends*, Volume 2013/2.

STOCK MARKET ACTIVITIES AND INDUSTRIAL PRODUCTION GROWTH: EVIDENCE FROM 20 INTERNATIONAL MARKETS

Thomas C. Chiang and Xiaoyu Chen

ABSTRACT

This study presents evidence on the relations of stock market performance and industrial production growth for a group of 20 industrial markets. Evidence supports the notion that an increase in stock returns or a rise in the market value of stocks contributes positively to industrial production growth. Evidence suggests that stock market risk has a significantly negative effect on production growth for advanced markets. The Granger test finds a unidirectional causality running from stock returns or stock volatility to industrial growth. However, the United States shows a bilateral causality between stock volatility and industrial production growth.

Keywords: Stock return; Chinese stock market; output growth; liquidity; implied volatility

JEL Classification: G14; G15

Advances in Pacific Basin Business, Economics and Finance, Volume 5, 39–75
Copyright © 2017 by Emerald Publishing Limited
All rights of reproduction in any form reserved
ISSN: 2514-4650/doi:10.1108/S2514-465020170000001003

1. INTRODUCTION

It is generally observed that stock market performance has the power of predicting investments and output growth (Barro, 1990; Fama, 1990; Schwert, 1990). Levine (1997) contends that this projection is essentially working through market functions to mitigate the effect of transactions, providing a mechanism for collecting and processing information on a wide array of firms' managers and investors. Gurley and Shaw (1997) emphasize the flows of fund mechanisms and argue that the stock market provides a vital role in channeling savings into investments (Gurley & Shaw, 1997), allocating funds from lenders to those borrowers for production. In essence, stock returns reflect information about corporate expectations of future cash flows and discount rates, which provide an effective signal to gauge the industrial production and investor's expectations (Fama, 1990; Schwert, 1990).[1]

Testing the relation between stock market performance and production growth, a number of studies find evidence to support a positive relation (Levine, 2003).[2] Particularly, Atje and Jovanovic (1993) investigate the value of stock market trading relative to GDP for 40 countries over the period 1980–1988 and find a significant positive relationship. Levine and Zervos (1998) use a cross-country regression model to examine a number of countries for the period 1976–1993. They show that equity market liquidity is positively and robustly correlated with contemporaneous and future rates of economic growth, capital accumulation, and productivity growth. Arestis, Demetriades, and Luintel (2001) apply time series data from several advanced countries based on Johansen's (1991) cointegration analysis and find a normalized vector depicting a positive association between stock market development, banking system development, and real GDP. This evidence supports the view that the stock market may be able to promote economic growth.[3]

Despite its positive contribution to output growth, the volatile behavior inherent in the stock market may produce a negative effect on economic activity. For instance, the evidence provided by Harris (1997) suggests that the stock market variable does not lend much support. Stock and Watson (1998) report that the relationship between stock returns and production growth has not remained stable over time. One possible argument is that even economic activity is positively related to stock market returns and the negative correlation between stock returns and volatility could lead to a negative effect on industrial growth. Schwert (1989a) notes that stock market volatility reflecting the future uncertainty of cash flows is likely to have a negative influence on investor decisions over the risk-return choice that interrupts future economic activity. Another linkage can be observed from the financing process through the equity market. That is, an increase in stock market volatility will raise the cost of financing to compensate investors for bearing higher risk. A higher cost of equity financing in the market would jeopardize business liquidity, which, in turn, interrupts industrial productions.

Several issues from the above studies merit comment. First, most empirical investigations focus on U.S. data (Barro, 1990; Fama, 1990; Schwert, 1990) or on other advanced markets (Choi, Hauser, & Kopecky, 1999). Very few studies have examined emerging markets, such as the BRICS and Asian markets. Given the rapid output growth of these emerging markets and ever rising savings, it is of interest to investigate whether stock market performance in emerging markets helps to promote output growth; it is also meaningful to compare their underlying behavior with that of advanced markets. Second, even though a large amount of empirical studies have used samples involving a large amount of cross-country data, the data under investigation were mainly quarterly or annually observations of GDP. No particular attention is paid to short-run output growth, such as monthly industrial production or manufacturing growth. Thus, the results mentioned above may be useful for a long run projection, however, it contains very little information advising for short run output growth. Third, although some studies employ time series methods in their empirical investigations, the underlying time series patterns have not been fully explored. As a result, the estimated parameters may be useful in explaining long-run economic growth. These parameters, however, may fail to serve for short-run predictions. Since the underlying time series patterns have been ignored, the estimated parametric relations may be biased, and thereby distort the statistical inference. Fourth, despite the fact that some studies incorporate cross-country effects and the uncertainty of the stock market into the empirical analysis (Rajan & Zingales, 1998; Arestis, et al., 2001), a systematic study of stock returns and, correspondingly, risk factors, has not been comprehensively addressed. The losses in industrial growth resulting from the 2008–2009 world financial crisis suggest that the impact of market volatility triggered by financial stress cannot be ignored and it should not be left out from the estimated equation. Otherwise, we are unable to see the full impact of the stock market on industrial production growth, leading to an overestimation of the stock market's contribution. Fifth, Fama (1990) reports that economic activity is positively related to lagged stock returns. Schwert (1990) and Chen (1991), however, show that fluctuations in the level of economic activity are a key determinant of the level of stock returns. These studies obviously point to two different causal directions between the stock market and economic activity. Thus, a further investigation of causality of this relation based on broader country data is needed. In our empirical study, the issues outlined above will be addressed.

This paper is organized as follows. Section "Data Description" describes the data. Section "The Model" constructs a transfer function model that contains time series properties and explanatory variables pertinent to explain industrial production. Section "Empirical Evidence" reports the empirical evidence using stock market returns or the growth of stock market value, respectively, as explanatory variables. Section "Does the Stock Market have Negative Effect?"

tests the impact of market return risk on industrial production growth. Section "Robustness Tests" conducts robustness tests using value-at-risk as an alternative measure of stock market risk. Section "Feedback of Industrial Production Growth to Stock Market" conducts causality tests on the relation between stock market variables and industrial production growth. Section "Concluding Remarks" contains concluding remarks.

2. DATA DESCRIPTION

The data in this study span January 2, 1995 through December 31, 2014, including both daily and monthly data for 20 markets. They are: G6 markets: United States (U.S.), Canada (CA), France (FR), Germany (GR), Italy (IT), and the United Kingdom (UK); Scandinavian markets: Denmark (DK), Finland (FN), Norway (NW), and Sweden (SD); BRICKS markets: Brazil (BZ), Russia (RS), India (ID), China (CN), and South Africa (SA); and Asian markets: South Korea (KO), Japan (JP), Singapore (SG), Taiwan (TW), and Thailand (TH). For measuring stock market performance, we employ the market return, market value, and the implied volatility for each country. For markets without implied volatility, we use daily stock return to construct the monthly absolute level of stock returns (French, Schwert, & Stambaugh, 1987). Industrial production growth is measured by the log-difference of the industrial production index times 100. For those markets with missing data, we replace the missing data with the manufacturing index. Stock returns are calculated as $((\log(p_t) - \log(p_{t-1}))\times 100$, where p_t denotes the monthly stock indices at the end of the month.[4] All data are taken from *Datastream International* for all markets except implied volatility for France, the United Kingdom, and Italy, which is taken from the *Bloomberg* database.

Table 1 reports a summary of statistics of stock returns and industrial production growth. Most emerging markets such as India, South Korea, Singapore, and Thailand have higher average growth rates in industrial production, while most advanced markets, such as France, Italy, the United Kingdom, and Japan, display relatively low or negatively average growth rates. With respect to the standard deviations of industrial production growth, advanced markets have relatively low variations as compared to the emerging markets. In regard to stock market performance, the BRICS countries have better performance led by South Africa and Brazil, while the Asian markets have relatively low performance, especially Thailand and Taiwan. However, the evidence indicates that stocks for China and Brazil exhibit the highest degree of variations as shown in the two greatest standard deviations of stock returns.

Figs. 1A to 4A are the time series plots of industrial production indices, Figs. 1B to 4B are, correspondingly, stock market price indices. Several observations are worth noting. First, industrial production indices across different

Table 1. A Summary of Statistics of Industrial Production Growth and Stock Returns.

	CA	FR	GM	IT	UK	US	DK	FN	NNW	SD
Pane A: Industrial output growth										
Mean	0.07	−0.02	0.15	−0.07	−0.02	0.19	0.05	0.13	0.10	0.01
Median	0.04	0.09	0.28	0.04	0.10	0.23	−0.09	0.10	0.10	0.31
Maximum	4.31	3.74	4.41	3.47	4.49	2.55	8.03	7.15	7.15	8.94
Minimum	−4.81	−6.43	−8.51	−4.19	−5.84	−3.59	−10.15	−13.20	−5.41	-8.42
Std. Dev.	1.17	1.41	1.57	1.29	1.02	0.76	3.01	2.06	1.60	2.56
Skewness	−0.16	−0.48	−0.80	−0.40	−0.74	−1.28	−0.02	−1.04	0.26	−0.19
Kurtosis	4.51	4.97	6.32	4.00	8.67	8.16	3.25	11.37	6.10	4.46
Jarque-Bera	21.46	47.92	135.67	16.40	343.43	331.68	0.49	743.92	99.12	17.04
SSD	292.09	474.51	589.87	400.72	249.40	139.75	1611.29	1016.45	614.55	1162.49
OBS	215.00	240.00	240.00	240.00	240.00	240.00	179.00	240.00	240.00	179.00

	BZ	RS	ID	CN	SA	SK	JP	SG	TH	TW
Mean	0.10	0.34	0.54	−0.04	0.10	0.51	−0.01	0.47	0.40	0.37
Median	0.31	1.02	0.43	−0.09	0.00	0.58	0.28	−0.20	0.32	0.40
Maximum	6.62	11.91	13.92	15.12	7.93	7.02	6.62	32.78	32.11	9.35
Minimum	−13.64	−20.88	−15.39	−14.39	−6.07	−11.33	−17.98	−27.76	−47.55	−15.54
Std. Dev	2.05	5.87	5.96	2.95	2.17	2.37	2.17	11.51	8.40	2.70
Skewness	−2.00	−1.20	−0.35	−0.21	−0.04	−0.90	−3.19	0.25	−1.01	−1.09
Kurtosis	15.58	5.31	3.57	13.14	3.67	7.04	24.85	3.16	8.89	10.37
Jarque-Bera	1742.27	82.39	3.92	1030.21	4.58	195.58	5181.03	2.69	308.67	559.38
SSD	999.75	6134.32	4080.37	2085.28	1130.54	1347.47	1124.28	31679.72	13399.76	1643.13
OBS	240.00	179.00	116.00	240.00	240.00	240.00	240.00	240.00	191.00	227.00

Table 1. *(Continued)*

	CA	FR	GM	IT	UK	US	DK	FN	NNW	SD
Pane B: Stock returns										
Mean	0.66	0.46	0.30	0.21	0.38	0.67	0.85	0.61	0.56	0.70
Median	1.27	1.27	1.12	0.25	1.01	1.57	1.19	1.28	1.46	1.32
Maximum	16.90	16.11	17.23	22.76	14.72	19.06	16.61	29.45	16.78	14.03
Minimum	−19.24	−17.13	−20.28	−20.31	−15.32	−17.83	−18.64	−25.36	−33.13	−23.39
Std. Dev.	4.51	5.45	6.32	6.24	4.43	4.87	5.28	8.54	6.37	5.06
Skewness	−0.83	−0.54	−0.62	−0.16	−0.59	-0.55	−0.82	−0.15	−1.08	−0.90
Kurtosis	6.20	3.68	3.76	3.87	4.81	5.00	4.68	4.57	6.57	5.62
Jarque-Bera	130.50	16.29	21.28	8.62	46.91	52.06	55.26	25.48	173.73	101.01
SSD	4856.34	7090.77	9557.71	9307.00	4695.20	5660.84	6669.73	17446.14	9695.47	6114.96
OBS	240.00	240.00	240.00	240.00	240.00	240.00	240.00	240.00	240.00	240.00

	BZ	RS	ID	CN	SA	SK	JP	SG	TH	TW
Mean	0.96	0.83	0.83	0.56	0.97	0.43	0.27	0.26	0.16	0.17
Median	1.03	1.18	1.18	0.60	1.06	0.67	0.40	0.54	0.40	0.70
Maximum	40.75	30.50	30.50	35.53	19.81	41.05	17.39	22.79	47.03	22.32
Minimum	−34.83	−26.99	−26.99	−26.31	−39.92	−30.68	−18.31	−19.91	−28.36	−27.36
Std. Dev.	9.44	8.35	8.35	9.77	5.89	8.38	5.46	5.97	9.28	7.24
Skewness	−0.10	−0.30	−0.30	0.10	−1.44	0.45	−0.12	−0.02	0.30	−0.15
Kurtosis	5.69	3.90	3.90	3.78	12.09	6.55	3.33	5.51	6.84	4.22
Jarque-Bera	72.92	11.72	11.72	6.38	909.13	133.89	1.69	62.92	150.83	15.86
SSD	21314.44	16655.38	16655.38	22831.90	8278.10	16774.98	0.43	8516.76	20589.83	12543.66
OBS	240.00	240.00	240.00	240.00	240.00	240.00	240.00	240.00	240.00	240.00

Note: This table reports a summary of statistics of industrial output growth and stock returns for 20 markets, including 10 North American and European advanced industrial markets, five BRICKS markets, and five major Asian markets.

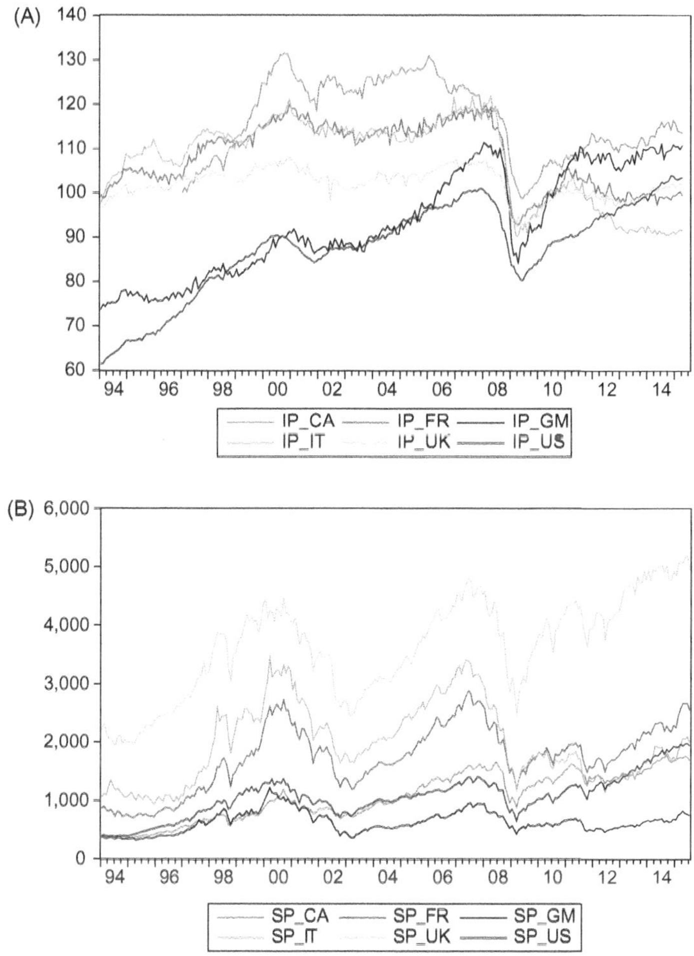

Fig. 1. (A) Industrial Production Indices for G6 Markets. (B) Stock Price Indices for G6 Markets.

countries exhibit some degree of comovements, although geographic segmentation of markets still plays a role. The real shock from the US market during the 2008–2009 crisis appears to have a global impact as shown by a dip in industrial production worldwide during the crisis period. Second, as shown in movements of stock price time series, the stock price indices also display in a similar fashion, comovements across markets and seem correlated with the industrial production indices. Obviously, we find the stock market plunge during the 2008–2009 financial crisis period. These observations motivated us to further

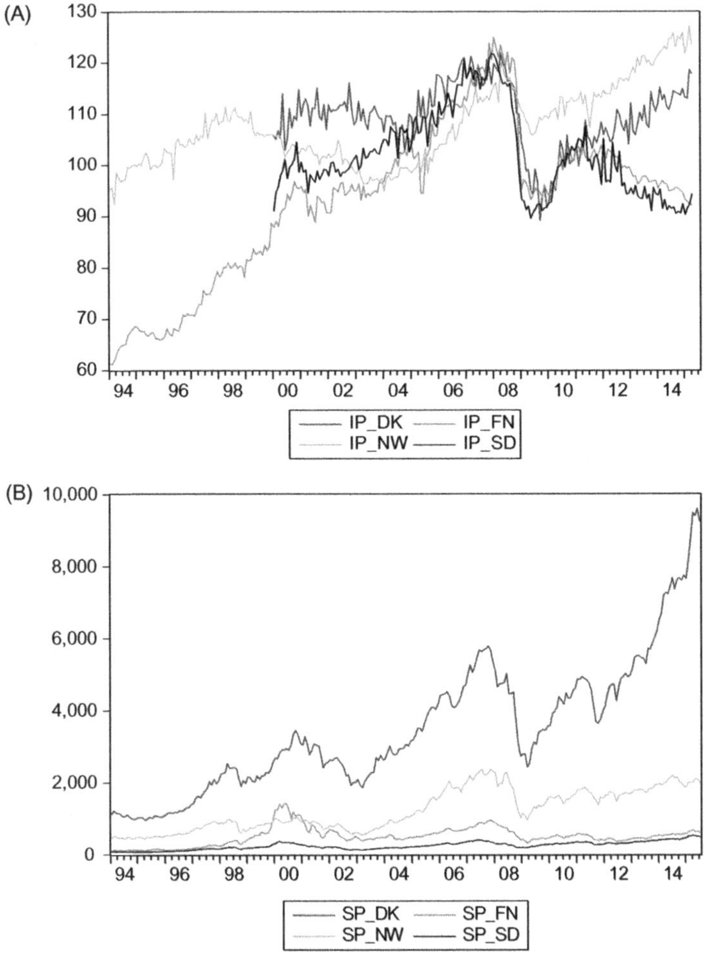

Fig. 2. (A) Industrial Production Indices for Scandinavia Markets. (B) Stock Price Indices for Scandinavia Markets.

investigate the dynamic relations between the stock market and real output production and their causal relations.[5]

3. THE MODEL

While conducting some pre-empirical investigations, we find that the series of industrial production growth for each market reveals either time series

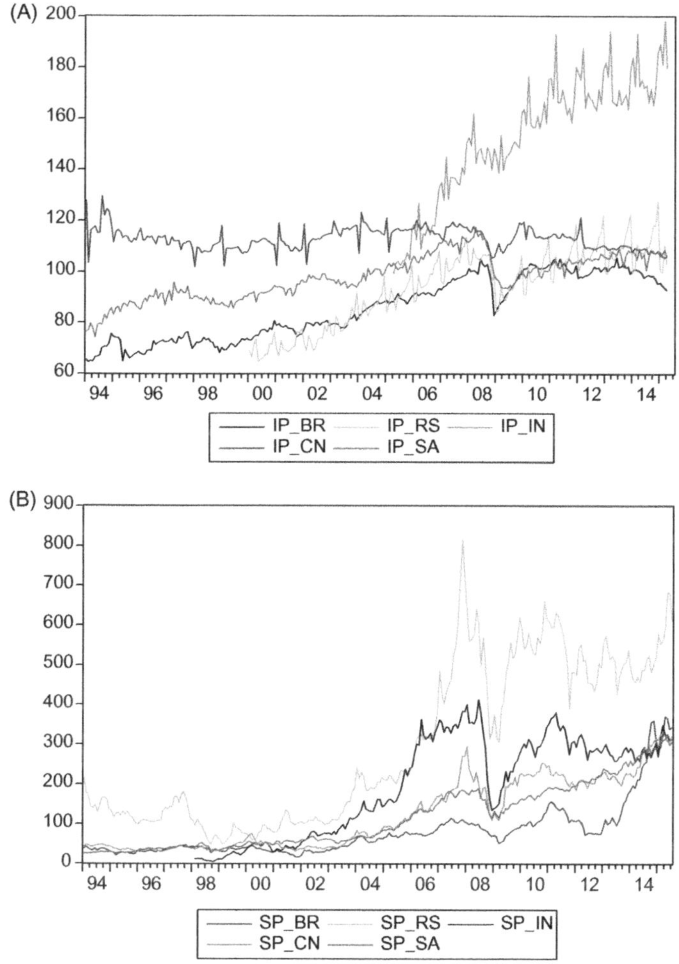

Fig. 3. (A) Industrial Production Indices for BRICS Markets. (B) Stock Price Indices for BRICS Markets.

patterns or seasonal fluctuations. It is appealing to specify the industrial production growth in a transfer function model and using stock market performance as an independent variable. Let Y_t be the industrial production index, which can be explained by X_t (stock price index) and a noise term, N_t. For nonstationary data, we take a log-difference for Y_t and X_t, leading to ΔY_t

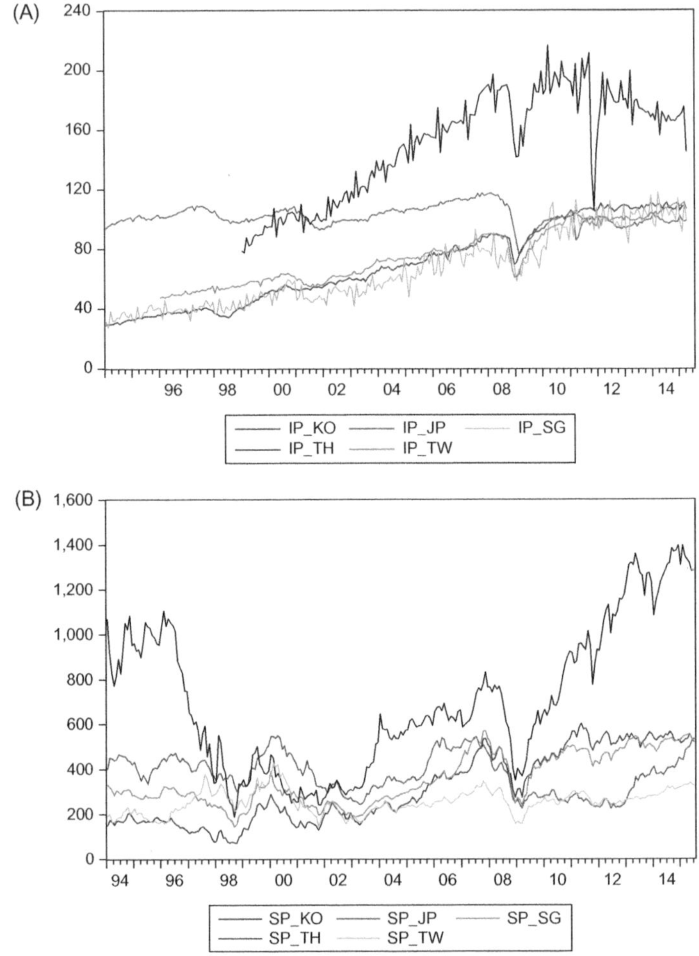

Fig. 4. (A) Industrial Production Indices for Asian Markets. (B) Stock Price Indices for Asian Markets.

(industrial output growth) and ΔX_t (stock return or other explanatory variables) to be stationary processes and specify an ARIMA model. The model is expressed as follows:

$$\Delta Y_t = C + \frac{\omega_s(B)}{\delta_r(B)} \Delta X_{t-b} + \frac{\theta_q(B)}{\varphi_p(B)} \varepsilon_t \tag{1}$$

where $\omega(B) = \omega_0 - \omega_1 B - \omega_2 B^2 - \cdots - \omega_s B^s$,

$$\delta(B) = 1 - \delta_1 B - \delta_2 B^2 - \cdots - \delta_r B^r$$

r, s, p, q, and b are constant parameters.

Series ΔY_t in Eq. (1) is explained by two parts: the causal effect of ΔX_t and the noise part, N_{ot}, which is modeled as $\theta(B)/\varphi(B)\varepsilon_t$. ΔY_t and ΔX_t are referred to as output and input variables, respectively. In terms of Eq. (1), ΔY_t denotes the industrial production growth, and ΔX_t refers to stock returns or stock market risk measured by implied volatility or value at risk (*VaR*). Since output growth may be subject to abrupt changes associated with economic innovation, an intervention variable, I_t, is also included in the model specification (Hamilton & Lin, 1996).

The evidence in Table 2 indicates that all the markets display some sort of time series patterns, some with lower orders of AR or MA components, and some present 12-(month) period lags. This indicates that industrial production growth does not simply exhibit an AR(1) process, but with a seasonal pattern, such as the 12-month lagged effect. In the test equation, the outliers or influential intervention dates are detected; thus, interventions are identified to control for unexpected abrupt shifts in the production growth series. The evidence shows that intervention variables, labelled by $I(1)$ and $I(2)$, are statistically significant for some markets. These occur more in Asian markets, while there is no evidence shown in the Scandinavian markets.

4. EMPIRICAL EVIDENCE

To test the effect of stock market performance on industrial production growth (IPG), in this section we use the stock return as an explanatory variable. A higher stock return is expected to have a positive signal for the future prospect of firm performance and, in turn, raising liquidity that facilitates production. Therefore, it is anticipated that the estimated coefficient on stock market performance is positive. Using a maximum likelihood method to estimate the test equation, results are reported in Table 3. The evidence indicates that all of the estimated coefficients present a positive sign and are statistically significant. These testing results are consistent with the finding reported by Levine and Zervos (1998) and Arestis, Demetriades, and Luintel (2001). The only exception is the case of the Japanese market. This result should not be surprising, since Japan's stock market has been in a depressed state since 1994. The low return of the Japanese stock market in conjunction with the inefficiency of the banking system has been impeding the Japanese economy from recovery. The depressed state of the economy is further hurting the banking system and stock market. It is these two-way links that bring about a long-run depression in the Japanese market (Hoshi & Kashyap, 2004).[6] The significance of the stock return

Table 2. Time Series Estimates of Industrial Production Growth.

Market	Constant	AR(p1)	AR(p2)	MA(q1)	MA(q2)	I(1)	I(2)	$\bar{R}^2$	*RMSE*
G6-markets									
CA(3)	0.0518 (0.47)	0.2850*** (3.38)						0.08	0.94
FR(1)	−0.0244 (0.29)	−0.2367*** (4.36)						0.05	0.94
GM(1)	0.1986** (2.61)	−0.2759*** (-5.09)				−10.703*** (6042)		0.18	1.32
IT(2,3; 12)	−0.0822 (1.19)	0.1912*** (3.00)	0.1936*** (3.06)		−0.5058*** (9.09)			0.17	0.65
UK(1,10)	0.0136 (0.33)			−0.2266*** (5.74)	−0.2133*** (3.19)			0.09	0.70
US(2,3)	0.1827 (1.45)	0.3278*** (6.73)	0.2943*** (4.74)			−1.7642*** (6.76)		0.30	0.66
Scandinavian markets									
DK(1,2; 12)	0.0208 (0.22)	−0.4985*** (-6.53)	−0.3115*** (4.47)		−0.1932** (2.06)			0.24	1.30
FN(1,12)	0.1591 (1.33)	−0.0944** (2.11)	−0.1980*** (3.83)					0.04	0.85
NW(1,2)	0.0812 (1.33)	−0.4279*** (8.59)	−0.1941*** (2.86)					0.15	1.10
SD(1,4)	0.0243 (0.14)			−0.2856*** (-5.41)	0.1547** (2.07)			0.10	2.33
BRICS markets									
BZ(1)	0.1856 (1.61)	−0.2031*** (4.10)				−14.293*** (2.95)		0.21	1.06
RS(1,12)	0.2298 (0.27)	−0.0816** (2.27)	0.8681*** (29.49)					0.77	2.18
IN(1,2; 12)	0.5000* (1.71)	−0.6527*** (7.16)	−0.2301* (1.78)		0.5199** (4.89)			0.54	3.99
CN(1,12)	−0.0149 (0.50)			−0.5773*** (11.99)	−0.2565*** (6.32)			0.36	0.96
SA(1,2)	0.1008 (1.19)	−0.4400*** (8.56)	−0.1721*** (2.88)					0.15	2.16
Asian markets									
KO(1,2)	0.6420*** (4.39)	−0.1064** (1.96)	0.1519*** (2.48)			−12.094*** (3.10)		0.23	2.01
JP(2,4)	0.2392* (1.84)	0.4145*** (5.97)			−0.1397* (1.75)	−20.610*** (33.55)	−9.864*** (13.06)	0.63	1.63
SG(1,2; 12)	0.4763 (1.43)	−0.6923*** (10.64)	−0.4367*** (7.30)		0.1919*** (2.98)			0.45	7.01
TH(2; 12)	0.7104 (0.85)	0.1475* (1.79)			0.3694*** (7.59)	−52.512*** (6.71)		0.34	3.63
TW(1; 12)	0.4923*** (3.67)	−0.221*** (5.17)				−14.092*** (13.16)		0.24	1.03

Note: This table reports the ARMA estimates of industrial output growth. The numbers in the parenthesis of each market denote orders of AR or/and MA, respectively. I(1) and I(2) are intervention dates or outliers. The absolute values of *t*-statistics are in parentheses. *RMSE* is the root mean squared error calculated by 12-month out-of-sample predictions from January to December, 2014.*, **, and *** indicate significance at the 10%, 5%, and 1% levels, respectively.

Table 3. Estimates of Stock Returns and Time Series Model on the Industrial Production Growth.

Market	Constant	AR(p1)	AR(p2)	MA(q1)	MA(q2)	I(1)	I(2)	$R_{m,t-1}$	$\bar{R}^2$	*RMSE*
G7-markets										
CA(3)	0.0328 (0.31)	0.2777*** (3.51)						0.0473*** (2.74)	0.11	0.98
FR(1)	−0.0503 (0.65)	−0.2919*** (5.48)						0.0577*** (3.84)	0.10	1.00
GM(1,2)	0.189*** (2.85)	−0.3530*** (5.82)	−0.1048* (1.79)			−11.095*** (8.65)		0.0412*** (3.03)	0.20	1.38
IT(2,3; 12)	−0.0872 (1.32)	0.1841*** (2.74)	0.1637** (2.48)		−0.5051*** (9.07)			0.0261*** (2.66)	0.19	0.65
UK(1,10)	0.0028 (0.08)			−0.269*** (6.38)	−0.211*** (2.87)			0.0332*** (2. 87)	0.11	0.70
US(2,3)	0.1695 (1.44)	0.3209*** (6.32)	0.2819*** (4.32)			−1.9398*** (6.65)		0.0217*** (2.83)	0.32	0.70
Scandinavian markets										
DK(1,2;12)	−0.0227 (0.26)	−0.5464*** (-6.75)	−0.3531*** (4.71)		−0.2282** (2.32)			0.0899*** (3.18)	0.28	1.17
FN(1,12)	0.1390 (1.22)	−0.1398*** (2.91)	−0.1956*** (3.54)					0.0349** (2.47)	0.06	0.87
NW(1,2)	0.0562(0.96)	−0.4415*** (8.96)	−0.2273*** (3.42)					0.0406*** (2.79)	0.15	0.18
SD(1,4)	0.0248 (0.14)			−0.3088*** (-5.61)	0.1618** (2.15)			0. 0555* (1.73)	0.10	2.59
BRICS markets										
BZ(1)	0.1669 (1.48)	−0.2347*** (4.46)				−14.1586*** (3.35)		0.0229** (2.29)	0.22	1.08
RS(1,12)	0.2008 (0.24)	−0.0878** (2.50)	0.8667*** (29.52)					0.0337*** (2.92)	0.78	2.15
IN(1,2;12)	0.3899 (1.44)	−0.7390*** (8.39)	−0.2984*** (2.73)		0.5643*** (4.92)			0.0755*** (2.29)	0.57	3.95
CN(1,12)	−0.0252 (1.04)			−0.6249*** (11.76)	−0.252*** (5.86)			0.0233** (2.27)	0.38	0.97
SA(1,2)	0.0434 (0.55)	−0.4531*** (8.14)	−0.2152*** (3.20)					0.0685*** (3.64)	0.18	2.92
Asian markets										
KO(1,2)	0.630*** (4.46)	−0.1064** (1.96)	0.1519*** (2.48)			−12.3651** (2.25)		0.0413*** (3.01)	0.24	1.71
JP(2;12)	0.265** (2.08)	0.4139*** (5.97)			−0.1647** (2.01)	−20.691*** (34.21)	−9.06*** (13.30)	0.0078 (0.47)	0.64	1.70
SG(1,2,12)	0.4763 (1.43)	−0.6923*** (10.64)	−0.4368*** (7.30)		0.2111*** (3.33)			0.1778*** (3.02)	0.44	7.13
TH(2;12)	0.5145 (0.61)	0.1859** (2.24)			0.4019*** (8.17)	−51.112*** (8.04)		0.2408*** (4.03)	0.39	3.79
TW	0.469*** (3.61)	−0.2511*** (6.04)				−13.225*** (12.76)		0.0613*** (2.65)	0.24	0.98

Note: This table reports the ARMA estimates of industrial output growth to be predicted by time series patterns and the lagged stock return. The numbers in the parenthesis of each market denote orders of AR or/and MA, respectively. The absolute values of t-statistics are in parentheses. *RMSE* is the root mean squared error calculated by 12-month out-of-sample predictions from January to December, 2014.*, **, and *** denote significance at the 10%, 5% and 1% levels, respectively.

coefficient for the other 19 markets confirms the hypothesis that stock market performance has a positive effect on industrial production growth.

In a globally integrated production process, the sharing of technology and the international division of labor in production will bring about some sort of production integration or interdependency in production modes. With its economic power in world trade, the U.S. influence (Masih & Masih, 1999) is indispensable. Thus, the inclusion of the U.S. industrial production growth into the test equation not only serves as a control variable, but helps to test the international industrial business cycle hypothesis. Table A1 in the Appendix reports the estimated results. The evidence indicates that the estimated coefficients of stock returns present a very comparable result despite adding a control variable of U.S. industrial production growth.[7]

Since the growth of market value, ΔMV_t, is an indicator for measuring the dynamic aspect of stock market capacity, it contains information for growth in prices and number of shares over time. It also represents growth in the wealth effect (Greenspan, 2000), giving rise to demand in consumption. Thus, it is appropriate to conduct a robustness test by using the growth in stock market value. The estimated results are reported in Table 4. In this table, we specify the model with the same time series patterns and intervention specification as before, but using the stock market value growth as an independent variable. The results show that no significant difference is found by using either stock return or market value growth as an independent variable to predict production growth. Overall, the simple regression estimations consistently show evidence that supports that stock market performance produces a positive impact on industrial production growth. The only exception is the case of the Japanese market.

5. DOES THE STOCK MARKET HAVE NEGATIVE EFFECT?

Although the evidence shows that a higher stock return (or growth in market value of the stock market) makes a positive contribution to production growth, Stock and Watson (1998) demonstrate that the relationship between stock returns and production growth has not been stable over time. In addition, stock market fluctuations are likely to produce a negative effect due to its erratic volatility, aggravating market sentiments (Baker & Wurgler, 2006). In the literature, a number of different proxies have been used to measure stock market risk. In empirical analysis, the implied volatility has been considered to be an efficient forecast of the market volatility (Bali & Engle, 2010; Schwert, 1990). For the U.S. market, the *VIX* is treated as a measure of the expected risk factor, which is calculated using the expected S&P 100 index option volatility by the Chicago Board Options Exchange (CBOE). We also use the *VIX* for measuring the Canadian stock market risk. For the French market, we use the

Table 4. Robustness Test of Stock Market Value Growth on Industrial Production Growth.

Market	Constant	AR(p1)	AR(p2)	MA(q1)	MA(q2)	I(1)	ΔMV_{t-1}	$\bar{R}^2$	*RMSE*
G6-markets									
CA(3)	0.0286 (0.27)	0.2523*** (3.02)					0.0345*** (2.36)	0.09	1.12
FR(1)	−0.0674 (0.88)	−0.2906*** (5.48)					0.0568*** (3.89)	0.10	1.05
GM(1,2)	0.177*** (2.70)	−0.3543*** (5.73)	−0.1148* (1.91)			−11.06*** (8.70)	0.0438*** (3.18)	0.20	1.38
IT(12)	−0.091* (1.95)				−0.4722*** (7.57)		0.0272*** (2.62)	0.14	0.74
UK(1,10)	0.028 (0.66)			−0.2845*** (6.16)	−0.2342*** (3.22)		0.0276** (2.40)	0.11	0.73
US(2,3)	0.1627 (1.39)	0.3183*** (6.21)	0.2831*** (4.31)			−1.9439*** (6.61)	0.0238*** (3.00)	0.32	0.70
Scandinavian markets									
DK(1,2; 12)	−0.0095 (0.12)	−0.5389*** (7.02)	−0.3536*** (4.93)		−0.2327** (2.54)		0.0812*** (3.19)	0.28	1.17
FN(1,12)	0.1332 (0.22)	−0.1429*** (2.98)	−0.1951*** (3.49)				0.0360*** (2.59)	0.06	0.87
NW(1,2)	0.0455 (0.05)	−0.4348*** (8.79)	−0.2237*** (3.35)				0.0360*** (2.56)	0.18	1.04
SD(1)	0.0114 (0.08)			−0.3004*** (5.14)			0. 0595** (2.25)	1.55	1.95
BRICS markets									
BZ(1)	0.1196 (1.08)	−0.2114*** (3.62)				−13.475*** (3.40)	0.0452** (3.46)	0.25	1.04
RS(1,12)	0.1738 (0.21)	−0.0877** (2.48)	0.8672*** (29.17)				0.0324*** (3.16)	0.78	2.16
IN(1,2; 12)	0.3696 (1.35)	−0.7301*** (8.40)	−0.2981*** (2.67)		0.5474** (4.93)		0.0748** (1.86)	0.57	4.02
CN(1,12)	−0.046 (1.43)			−0.6132*** (13.02)	−0.2914*** (5.99)		0.01159* (1.72)	0.38	0.97
SA(1,2)	0.0457 (0.56)	−0.4345*** (7.61)	−0.1898*** (2.83)				0.0611*** (3.29)	0.18	2.92

Table 4. *(Continued)*

Market	Constant	AR(p1)	AR(p2)	MA(q1)	MA(q2)	I(1)	ΔMV_{t-1}	$\bar{R}^2$	*RMSE*
Asian markets									
KO(1,2)	0.585*** (4.64)	−0.607*** (2.93)				−12.043* (1.81)	0.0455*** (3.52)	0.24	2.03
JP(2,4)	0.2707* (1.82)			0.4257*** (5.96)	0.2484*** (3.53)	−20.521*** (32.76)	−0.0197 (1.46)	0.64	1.64
SG(1,2; 12)	0.4165 (1.22)	−0.6910*** (10.55)	−0.4312*** (7.09)		0.2166*** (3.42)		0.1861*** (3.17)	0.44	7.13
TH(2; 12)	0.3633 (0.43)	0.1894** (2.31)			0.4006*** (7.98)	−51.126*** (8.23)	0.2444*** (4.17)	0.39	3.82
TW	0.441*** (3.39)	−0.2467*** (5.95)				−13.316*** (12.76)	0.0546*** (2.66)	0.26	0.97

Note: This table reports evidence of the time series patterns of each industrial output growth, the lagged market value change, and the lagged US industrial output growth on domestic industrial output growth. The numbers in the parenthesis besides each country name denote orders of AR or/and MA, respectively. The absolute values of t-statistics are in parentheses. *RMSE* is the root mean squared error calculated by 12-month out-of-sample predictions.*, **, and *** denote significance at the 10%, 5%, and 1% levels, respectively.

VCAC, and proxy for the UK market with the VFTSE. For the German market, stock volatility is measured by *VADX*, which is calculated using the DAX option contract, including 30 major German stocks traded on the Frankfurt stock exchange. Since not all markets have implied volatilities, we apply *VDAX* for Italy, Denmark, Finland, Norway, and Sweden. For the United Kingdom, we employ the VFTSE, which is based on the FTSE 100 index, and for France it is the VCAC, which is derived from CAC40.[8] With respect to other markets without implied volatility, we use daily stock returns to construct the market volatility proposed by French et al. (1987).

Table 5 reports the estimates by regressing industrial product growth on stock returns with stock volatility as a control variable. The evidence shows that except for the Swedish market, the coefficients on stock returns remain positive and statistically significant, supporting the hypothesis that better stock market performance leads to higher production growth.

With respect to the *VIX* variable, all estimated coefficients for the G6 and Scandinavian countries are negative and highly significant, suggesting a destructive effect on production growth. However, the level of significance of the volatility coefficient for most Asian markets is insignificant, implying that the negative effect on industrial production growth is less for most of the Asian markets. After replacing the lagged market value growth (ΔMV_{t-1}) for the lagged stock return ($R_{m,t-1}$) of each country, we achieve a similar result as shown in Table 6 although the coefficients of the United Kingdom and Norway become insignificant.[9]

Comparing with the existing literature, two important findings are worth noting. First, empirical estimations of the test relation include only the stock return as an explanatory variable without considering the volatility effect that can produce a biased estimator. As a result, the contribution of stock market performance on production growth may be overestimated. Second, the volatility effect in advanced markets on industrial production growth is more profound and significant than in emerging markets. This is consistent with the notion that output productions in the emerging market are less sensitive to stock volatility. This is so because the sources of loanable funds for an emerging market are mainly coming from bank financing, rather than equity financing. As a result, the negative effect of market volatility is more severe for advanced markets than for emerging markets. This evidence is consistent with studies by Hamilton and Lin (1996) and Schwert (1989), who find that high stock market volatility is often associated with periods of recession.

6. ROBUSTNESS TESTS

Using volatility as an independent variable tends to ignore the asymmetric effect from the downside risk. The experience of the world finance crisis of

Table 5. Estimates of the Industrial Production Growth Predicted by Stock Returns and VIX.

Market	Constant	AR(p1)	AR(p2)	MA(q1)	MA(q2)	I(1)	$R_{m,t-1}$	VIX_{t-1}	$\bar{R}^2$	*RMSE*
G6 market										
CA(3)	0.6402** (2.59)	0.2755*** (3.39)					0.056*** (3.20)	−0.0278*** (3.22)	0.13	0.96
FR(1)	0.4546* (1.66)	−0.2424*** (3.49)					0.0525** (2.42)	−0.0225** (2.09)	0.10	1.04
GM(1,2)	0.643*** (3.37)	−0.3605*** (5.88)	−0.1052* (1.76)			−10.07*** (7.68)	0.0260* (1.94)	−0.0205*** (2.80)	0.22	1.36
IT(12)	0.2738 (1.38)				−0.51*** (8.79)		0.028** (2.57)	−0.0142*** (4.04)	0.17	0.72
UK(1,10)	0.4073*** (3.42)			−0.382*** (5.93)	−0.27*** (2.85)		0.0356*** (2.76)	−0.0217*** (3.99)	0.18	0.66
US(2)	0.702*** (4.77)		0.2877*** (5.01)			−3.035*** (3.57)	0.0170* (1.91)	−0.0248*** (4.43)	0.29	0.66
Scandinavian market										
DK(1,2; 12)	0.4838 (0.54)	−0.548*** (7.71)	−0.3644*** (5.11)		−0.285*** (4.07)		0.0653** (2.16)	−0.6354* (1.67)	0.30	1.19
FN(1,12)	0.9005*** (2.84)	−0.1583*** (3.13)	-0.1845*** (3.06)				0.0300** (2.09)	−0.0336*** (2.55)	0.08	1.07
NW(1,2)	0.5357*** (2.88)	−0.4738*** (7.26)	−0.2511*** (3.84)				0.0233* (1.66)	−0.0208*** (2.70)	0.21	1.02
SD(1,4)	0.7607* (1.79)			−0.3231*** (5.17)	0.1581** (2.15)		0. 0361 (1.01)	−0.0288** (2.01)	0.11	1.83
BRICS market										
BZ(1)	0.3954** (2.37)	−0.2434*** (4.69)				−14.091*** (3.52)	0.0217** (2.15)	−0.0333** (2.11)	0.23	1.16
RS(1,12)	1.1689 (1.38)	−0.0784*** (2.71)	0.8848*** (33.94)				0.0302** (2.31)	−0.1296*** (5.76)	0.82	2.33
IN(1,2; 12)	0.2850 (0.73)	−0.7491*** (8.49)	−0.3135*** (2.80)		0.5605** (4.91)		0.0789** (2.46)	0.0198 (0.41)	0.57	3.95
CN(1,12)	0.0013 (0.01)			−0.6089*** (10.81)	−0.26*** (5.75)		0.0202** (1.96)	−0.0027 (0.15)	0.37	0.99
SA(1,2)	0.3563*** (2.63)	−0.4756*** (8.25)	−0.2468*** (3.39)				0.062*** (3.27)	−0.0699*** (2.82)	0.20	2.93

Asian market										
KO(1,2)	0.8848*** (4.15)	-0.1506*** (2.71)	0.1039* (1.69)			−12.088** (3.52)	0.047*** (3.22)	−0.0423* (1.84)	0.25	2.11
JP(2,4)	0.3502* (1.74)			0.4058*** (5.51)	0.2513*** (3.48)	−20.65*** (33.18)	0.0039 (0.23)	−0.0196 (0.73)	0.64	1.64
SG(1,2; 12)	0.7452 (1.40)	−0.6936*** (10.59)	−0.4337*** (7.11)		0.2126*** (3.28)		0.176*** (2.94)	−0.0597 (1.09)	0.39	7.16
TH(2; 12)	0.9928 (1.06)	0.1728** (1.99)			0.4091*** (8.35)	−50.13*** (7.17)	0.238*** (3.76)	−0.0709 (0.09)	0.39	3.92
TW	0.523** (2.23)	−0.2502*** (5.92)				−13.145*** (12.55)	0.061*** (2.66)	−0.0095 (0.30)	0.27	0.99

Note: This table reports the estimates of industrial output growth in relation to stock return and stock market risk. The numbers in parenthesis besides each country name denote orders of AR or/and MA, respectively. The absolute values of t-statistics are in parentheses. ***RMSE*** is the root mean squared error calculated by 12-month out-of-sample predictions.*, **, and *** indicate significance at the 10%, 5%, and 1% levels, respectively.

Table 6. Estimates of the Industrial Production Growth Predicted by Stock Market Growth and VIX.

Market	Constant	AR(p1)	AR(p2)	MA(q1)	MA(q2)	I(1)	ΔMV_{t-1}	VIX_{t-1}	$\overline{R}^2$	*RMSE*
G6-markets										
CA(3)	0.4967** (2.00)	0.2711*** (3.20)					0.0029 (0.20)	−0.0204** (2.27)	0.08	1.01
FR(1)	0.4675* (1.69)	−0.2398*** (3.43)					0.0478** (2.23)	−0.0234** (2.17)	0.09	1.04
GM(1,2)	0.6835*** (3.30)	−0.3510*** (5.49)	−0.1005* (1.65)			−10.525*** (7.29)	0.0272* (1.90)	−0.0221** (2.27)	0.22	1.37
IT(0,0; 12)	0.33338 (1.71)				−0.4833*** (7.84)		0.0205* (1.93)	−0.0168*** (4.10)	0.16	0.74
UK(1,10)	0.2592*** (4.58)			−0.3869*** (5.93)	−0.2755*** (2.91)		0.0383*** (3.04)	−0.0219*** (3.01)	0.16	0.65
US(2)	0.6888*** (4.69)		0.3087*** (5.20)			−3.0386*** (3.51)	0.01908** (2.11)	−0.0244*** (4.37)	0.29	0.66
Scandinavia markets										
DK(1,2; 12)	0.5353* (1.71)	−0.5463*** (7.68)	−0.3645*** (5.12)		−0.2926*** (4.04)		0.0560* (1.90)	−0.0241* (1.82)	0.30	1.20
FN(1,12)	0.8886*** (2.82)	−0.1610*** (3.20)	−0.1844*** (3.04)				0.0313** (2.25)	−0.0333** (2.55)	0.08	1.06
NW(1,2)	0.5504*** (2.72)	−0.4704*** (9.56)	−0.2473*** (3.78)				0.0192 (1.32)	−0.0217** (2.32)	0.20	1.02
SD(1,4)	0.7065* (1.78)			−0.3179*** (4.24)			0. 0471* (1.75)	−0.0272** (2.01)	0.11	1.63

BRICS markets	Constant	AR(p1)	AR(p2)	MA(q1)	MA(q2)	I(1)	$R_{m,t-1}$	VAR_{t-1}	$\overline{R}^2$	*RMSE*
BZ(1)	0.2902* (1.79)	−0.2220*** (3.87)				−13.505*** (3.56)	0.04088** (3.07)	−0.0239 (1.51)	0.25	1.09
RS(1,12)	1.1608 (1.38)	−0.0786*** (2.74)	0.8859*** (34.05)				0.0339*** (3.19)	−0.1328*** (6.40)	0.82	2.34
IN(1,2; 12)	0.2333 (0.59)	−0.7370*** (8.32)	−0.3041*** (2.69)		0.5476** (4.89)		0.0764** (2.14)	0.0211 (0.43)	0.57	4.02
CN(1,12)	−0.0141 (0.08)			−0.6112*** (11.47)	−0.2658*** (5.60)		0.0144 (1.35)	−0.0037 (0.19)	0.37	0.97
SA(1,2)	0.3710*** (2.67)	−0.4528*** (7.88)	−0.2247*** (3.16)				0.0568*** (3.18)	−0.0732*** (2.93)	0.20	2.92

Asian markets										
KO(1)	0.8547*** (4.45)	−0.1742*** (3.17)				−11.719*** (3.52)	0.0517*** (3.58)	−0.0433** (2.03)	0.25	2.09
JP(2,4)	0.3550* (1.78)			0.4252*** (5.91)	0.2499*** (3.58)	−20.613*** (32.18)	-0.0201 (1.49)	−0.0199 (0.76)	0.64	1.66
SG(1,2; 12)	0.6824 (1.27)	−0.6939*** (10.63)	−0.4317*** (7.08)		0.2178*** (3.38)		0.1866*** (3.16)	−0.0609 (0.67)	0.44	7.16
TH(2; 12)	0.8899 (0.95)	0.1767** (2.03)			0.4089*** (3.19)	−50.038*** (7.29)	0.2429*** (3.92)	−0.0781 (1.22)	0.39	3.96
TW	0.5178** (2.21)	−0.2457*** (5.83)				−13.196*** (12.42)	0.0552*** (2.65)	−0.0135 (0.43)	0.26	0.98

Note: This table reports the estimates of industrial output growth in relation to growth of market value and stock market risk. The numbers in the parenthesis of each country denote orders of AR or/and MA, respectively. The absolute values of *t*-statistics are in parentheses. *RMSE* is the root mean squared error calculated by 12-month out-of-sample predictions.*, **, and *** denote significance at the 10%, 5%, and 1% levels, respectively.

2007–2008 produced substantial economic losses in industrial production. In recent years, influenced by significant changes in stock return volatility triggered by financial market crises, the U.S. subprime crisis (2007–2009) and the European sovereign risk (2009–2011) crisis, investors are more sensitive to market risk involving extreme losses. As a result, much attention has been paid to *Value-at-risk* (*VaR*), which measures the maximum loss expected on a portfolio of assets over a specific time frame at a given level of probability. The probability of the loss that lies on the negative side of the return distribution, referred to as a "worst case" scenario for an investment, is usually called the downside risk (Embrechts, Klueppelberg, & Mikosch, 1997). There are good reasons for using downside risk in examining industrial production growth. First, downside risk is a useful tool for estimating the exposure to stock market risks. There is a long literature (Roy, 1952) on safety first for investors who minimize the probability of big losses. Highly risk-averse behavior under extreme market conditions is more revealing in downside risk. Second, banks and financial institutions need a good measure to quantify, reveal, and monitor the amount of risk for their portfolios should losses occur. VaR provides a useful tool for measuring downside risk, since it measures the maximum potential loss on a firm's trading portfolio if the lowest 1% (or 5%) quantile return occurs. Capital adequacy thus can be judged on the basis of the amount of this expected loss over a specific time frame (Bali, Demirtas, & Levy, 2009). Third, since VaR emphasizes negative and big breaks in stock returns, it provides insights into the interpretation of the economic sources of model instability (Pettenuzzo & Timmermann, 2011).

Recognizing the fact that most stock returns are likely to be skewed, peaked around the mode, display fat tails, shows that extreme events series occur much more frequently than predicted by the Gaussian distribution. It follows that the standard measures of symmetric market risk (e.g., variance or return square) appear to be irrelevant in approximating the maximum loss that a market expects to anticipate under highly volatile time periods or environments. As a result, we need a more precise measure to proxy for recent market risk. Following Bali et al. (2009), VaR series in this study for each market are defined as (−1) times the minimum market index return observed in the last month as of the end of each month t. Each month is assumed to have 22 stock returns.[10]

Table 7 reports regression results of industrial production growth predicted by stock returns and VaR. Evidence suggests that coefficients on stock returns are positive, however, the significance level has been reduced from 19 to 16 markets. Among them, Sweden, Brazil, Russia, and Japan are insignificant. Coefficients for other markets remain positive and significant. However, the risk factor measured by VaR appears to be more significantly negative for G6 markets and Sweden, Brazil, Russia, and South Africa, indicating that these markets are more sensitive to downside risk. The negative relation between downside risk and industrial production growth is consistent with the evidence

Table 7. Estimates of the Industrial Production Growth Predicted by Stock Returns and VaR.

Market	Constant	AR(p1)	AR(p2)	MA(q1)	MA(q2)	I(1)	$R_{m,t-1}$	VaR_{t-1}	$\overline{R}^2$	*RMSE*
G6-markets										
CA(3)	0.3636** (2.43)	0.2735*** (3.50)					0.0510*** (2.98)	−0.1694*** (4.29)	0.16	0.95
FR(1)	0.4780*** (3.16)	−0.3231*** (5.57)					0.02856* (1.67)	−0.2266*** (4.01)	0.14	1.03
GM(1,2)	0.5239*** (4.36)	−0.347*** (5.98)				-10.464*** (6.64)	0.0249** (2.00)	−0.1992*** (3.80)	0.24	1.31
IT(0,0,12)	0.1867 (1.30)				−0.4999*** (8.80)		0.0234* (1.93)	−0.1111** (2.01)	0.16	0.68
UK(1,10)	0.2591*** (3.92)			−0.4179*** (7.38)	−0.3204*** (5.54)		0.0321*** (3.18)	−0.1444*** (6.14)	0.18	0.53
US(2)	0.3934*** (3.78)		0.2738*** (4.29)			−3.091*** (3.53)	0.0214** (2.55)	−0.1038*** (3.17)	0.28	0.69
Scandinavian markets										
DK(1,2; 12)	0.3636 (1.38)	−0.5616*** (7.88)	−0.3698*** (5.20)		−0.3226*** (4.50)		0.0614* (1.88)	−0.1761 (1.54)	0.30	1.16
FN(1,12)	0.2996*** (1.18)	−0.1333*** (2.76)	−0.1956*** (3.57)				0.0312** (2.03)	−0.0461 (0.76)	0.06	0.91
NW(1,2)	0.1089*** (0.78)	−0.4469*** (6.84)	−0.2303*** (3.52)				0.0371** (2.40)	−0.0212 (0.42)	0.18	0.87
SD(1,4)	0.7291* (1.92)			−0.3222*** (5.32)			0. 0092 (0.21)	−0.2555** (2.15)	0.09	1.71
BRICS markets										
BZ(1)	0.3206*** (3.91)	−0.2602*** (4.63)				−12.967*** (4.09)	0.0006 (0.05)	−0.2249*** (4.09)	0.26	1.15
RS(1,12)	1.1156 (1.29)	−0.0861*** (2.83)	0.8778*** (32.04)				0.0088 (0.59)	−0.2240*** (4.76)	0.82	2.32
CN(1,12)	0.1243 (0.93)			−0.6678*** (13.42)	−0.2291*** (5.25)		0.0207* (1.86)	−0.0459 (1.16)	0.38	1.05
IN(1,2; 12)	0.4601 (1.02)	−0.7412*** (8.51)	−0.3072*** (2.78)		0.5621** (4.88)		0.0763** (2.14)	−0.0171 (0.12)	0.57	3.94
SA(1,2)	0.4532** (2.49)	−0.4860*** (8.24)	−0.2442*** (3.50)				0.0375*** (1.46)	−0.1807** (2.54)	0.19	2.91

Table 7. *(Continued)*

Market	Constant	AR(p1)	AR(p2)	MA(q1)	MA(q2)	I(1)	$R_{m,t-1}$	VaR_{t-1}	$\bar{R}^2$	*RMSE*
Asian markets										
KO(1,2)	0.6955** (2.36)	−0.1410** (2.56)	0.1037* (1.72)			−12.264** (2.14)	0.0405*** (2.86)	−0.0194 (0.28)	0.24	2.06
JP(2,4)	0.4068* (1.93)			0.4121*** (5.77)	0.2497*** (3.51)	−20.54*** (33.30)	-0.0037 (0.20)	−0.0594 (1.05)	0.64	1.63
SG(1,2; 12)	0.5407 (0.73)	−0.6922*** (10.60)	−0.4370*** (7.29)		0.2110*** (3.32)		0.1752*** (2.62)	−0.0314 (0.10)	0.44	7.14
TH(2; 12)	0.9899 (0.77)	0.1836** (2.19)			0.4036*** (8.13)	−50.433*** (7.65)	0.2399*** (3.64)	−0.1705 (0.46)	0.39	3.93
TW	0.7472* (1.81)	−0.2496*** (5.95)				−12.971** (12.20)	0.0555** (2.27)	−0.0964 (0.79)	0.27	0.97

Note: This table reports the estimates of industrial output growth in relation to stock return and stock market risk. The numbers in the parenthesis of each country denote orders of AR or/and MA, respectively. The absolute values of *t*-statistics are in parentheses. *RMSE* is the root mean squared error calculated by 12-month out-of-sample predictions.*, **, and *** denote significance at the 10%, 5%, and 1% levels, respectively.

reported by Schwert (1989) and Hamilton and Lin (1996). In their studies of the U.S. market, the correlations of stock return volatility and industrial production growth are higher in recessions. Our study suggests that even though the stock market can bring a positive effect to production growth, the adverse effect attributed to downside risk may cause a substantial setback on output growth. This finding offers a rational for policy makers to maintain financial market stability.

An interesting issue emerging from our empirical study is that although the stock returns (or growth of market value) and stock volatility, respectively, have incremental explanatory power relative to the time series model in the estimated sample period, however, we cannot yield a compatible power as we expected in the out-of-sample predictions. This can be seen by comparing the adjusted *R*-squares ($\overline{R}^2$) in Table 2 with those shown in Tables 3–7, where we find that the values of $\overline{R}^2$are higher by adding the argument of stock returns or/and stock market volatility. However, there are no comparable performances while evaluating the model by using root mean square errors (RMSE) from the out-of-sample predictions for the period of January 2014 to December 2014. One possible explanation is that, as noted by Rossi and Sekhposyan (2011), there is estimation uncertainty which makes models' in-sample fit not informative about their out-of-sample forecasting ability. Since the stock returns and variance are inherently more sensitive and venerable to random shocks, time-varying forecasting ability might be disturbed by changes in the parameters of the models as well as by unmodeled changes in the stochastic processes generating the variables. Given this stochastic nature, the forecasting ability in out-of-sample will be tied closely to the future stability of the stock market.[11]

7. FEEDBACK OF INDUSTRIAL PRODUCTION GROWTH TO STOCK MARKET

In his study of the U.S. market, Schwert (1989) examines several major economic factors and finds that the level of real economic activity is the most important indicator that determines the conditional variance of stock returns. Campbell, Kim, and Lettau (1993) also reach a similar conclusion. The causal direction in these studies is in contrast to the one we presented in previous sections. To address this issue, we conduct the Granger causality test, which examines the prediction efficiency of an incremental variable. Typically, the Granger causality test is designed for detecting the causal relations between stock returns ($R_{m,t}$) and industrial production growth (ΔY_t=IPG$_t$). The test involves the following two equations:

$$R_{m,t} = \alpha(s_t) + \sum_{s=1}^{n} \varphi_s R_{m,t-s} + \sum_{s=1}^{n} \lambda_s \Delta Y_{t-s} + \varepsilon_{1,t} \quad (2)$$

H_0: $\lambda_s = 0$ (IPG does not Granger cause R_m), H_1: $\lambda_s \neq 0$

$$\Delta Y_t = c_2 + \sum_{s=1}^{n} \delta_s \Delta Y_{t-s} + \sum_{s=1}^{n} \gamma_s R_{m,t-s} + \varepsilon_{2,t} \quad (3)$$

H_0: $\gamma_s = 0$ (R_m does not Granger cause IPG), H_1: $\gamma_s \neq 0$
where $R_{m,t}$ and ΔY_t denote stock returns and industrial production growth (*IPG*) at time *t*, respectively, $\varepsilon_t = (\varepsilon_{1,t}, \varepsilon_{2,t})'$ is a vector of error terms, and *s* is the optimal lag length obtained by using the minimum final prediction error (Hsiao, 1981). The null hypothesis that the *IPG* does not Granger cause R_m is equivalent to testing the restriction that $\lambda_s = 0$ for all *s* in Eq. (2); conversely, the null hypothesis that the R_m does not Granger cause *IPG* is equivalent to testing the restriction that $\gamma_s = 0$ for all *s* in Eq. (3). The restrictions are tested by using *F*-statistics. If the null $\lambda_s = 0$ is rejected and $\gamma_s = 0$ cannot be rejected, we conclude that industrial production growth causes stock returns (*IPG* $\rightarrow$ *Rm*); if the restriction $\lambda_s = 0$ cannot be rejected and $\gamma_s = 0$ is rejected, we conclude that stock returns cause industrial production (*Rm* $\rightarrow$ *IPG*); if both $\lambda_s = 0$ and $\gamma_s = 0$ are rejected, we conclude that there are two-way causations; if both $\lambda_s = 0$ and $\gamma_s = 0$ cannot be rejected, we conclude that there is no causation.

Table 8 reports the Granger causality test. The numbers in parentheses of the first column are the optimal lag in the specification of the Granger test; the *F*-values are the statistics testing the incremental efficiency after the autocorrelation lags are included. The evidence in Table 8 consistently concludes that the null hypothesis that $R_{m,t}$ does not Granger cause IPG_t is rejected for all the G6, Scandinavia, and Asian markets plus South Africa, indicating a unidirectional causation from stock returns to industrial production growth. However, for the BRICS group, four out of five markets cannot find evidence for rejection of the null, meaning no causation occurs in either direction.

We also conduct the Granger causality test for the relations between stock market risk (σ_m) and industrial production growth (*IPG*). The underlying idea is to test whether prior negative shocks measured by the value at risk, VaR, could cause a negative effect on the subsequent industrial production growth; conversely, we test whether the setback of industrial production growth leads to a negative shock on the stock market risk.

Table 9 reports the results. The evidence consistently shows the null hypothesis: σ_m does not Granger cause IPG, is strongly rejected for all G6, Asian, and South Africa markets, suggesting that the extreme downside risk in these stock markets will produce a negative impact on their industrial production growth. However, there is no significant evidence to show a reverse causation, except in

Table 8. Statistics of the Granger Test between Stock Returns and Industrial Production Growth.

Market	Null Hypothesis	*F*-Statistic	Causal Decision
Group 6 advanced market			
CA(1)	*IPG* does not Granger Cause *Rm*	0.427	—
	Rm does not Granger Cause *IPG*	9.159	*Rm* → *IPG*
FR(1)	*IPG* does not Granger Cause *Rm*	1.330	—
	Rm does not Granger Cause *IPG*	7.756	*Rm* → *IPG*
GM(3)	*IPG* does not Granger Cause *Rm*	1.621	—
	Rm does not Granger Cause *IPG*	3.772	*Rm* → *IPG*
IT(1)	*IPG* does not Granger Cause *Rm*	0.057	—
	Rm does not Granger Cause *IPG*	16.063	*Rm* → *IPG*
UK(6)	*IPG* does not Granger Cause *Rm*	1.995	—
	Rm does not Granger Cause *IPG*	2.392	*Rm* → *IPG*
US(1)	*IPG* does not Granger Cause *Rm*	1.205	
	Rm does not Granger Cause *IPG*	11.127	*Rm* → *IPG*
Scandinavian market			
DK(2)	*IPG* does not Granger Cause *Rm*	0.561	—
	Rm does not Granger Cause *IPG*	4.379	*Rm* → *IPG*
FN(2)	*IPG* does not Granger Cause *Rm*	2.579	—
	Rm does not Granger Cause *IPG*	5.479	*Rm* → *IPG*
NW(2)	*IPG* does not Granger Cause *Rm*	1.156	—
	Rm does not Granger Cause *IPG*	4.447	*Rm* → *IPG*
SD (2)	*IPG* does not Granger Cause *Rm*	0.546	—
	Rm does not Granger Cause *IPG*	2.561	*Rm* → *IPG*
BRICS			
BR(1)	*IPG* does not Granger Cause *Rm*	0.014	—
	Rm does not Granger Cause *IPG*	0.595	—
RS(1)	*IPG* does not Granger Cause *Rm*	0.065	—
	Rm does not Granger Cause *IPG*	2.345	—
ID(1)	*IPG* does not Granger Cause *Rm*	0.110	—
	Rm does not Granger *Cause* *IPG*	0.043	—
CN(1)	*IPG* does not Granger Cause *Rm*	1.848	—
	Rm does not Granger Cause *IPG*	0.177	—
SA(1)	*IPG* does not Granger Cause *Rm*	0.022	—
	Rm does not Granger Cause *IPG*	10.827	*Rm* → *IPG*

Table 8. (*Continued*)

Market	Null Hypothesis	F-Statistic	Causal Decision
Asian market	*IPG* does not Granger Cause *Rm*	0.427	—
	Rm does not Granger Cause *IPG*	9.159	*Rm* → *IPG*
KO(1)	*IPG* does not Granger Cause *Rm*	0.407	—
	Rm does not Granger Cause *IPG*	10.057	*Rm* → *IPG*
JP (3)	*IPG* does not Granger Cause *Rm*	1.794	—
	Rm does not Granger Cause *IPG*	3.340	*Rm* → *IPG*
SG(1)	*IPG* does not Granger Cause *Rm*	2.469	—
	Rm does not Granger Cause *IPG*	3.455	*Rm* → *IPG*
TH(1)	*IPG* does not Granger Cause *Rm*	0.663	—
	Rm does not Granger Cause *IPG*	14.012	*Rm* → *IPG*
TW(3)	*IPG* does not Granger Cause *Rm*	1.059	—
	Rm does not Granger Cause *IPG*	4.278	*Rm* → *IPG*

Note: The "→" denotes causal relationship. "—" denotes no causation. The test is at 5% level of significance.

the United States and South Africa. The test also concludes that there is no significant causation for the Scandinavian or BRICS countries (except SA), showing that these markets are lacking significant links between downside risk and output growth. Overall, this section decisively concludes that the stock market performance, whether it is measured by stock market returns or downside risk, presents a unidirectional causation from the stock market to industrial production growth, not the other way around. The exceptions are the United States and South Africa, where the United States displays strong bilateral causations between downside risk and industrial production growth. This means that any countries outside of the United States using the empirical evidence from the U. S. market to infer their stock risk and industrial production growth relation can be misleading.

8. CONCLUDING REMARKS

This study presents empirical evidence to investigate the effect of stock market performance on industrial production growth. The sample includes monthly observations for the period from January 1994 to December 2014. The data cover six advanced industrial markets: Canada, France, Germany, Italy, the

Table 9. Statistics of the Granger Test between Stock Return Volatility and Industrial Production Growth.

Market	Null Hypothesis	*F*-Statistic	Causal Decision
Group 6 advanced market			
CA(1)	*IPG* does not Granger Cause σ_m	1.497	—
	σ_m does not Granger Cause *IPG*	5.387	$\sigma_m \rightarrow IPG$
FR(1)	*IPG* does not Granger Cause σ_m	0.735	—
	σ_m does not Granger Cause *IPG*	18.94	$\sigma_m \rightarrow IPG$
GM(1)	*IPG* does not Granger Cause σ_m	2.489	—
	σ_m does not Granger Cause *IPG*	8.085	$\sigma_m \rightarrow IPG$
IT(1)	*IPG* does not Granger Cause σ_m	2.489	—
	σ_m does not Granger Cause *IPG*	8.085	$\sigma_m \rightarrow IPG$
UK(3)	*IPG* does not Granger Cause σ_m	2.489	—
	σ_m does not Granger Cause *IPG*	8.085	$\sigma_m \rightarrow IPG$
US(1)	*IPG* does not Granger Cause σ_m	15.65	$\sigma_m \leftarrow IPG$
	σ_m does not Granger Cause *IPG*	18.65	$\sigma_m \rightarrow IPG$
Scandinavian market			
DK(2)	*IPG* does not Granger Cause σ_m	1.308	—
	σ_m does not Granger Cause *IPG*	0.675	—
FN(1)	*IPG* does not Granger Cause σ_m	0.205	—
	σ_m does not Granger Cause *IPG*	2.846	—
NW(1)	*IPG* does not Granger Cause σ_m	0.619	—
	σ_m does not Granger Cause *IPG*	1.425	—
SD (1)	*IPG* does not Granger Cause σ_m	0.012	—
	σ_m does not Granger Cause *IPG*	5.782	$\sigma_m \rightarrow IPG$
BRICS			
BR(1)	*IPG* does not Granger Cause σ_m	0.866	—
	σ_m does not Granger Cause *IPG*	15.94	—
RS(1)	*IPG* does not Granger Cause σ_m	0.551	—
	σ_m does not Granger Cause *IPG*	1.142	—
ID(1)	*IPG* does not Granger Cause σ_m	0.375	—
	σ_m does not Granger Cause *IPG*	0.505	—
CN(1)	*IPG* does not Granger Cause σ_m	0.611	—
	σ_m does not Granger Cause *IPG*	0.003	—
SA(1)	*IPG* does not Granger Cause σ_m	4.324	$\sigma_m \leftarrow IPG$
	σ_m does not Granger Cause *IPG*	4.106	$\sigma_m \rightarrow IPG$

Table 9. *(Continued)*

Market	Null Hypothesis	*F*-Statistic	Causal Decision
Asian market			
KO(1)	*IPG* does not Granger Cause σ_m	0.002	—
	σ_m does not Granger Cause *IPG*	5.699	$\sigma_m \rightarrow IPG$
JP (3)	*IPG* does not Granger Cause σ_m	1.794	—
	σ_m does not Granger Cause *IPG*	5.989	$\sigma_m \rightarrow IPG$
SG(3)	*IPG* does not Granger Cause σ_m	1.742	—
	σ_m does not Granger Cause *IPG*	3.760	$\sigma_m \rightarrow IPG$
TH(2)	*IPG* does not Granger Cause σ_m	0.075	—
	σ_m does not Granger Cause *IPG*	2.900	$\sigma_m \rightarrow IPG$
TW(1)	*IPG* does not Granger Cause σ_m	0.673	—
	σ_m does not Granger Cause *IPG*	7.544	$\sigma_m \rightarrow IPG$

Note: The "→" denotes causal relationship,"—" denotes no causation. The test is at 5% level of significance.

United Kingdom, and the United States; four Scandinavian markets: Denmark, Norway, Finland, and Sweden; five large growing emerging markets (BRICS): Brazil, Russia, India, China, and South Africa; and five industrial/semi-industrial Asian markets: South Korea, Japan, Singapore, Thailand, and Taiwan. Our analysis provides important empirical evidence. First, all of the markets present some sort of time serial patterns in production growth, some of them exhibit seasonal regularity and unusual outliers. These time series patterns are revealing in the *R*-squares and the root mean squared errors are a very powerful property in describing the industrial output growth for the BRICS and Asian markets (including Japan) relative to that of the European markets (G6 advanced and Scandinavian markets). Without appropriate controls for the underlying time series patterns, the estimated coefficients of stock returns on industrial production growth can be misleading.

Second, by adding stock returns to the test equation, the stock return variable makes a marginal contribution in supporting the hypothesis that a rise of stock returns will help predict an increase in the industrial production growth. The evidence is consistent with the existing literature documented by Levine and Zervos (1998) and Arestis, Demetriades, and Luintel (2001). However, our finding is pertinent to describe the short-run industrial production growth.

Third, evidence suggests that U.S. industrial production growth has an incremental explanatory power for explaining the industrial output growth in all of the European advanced markets, showing some degree of comovements of the international business cycle. However, no comparable influence is found on the BRICS and Asian markets (expect Russia, South Africa, and Taiwan). This may stem from a lack of industrial ties between the United States and these markets.

Fourth, this study incorporates the volatility effect of the stock market into the test equation. Using implied volatility or stock variance as an argument conforms that stock market risk tends to produce uncertainty about the future cash flows that adversely effects industrial production. This negative effect appears to be stronger for more advanced markets.

Fifth, the negative effect is more profound when stock market risk is measured by value at risk (VaR). Again, its negative impact on industrial growth appears to be more severe for advanced markets as compared to the BRICS or Asian markets. This could result from the fact that industrial production in advanced markets is tied more closely to the equity finance, while the group in the less advanced markets relies more on the bank finance.

Finally, the Granger causality test finds a unidirectional causation running from stock returns to industrial growth. A similar finding of causation holds true for stock volatility; however, it is with a negative sign. Exceptions are the United States and South Africa. These two markets present bilateral causations between stock volatility and industrial production growth. In sum, the effect of stock volatility on industrial production is highly significant. Without incorporating this risk factor into the test equation of industrial production growth, studies tend to overestimate the stock market's contribution.

NOTES

1. Mauro (2000) provides a good review on the relationship between stock returns and economic activity.
2. Levine (2003) offers a survey on empirical studies of finance and growth. Levine, Loayza, and Beck (2000) employ data from 71 countries and find a very strong connection between the exogenous components of financial intermediary development and economic growth.
3. Arestis, Demetriades, and Luintel (2001) argue that using the logarithm of the stock market capitalization ratio (stock market value to GDP), the logarithms of the ratio of total stock market transactions to GDP (TRY) and the ratio of total stock market transactions to market valuation (TRMV) to measure stock market development yields similar empirical conclusions. However, compared with bank financing, stock market financing is relatively less powerful.
4. Since the series of industrial production index is given by the end of the month, so does the stock price index.
5. The comovement behavior of stock markets during the crisis periods can be found in Forbes and Rigobon (2002), Pericoli and Sbracoa (2003) and Chiang, Jeon, and Li (2007).
6. The Japanese Nikkei index (weekly data) hit a bottom of 7,173 points on March 6, 2009, and did not consistently rebound until November 9, 2012. The sample covers most of the time period of the depressed state of the Japanese economy.

7. The estimates for the coefficient on industrial growth are positive. Among them, all of the G6 countries and Scandinavian countries are statistically significant. For the emerging markets, only Russia, South Africa, and Taiwan are significant, indicating that the international business cycle hypothesis for industrial production gains more support for the advanced countries. This implies that a better coordination/cooperation between the two countries helps to promote economic stability and industrial growth.

8. The data of implied volatility for various markets are obtained from a data basis of the *Bloomberg*.

9. Additional tests are conducted by adding credit growth and money supply growth in the test equation. However, we cannot find any consistent supportive evidence owing to either statistically insignificant or even a wrong sign. For these reasons, we did not report the results. The estimated results are available upon request.

10. Bali et al. (2009) briefly summarize different measures of estimating downside risk. Detailed elaborations can be found in Jorion (2006).

11. A thorough discussion is referred to in Rossi and Sekhposyan (2011), where they propose a technique involving a decomposition of the existing measures of forecasting performance into components and test for assessing the significance of each component.

REFERENCES

Arestis, P., Demetriades, P. O., & Luintel, K. B. (2001). Financial development and economic growth: The role of stock markets. *Journal of Money, Credit and Banking*, *33*, 16–41.

Atje, R., & Jovanovic, B. (1993). Stocks markets and development. *European Economic Review*, *37*, 632–640.

Baker, M., & Wurgler, J. (2006). Investor sentiment and the cross-section of stock returns. *Journal of Finance*, *61*, 1645–1680.

Bali, T. G., & Engle, R. F. (2010). The intertemporal capital asset pricing model with dynamic conditional correlations. *Journal of Monetary Economics*, *57*, 377–390.

Bali, T. G., Demirtas, K., & Levy, H. (2009). Is there an intertemporal relation between downside risk and expected returns? *Journal of Financial and Quantitative Analysis*, *44*, 883–909.

Barro, R. J. (1990). The stock market and investment. *The Review of Financial Studies*, *3*, 115–131.

Campbell, J. Y., Kim, S., & Lettau, M. (1993). *Dispersion and volatility in stock returns: An empirical investigation*. Working paper, Princeton University.

Chen, N. (1991). Financial investment opportunities and the macroeconomy. *Journal of Finance*, *46*, 529–554.

Chiang, T. C., Jeon, B. N., & Li, H. (2007). Dynamic correlation analysis of financial contagion: Evidence from Asian markets. *Journal of International Money and Finance*, *26*, 1206–1228.

Choi, J. J., Hauser, S., & Kopecky, K. (1999). Does the stock market predict real activity? Time series evidence from the G-7 countries. *Journal of Banking and Finance*, *23*, 1771–1792.

Embrechts, P., Klueppelberg, C., & Mikosch, T.(1997). *Modeling extremal events for insurance and finance*. Berlin: Springer Verlag.

Fama, E. F. (1990). Stock returns, expected returns, and real activity. *Journal of Finance*, *45*, 1089–1108.

Forbes, K., & Rigobon, R. (2002). No contagion, only interdependence: Measuring stock market comovements. *Journal of Finance*, *57*, 2223–2261.

French, K. R., Schwert, G. W., & Stambaugh, R. F. (1987). Expected stock returns and volatility. *Journal of Financial Economics*, *19*, 3–29.

Greenspan, A. (2000). Technology and the economy. Before the Economic Club of New York. New York, NY, January 13, Federal Reserve Board of Governor. http://www.federalreserve.gov/boarddocs/speeches/2000/200001132.htm

Gurley, J., & Shaw, E. (1997). Financial aspects of economic development. *American Economic Review*, *41*, 139–146.

Hamilton, J., & Lin, G. (1996). Stock market volatility and the business cycle. *Journal of Applied Econometrics*, *11*, 573–593.

Harris, R. (1997). Stock markets and development: A reassessment. *European Economic Review*, *41*, 139–146.

Hoshi, T., & Kashyap, A. K. (2004). Japan's financial crisis and economic stagnation. *Journal of Economic Perspectives*, *18*, 3–26.

Hsiao, C. (1981). Autoregressive modeling and money-income causality detection. *Journal of Monetary Economics*, *7*, 85–106.

Johansen, S. (1991). Estimation and hypothesis testing of cointegration vectors in Gaussian vector autoregressive models. *Econometrica*, *59*, 1551–1580.

Jorion, P. (2006). *Value at Risk: The New Benchmark for Managing Financial Risk* (3rd ed.), New York, N.Y.: McGraw Hill.

Levine, R. (1997). Financial development and economic growth: Views and agenda. *Journal of Economic Literature*, *35*(2), 688–726.

Levine, R. (2003). More on finance and growth: More finance, more growth? Review, Federal Reserve Bank of St. Louis, July/August, 31–46.

Levine, R., Loayza, N., & Beck, T. (2000). Financial intermediation and growth: Causality and causes. *Journal of Monetary Economics*, *46*, 31–77.

Levine, R., & Zervos, S. (1998). Stock markets, banks, and economic growth. *American Economic Review*, *88*, 537–558.

Masih, A., & Masih, R. (1999). Are Asian market fluctuations due mainly to intra-regional contagion effects? Evidence based on Asian emerging stock markets. *Pacific-Basin Finance Journal*, *7*, 251–282.

Mauro, P. (2000). Stock returns and output growth in Emerging and advanced economies. IMF working paper, WP/00/89.

Pericoli, M., & Sbracia, M. (2003). A primer on financial contagion. *Journal of Economic Surveys*, *17*, 571–608.

Pettenuzzo, D., & Timmermann, A. (2011). Predictability of stock returns and asset allocation under structural breaks. *Journal of Econometrics*, *164*, 60–78.

Rajan, R. G., & Zingales, L. (1998). Financial dependence and growth. *American Economic Review*, *88*, 559–586.

Rossi, B., & Sekhposyan, T. (2011). Understanding models' forecasting performance. *Journal of Econometrics*, *164*, 158–172.

Roy, A. D. (1952). Safety first and the holding of assets. *Econometrica*, *20*, 431–449.

Schwert, G. W. (1989). Business cycles, financial crises, and stock volatility. *Carnegie Rochester Conference Series on Policy*, *31*, 83–126.

Schwert, G. W. (1990). Why does stock market volatility change over time? *Journal of Finance*, *44*, 1115–1153.

Stock, J. H., & Watson, M. W. (1998). Business cycle fluctuations in U.S. macroeconomic time series. NBER Working Paper No. 6528. National Bureau of Economic Research: Cambridge, MA.

APPENDIX A. ESTIMATES OF STOCK MARKET PERFORMANCE WITH THE US INDUSTRIAL PRODUCTION GROWTH

Table A1. Estimates of Stock Returns and Time Series Model of Industrial Production Growth.

Market	Constant	AR(p1)	AR(p2)	MA(q1)	MA(q2)	I(1)	$R_{m,t-1}$	$\Delta y_{US,t-1}$	$\bar{R}^2$	*RMSE*
G6-markets										
CA(3)	−0.0188 (0.20)	0.1917** (2.43)					0.0387** (2.09)	0.3582*** (3.92)	0.14	1.09
FR(1)	−0.1544** (2.59)	−0.4065*** (8.34)					0.03678** (2.37)	0.6436*** (8.83)	0.24	1.13
GM(1,2)	0.0904* (1.67)	−0.4456*** (7.14)	−0.198*** (2.87)			−8.841*** (4.33)	0.0316** (2.51)	0.5171*** (3.03)	0.28	1.48
IT(2,3; 12)	−0.138*** (3.16)				−0.4835*** (7.99)		0.0305*** (3.68)	0.3325*** (3.68)	0.19	0.55
UK(1,10)	−0.081*** (3.84)			−0.479*** (8.47)	−0.2318*** (3.71)		0.0224** (2.58)	0.4139** (8.11)	0.22	0.67
US(2,3)	0.1632 (1.63)	0.2877*** (5.01)	0.2614*** (3.77)			−2.2072*** (6.29)	0.0204*** (2.70)	0.1118*** (3.68)	0.33	0.70
Scandinavia markets										
DK(1,2;12)	−0.0452 (0.54)	−0.5832*** (-7.28)	−0.3880*** (5.27)		−0.1898** (1.96)		0.0524* (1.72)	0.6354*** (3.40)	0.32	1.22
FN(1,12)	0.0384 (0.38)	−0.2143*** (3.45)	−0.1853*** (3.28)				0.0267* (1.81)	0.5911*** (3.91)	0.10	1.05
NW(1,2)	0.0155 (0.24)	−0.4670*** (9.43)	−0.2462*** (3.62)				0.0286* (1.86)	0.2711* (2.20)	0.21	1.13
SD(4;1)	−0.0437 (0.37)	−0.1434** (1.99)		−0.4643*** (7.12)			0. 0495* (1.70)	0.945*** (4.56)	0.19	1.95
BRICS markets										
BZ(1)	0.1521 (1.34)	−0.2345*** (4.42)				−13.982*** (3.51)	0.0232** (2.31)	0.0876 (0.58)	0.22	1.09
RS(1,12)	0.1626 (0.20)	−0.0896*** (2.70)	0.8697*** (30.94)				0.0245** (2.03)	0.4678** (2.44)	0.79	2.13
IN(1,2;12)	0.4021 (1.49)	−0.7411*** (8.58)	−0.3068*** (2.79)		0.5558** (5.08)		0.0739** (2.19)	0.1783 (0.66)	0.57	3.95
CN(1,12)	−0.0426 (1.58)			−0.6399*** (11.07)	−0.2767*** (6.09)		0.0265** (2.50)	0.1243 (1.24)	0.38	1.06
SA(1,2)	−0.0397 (0.57)	−0.5315*** (8.99)	−0.2950*** (4.16)				0.0522*** (2.66)	0.5619*** (4.82)	0.25	2.92

Asian markets									
KO(1,2)	0.605*** (4.02)	−0.1386** (2.42)	0.1065* (1.80)			−12.0023** (2.43)	0.0404*** (2.93)	0.1278 (0.61)	0.24	2.05
JP(2,4)	0.2663* (1.80)			0.4064*** (5.63)	0.2497*** (3.39)	−20.559*** (33.39)	0.0029 (0.17)	0.0069 (0.04)	0.64	1.62
SG(1,2;12)	0.4763 (1.43)	−0.6923*** (10.64)	−0.4368*** (7.30)		0.2125*** (3.26)		0.1643** (2.55)	0.3005 (0.66)	0.44	7.06
TH(2;12)	0.5063 (0.55)	0.1836** (2.22)			0.4019*** (8.11)	−51.109*** (8.01)	0.2403*** (4.03)	0.0865 (0.09)	0.39	3.80
TW	0.431*** (3.22)	−0.248*** (6.05)				−13.005*** (12.77)	0.0856** (2.49)	0.2334** (2.08)	0.27	1.01

Note: This table reports the industrial output growth influenced by its own time series pattern, seasonal factor, the lagged stock return, and the lagged US output growth. The numbers in the parenthesis of each market denote orders of AR or/and MA, respectively. The absolute values of t-statistics are in parentheses. *RMSE* is the root mean squared error calculated by 12-month out-of-sample predictions. *,**, and *** denote significance at the 10%, 5%, and 1% levels, respectively.

Table A2. Robustness Test of Stock Market Value Growth on Industrial Production Growth.

Market	Constant	AR(p1)	AR(p2)	MA(q1)	MA(q2)	I(1)	ΔMV_{t-1}	$\Delta y_{US,t-1}$	$\bar{R}^2$	*RMSE*
G6-markets										
CA(3)	−0.0278 (0.30)	0.1661** (2.06)					0.0303* (1.77)	0.3868*** (367)	0.15	1.16
FR(1)	−0.163*** (2.71)	−0.4039*** (8.89)					0.0352** (2.36)	0.6438*** (8.29)	0.24	1.09
GM(1,2)	0.0781 (1.49)	−0.4440*** (7.36)	−0.1991*** (2.94)			−8.9568*** (4.53)	0.0305** (2.35)	0.4925*** (6.17)	0.27	1.47
IT(2,3;12)	−0.142*** (3.09)				−0.4582*** (7.12)		0.0193* (1.84)	0.3423*** (3.85)	0.18	0.69
UK(1,10)	−0.062** (2.60)			−0.4359*** (8.66)	−0.1747*** (3.29)		0.0222*** (2.83)	0.4045** (8.99)	0.22	0.68
US(2,3)	0.1584 (1.58)	0.2865*** (4.96)	0.2631*** (3.79)			−2.2007*** (6.24)	0.0204*** (2.70)	0.1082** (2.32)	0.33	0.71
Scandinavia markets										
DK(1,2;12)	−0.0633 (0.98)	−0.5389*** (8.38)	−0.4058** (2.13)		−0.2435*** (3.66)		0.0492** (2.13)	0.6756*** (4.08)	0.32	1.16
FN(1,12)	0.0164 (0.22)	−0.3647*** (4.61)	−0.1009* (1.65)				0.0244* (1.83)	0.8622*** (7.51)	0.08	1.18
NW(1,2)	−0.0034 (0.05)	−0.4620*** (9.36)	−0.2381*** (3.69)				0.0257* (1.83)	0.301*** (2.86)	0.21	0.99
SD(4;1)	−0.0465 (0.40)	−0.1304* (1.82)		−0.4602*** (7.05)			0. 0495* (1.70)	0.945*** (4.56)	0.19	1.95
BRICS markets										
BZ(1)	0.1196 (1.07)	−0.2114*** (3.61)				−13.475*** (3.44)	0.00452*** (3.44)	0.0004 (0.01)	0.24	1.04
RS(1,12)	0.1365 (0.17)	−0.0893*** (2.70)	0.8702*** (30.44)				0.0268** (2.61)	0.4736** (2.58)	0.79	2.13
IN(1,2;12)	0.3647 (1.32)	−0.7282*** (8.40)	−0.2968*** (2.66)		0.5479** (5.04)		0.0705* (1.86)	0.1659 (0.59)	0.57	4.03
CN(1,12)	−0.051*** (4.21)			−0.7399*** (39.46)	−0.2471*** (16.00)		0.0111** (2.58)	0.0902** (2.38)	0.37	1.02
SA(1,2)	−0.0284 (0.39)	−0.5118*** (8.68)	−0.2735*** (3.80)				0.0468* (1.81)	0.9350*** (4.33)	0.19	1.89

Asian markets										
KO(1,2)	0.581*** (3.85)	−0.1390** (2.43)	0.1008* (1.70)			−12.009** (2.27)	0.0389*** (2.80)	0.1222 (0.56)	0.24	2.04
JP(2,4)	0.2689* (1.81)			0.4249*** (5.94)	0.2472*** (3.39)	−20.510*** (32.45)	−0.0197 (1.43)	0.0108 (0.06)	0.64	1.64
SG(1,2;12)	0.3687 (1.05)	−0.6897*** (10.46)	−0.4310*** (7.13)		0.2182*** (3.35)		0.1732*** (2.73)	0.3183 (0.70)	0.44	7.06
TH(2;12)	0.3595 (0.69)	0.1889** (2.30)			0.4007*** (7.93)	−51.124*** (8.21)	0.2442*** (4.16)	0.0420 (0.04)	0.38	3.83
TW	0.403*** (2.98)	−0.2443*** (5.96)				−13.082*** (12.78)	0.0522** (2.46)	0.2453** (2.16)	0.27	1.01

Note: This table reports evidence of the time series patterns of each industrial output growth, the lagged market value change, and the lagged US industrial output growth on domestic industrial output growth. The numbers in the parenthesis of each country denote orders of AR or/and MA, respectively. The absolute values of t-statistics are in parentheses. *RMSE* is the root mean squared error calculated by 12-month out-of-sample predictions.*,**, and *** denote significance at the 10%, 5%, and 1% levels, respectively.

BANK CAPITAL STANDARDS AND SUBORDINATED DEBT PRICES

Jin-Ping Lee, Edward M.H. Lin, Min-Teh Yu and Yang Zhao

ABSTRACT

This study develops a multi-period structural model to value bank subordinated debt (subdebt) under different regulatory policies. The model provides a complete framework for analyzing how various factors, such as credit and interest rate risks, bank characteristics, and regulatory policies, affect subdebt prices and yield spreads. It finds that the implementation of Prompt Corrective Action (PCA) will raise subdebt prices and lower subdebt spreads, while capital forbearance will have the opposite effects. Also, subdebt spreads are less sensitive to bank risk when PCA is imposed than when capital forbearance occurs. The results of the paper suggest that enhancing market discipline through giving subdebt investors more rights to force timely reorganization of weak banks will reduce the subdebt spreads required by investors.

Keywords: Bank subordinated debt; capital standard; prompt corrective action; capital forbearance; moral hazard

JEL classifications: G20; G28; G21

Advances in Pacific Basin Business, Economics and Finance, Volume 5, 77–99
Copyright © 2017 by Emerald Publishing Limited
All rights of reproduction in any form reserved
ISSN: 2514-4650/doi:10.1108/S2514-465020170000001004

1. INTRODUCTION

Market discipline has been proposed by the Basel Capital Accord as one of the three pillars for promoting the safety and soundness of banks.[1] One way to enforce market discipline is to require banks to issue subordinated debt (subdebt, hereafter). Subdebt holders get paid only after all senior creditors receive full payments. The junior status of subdebt makes it more risk-sensitive than bank deposits and other uninsured debt instruments. Proponents of subdebt suggest that it will increase market discipline because riskier banks have to pay higher interest rates on the subdebt. Also, subdebt prices provide supplementary information to supervisors for determining when to take Prompt Correction Action (PCA).

Subdebt has become an important funding source for banks, especially for large ones. According to Basel Committee on Banking Supervision (2003), subdebt issuance has been widespread in the largest European countries, Japan, and the United States over the period 1990–2002. The report shows that the subdebt of banks is on average about 3.63 of risk-weighted assets (RWA). When considering only the 50 largest issuers, the average share of subdebt is 5.33 of RWA. It also shows that the vast majority of issues have an initial term to maturity of between 5 and 15 years with an average of 11.4 years. Pennacchi (2010) states that for the 20 largest domestic bank holding companies in the United States, subdebt was equal to 2.23 of total assets in June 2007. Flannery (2016) reports that for the 14 traditional bank holding companies in the Supervisory Capital Assessment Program, the ratio of subordinated debentures to total risky assets was 4.893 on average at the end of 2008.

There have been a lot of papers empirically investigating the market discipline effects of subdebt. Most papers find that subdebt spreads increase as a bank's risk rises, which implies the spreads can signal a bank's risk profile. For example, Flannery and Sorescu (1996) and Goyal (2005) find that bank risk measures are correlated with subdebt yields. Black, Correa, Huang, and Zhou (2016) propose that Credit Default Swap (CDS) spreads on subdebt is a crude proxy to estimate banks' risk-neutral Probability of Default (PD). Chen, Robinson, and Siems (2004) show that subdebt holdings are sensitive to risk measures and can enhance market discipline on a bank. DeYoung, Flannery, Lang, and Sorescu (2001) support that mandatory subdebt issuance generates helpful market signals about a bank's financial condition to regulators. Evanoff and Wall (2001, 2002) provide evidence that subdebt spreads are better risk measures than the risk-based capital adequacy ratios in terms of predicting supervisory examination ratings, and they suggest subdebt spreads can become an integral part of the regulatory process to trigger PCA. Sironi (2003) also finds that the spreads are sensitive to bank risk for European banks. Nguyen (2013) provides evidence that subdebt has a mitigating effect on bank risk taking.

Others find little support for the presence of market discipline in the subdebt market. For example, Avery, Belton, and Goldberg (1988), and Gorton and Santomero (1990) offer no relation between balance sheet risks and subdebt pricing. Osterberg and Thomson (1991) show that a mandatory subdebt requirement may reduce the deposit insurance subsidy, but cannot fully reflect the risk exposure. Levonian (2001) uses a standard contingent-claim model to show that subdebt has no advantages over equity, either as a form of bank capital or as a source of market discipline. Hanweck and Spellman (2003) find that lengthy forbearance expectations prevent subdebt spreads from being effective as signals for insolvency detection and deposit insurance pricing. Krishnan, Ritchken, and Thomson (2005) also find that changes in credit spreads of subdebts do not consistently reflect changes in bank risk. Miller, Olson, and Yeager (2015) show that subdebt spreads are extremely poor predictors of bank distress because the spreads are distorted by too-big-to-fail subsidies.

To study the disciplining role of subdebt, it is important to understand how subdebt spreads are determined. The aim of this paper is to establish a multi-period structural model to value subdebt. In the model, the bank's asset return due to credit risk, interest rate, and deposits are all stochastic. The bank's risk-taking behavior under regulatory forbearance is also considered. The bank that issues subdebt is audited by regulators at the end of each period, and it will be reorganized if the ratio of its total assets to its total debts falls short of the cut-off value pre-specified by regulators. This model allows us to examine how regulatory policies (PCA and capital forbearance) and the bank's risk-taking problem affect the spreads of subdebt.

To our knowledge, not many studies in the literature develop valuation models for subdebt and examine how subdebt spreads are determined. Gorton and Santomero (1990), Schellhorn and Spellman (1996), Fan, Haubrich, Ritchken, and Thomson (2003), and Pennacchi (2010) are all that we can find. These papers can be considered as single-period models in nature that cannot sufficiently explore the interplay among the enforcement of capital standards, regulatory forbearance, and the potential risk-taking behavior of a bank, which can significantly affect subdebt yields.

The rest of the paper is organized as follows. The following section presents the model. Section 3 states the payoffs of subdebt under various scenarios. Section 4 introduces the methodology for the numerical analysis and specifies parameter values. Section 5 reports and discusses the results of the numerical analysis. The conclusion follows in Section 6.

2. A MODEL FOR PRICING SUBDEBT

Our model extends Merton's (1974) structural approach to value subdebt. The structural approach allows us to link the valuation of financial claims to economic fundamentals of the issuing firm such as the firm's assets and capital structure, and default in a structural model is endogenously determined.[2]

Since subdebt is junior to deposits in claim payment and can be treated as capital for regulatory purposes, this study considers it as a special category of equity for ease of presentation. Subdebts are assumed to be zero-coupon bonds and are fully paid if the bank is solvent at maturity; otherwise, shareholders default, and the subdebt holders absorb the loss and become the residual claimants. In order to value subdebt, we first specify the asset and interest rate dynamics and then present the corresponding payoffs for subdebt holders under different scenarios.

2.1. Asset Dynamics

In the literature, the typical way to model a bank's asset value dynamic is to assume a lognormal diffusion process.[3] This modeling approach fails to explicitly take into account the impact of stochastic interest rates on the asset's value. This shortcoming is particularly important for modeling a bank's assets, because it is common for banks to hold a large portion of interest-rate-sensitive assets. In order to measure the effect of the interest rate risk on valuing subdebt, we thus follow Duan, Moreau, and Sealey (1995) to describe the bank's asset value as consisting of two risk components – interest rate and credit risks. The term "credit risk" refers to all risks that are orthogonal to the interest rate risk. Specifically, the value of a bank's assets is governed by the following process:

$$dA_t = (\mu_A A_t + \eta D_t)dt + \phi_A A_t dr_t + \sigma_A A_t dW_{A,t} \tag{1}$$

where A_t is the value of the bank's total assets at time t; μ_A is the instantaneous drift due to the credit risk; η is the net rate of increment in deposits; D_t denotes the total deposits of the bank at time t; r_t is the instantaneous interest rate at time t; ϕ_A is the instantaneous interest rate elasticity of the bank's assets; and $W_{A,t}$ is the Wiener process that represents credit risk.

The instantaneous interest rate is assumed to follow the squared-root process of Cox, Ingersoll, and Ross (1985). This setting avoids the negative interest rate that may appear in Vasicek's model (1977). The instantaneous interest rate process can be written as:

$$dr_t = \kappa(m - r_t)dt + \upsilon\sqrt{r_t}\, dZ_t \tag{2}$$

where κ is the mean-reverting force measurement; m is the long-run mean of the interest rate;υ is the volatility parameter for the interest rate; and Z_t is a Wiener process independent of $W_{A,t}$. Combining (1) and (2), the asset dynamics can be described as follows:

$$dA_t = [(\mu_A + \phi_A \kappa m - \phi_A \kappa r_t)A_t + \eta D_t]dt + \phi_A A_t \upsilon \sqrt{r_t} dZ_t + \sigma_A A_t dW_{A,t} \tag{3}$$

For derivative pricing, it is standard to use the device of risk-neutralization. The dynamics for the interest rate process under the risk-neutral pricing measure, denoted by Q, can be written as:

$$dr_t = \kappa^*(m^* - r_t)dt + \upsilon\sqrt{r_t}\, dZ_t^* \tag{4}$$

where κ^*, m^*, and Z_t^* are defined as:

$$\kappa^* = \kappa + \lambda$$
$$m^* = \frac{\kappa m}{\kappa + \lambda}$$
$$Z_t^* = dZ_t + \frac{\lambda\sqrt{r_t}}{\upsilon} dt$$

The term λ can be interpreted as the market price of interest rate risk and is a constant under Cox et al. (1985); Z_t^* is a Wiener process under Q. Thus, the bank's asset dynamics can be risk-neutralized to become:

$$dA_t = (r_A A_t + \eta D_t)dt + \phi_A A_t \upsilon \sqrt{r_t}\, dZ_t^* + \sigma_A A_t\, dW_{A,t}^* \tag{5}$$

where $W_{A,t}^*$ is defined as:

$$dW_{A,t}^* = dW_{A,t} + \left(\frac{\mu_A - r_t}{\sigma_A}\right)dt$$

Here, $W_{A,t}^*$ is a Wiener process under Q and is independent of Z_t^*. The above expression states that the bank's assets, excluding the net increment in new deposits, are expected to earn a risk-free rate of interest in a risk-neutral world.

2.2. Deposit Dynamics

We assume that all the deposits are covered by deposit insurance. Also, we follow Pennacchi (1987) to assume that the bank keeps the average time to maturity of its total deposits constant over time and deposits earn a rate of return equal to that of a risk-free discount bond with the same maturity. This is the same as assuming that the variance of the return on deposits is constant over time and equals the variance of the return on a risk-free discount bond with the same maturity. The assumption that the bank's average deposit maturity stays constant over time attempts to model the fact that most banks have a fairly constant turnover of deposits. This specification can be used to analyze how a bank's interest rate risk exposure affects subdebt prices.

In the case where the instantaneous interest rate follows the framework of Cox et al. (1985), the bank deposit dynamics, under the risk-neutral measure Q, can be described as follows:

$$dD_t = (r_A(1 - \lambda B(T_D)) + \eta)D_t\, dt - B(T_D)D_t \upsilon \sqrt{r_t}\, dZ_t^* \tag{6}$$

$$B(T_D) = \frac{2(e^{\gamma T_D} - 1)}{(\gamma + \kappa + \lambda)(e^{\gamma T_D} - 1) + 2\gamma}$$

$$\gamma = [(\kappa + \lambda)^2 + 2\upsilon^2]^{\frac{1}{2}}$$

where D_t denotes the value of total interest-bearing bank deposits at time t; r_t is the instantaneous interest rate; η is the net rate of new deposits coming to the bank; T_D denotes the average deposit maturity; and λ, κ, and υ are parameters of interest rate dynamics that have been described in the previous section.

3. PRICING SUBDEBT

Once the risk-neutralized process of the asset, interest rate, and deposit dynamics are known, one can value a subdebt by discounting the expected values of its payoffs in the risk-neutral world. This section specifies the subdebt's payoffs under alternative scenarios. It first presents the one-period case, in which bank is audited by regulators only when the debt matures. It then looks into the multi-period case where periodic audits take place and banks may pay dividends, be reorganized, or take more risk before the subdebt matures.

3.1. One-Period Subdebt

Consider the case where the bank is audited only at the time when the subdebt matures. Our model thus can be simplified and the debt can be valued in a one-period case like Gorton and Santomero (1990), Schellhorn and Spellman (1996), Levonian (2001), and Pennacchi (2010). In this case, bank capital regulation is irrelevant to the valuation of subdebt. The payoffs of the subdebt (PO) at maturity (T_{SD}) are as follows:

$$PO_{T_{SD}} = \begin{cases} SD & \text{if } A_{T_{SD}} > SD + D_{T_{SD}} \\ A_{T_{SD}} - D_{T_{SD}} & \text{if } SD + D_{T_{SD}} \geq A_{T_{SD}} > D_{T_{SD}} \\ 0 & \text{otherwise} \end{cases} \tag{7}$$

where SD is the face amount of subdebt.

We can apply the risk-neutral approach of Harrison and Pliska (1981) to price the subdebt with the payoffs specified in Eq. (7). More specifically, under the risk-neutralized pricing measure Q, the value of subdebt on the issuing date (i.e., time 0) can be written as follows:

$$P_{SD}(0) = \frac{1}{SD} E^* \left[e^{-\int_0^{T_{SD}} r_s ds} PO_{T_{SD}} \right] \tag{8}$$

where $P_{SD}(0)$ is the subdebt price at time 0 and E^* denotes expectations in a risk-neutral world.

3.2. *Multi-Period Subdebt*

As mentioned in Section 1, the average maturity of the subdebts in the sample of Basel Committee on Banking Supervision (2003) is over 11 years. The financial characteristics of the issuing bank may change substantially during such a long period of time. The issuing bank may fail and be reorganized, suffer a loss, and become weakly capitalized, or withdraw the profits by paying dividends. When valuing a bank's long-term subdebt, it is necessary to consider these potential changes. This study follows the framework of Lee and Yu (2002), Duan and Yu (2005), and Chang and Yu (2017) to model the interactions between capital standards and bank failure resolutions. It values the subdebt taking into account the impacts of PCA, forbearance, the bank's risk-taking behavior, and other characteristics of the bank and subdebt.[4]

3.2.1. Capital Standards and Reorganization

In the model, when a bank is audited, its assets will be adjusted under two circumstances. First, if the ratio of the bank's assets to its deposits is lower than k at the time of the audit, the bank is taken over and reorganized by the regulatory authority, where k is pre-specified by the regulatory authority. For a reorganized bank, its assets are adjusted so that the after-adjustment asset value equals q_l times its deposits. The parameter q_l reflects the capital standard set by the regulatory authority on the minimum amount of capital a bank should keep. According to the Basel Accord, a bank's total capital should be no less than 83 of its total risk-adjusted assets. This capital standard is equivalent to requiring that q_l =1.087. The k is the threshold value of bank capital that will trigger the reorganization of the bank. We assume that, depending on the regulatory authority's policy, k is equal to either q_l or p, where p is a parameter representing the degree of capital forbearance and its value is between 0 and 1. Because $q_l > 1 > p$, the bank is reorganized before it exhausts its capital when k equals q_l, and is allowed to keep operating with a negative equity value when k equals p. We will say that the regulatory authority imposes PCA if k is equal to p, and that it allows capital forbearance to occur if k is equal to p.[5] In the case of capital forbearance, an insolvent bank will not face intervention as long as it remains within the capital forbearance range. Once a bank breaks the forbearance threshold level at the time of the audit, it becomes intolerable and is reorganized immediately. Although the threshold value for triggering bank reorganization in the forbearance case is lower than that in the PCA case, the adjustment of bank assets will, if it takes place, fully restore the asset to the level required by the capital standard. It is clear that when capital forbearance occurs, the bank's asset value must have already breached the capital standard.

Second, at the time of the audit, if a bank is so profitable that the ratio of its assets to its deposits exceeds (q_u), its equity holders withdraw excessive capital by paying themselves dividends until the bank's asset value equals q_u times its deposits, where q_u is a parameter with $q_u > q_l$. In the model,q_u represents the dollar amount of capital that the equity holders of a profitable bank has to leave with the bank for each dollar's asset. We assume $q_u > q_l$ because subdebts may contain protective covenants that prohibit the bank from paying excessive dividends to equity holders.

Given the asset value adjustment mechanism stated above, the bank's asset value at the time of audit after the adjustments are made can be written as:

$$A_{t_i} = \begin{cases} q_u D_{t_i} & \text{if } A^*_{t_i} > q_u D_{t_i} \\ A^*_{t_i} & \text{if } q_u D_{t_i} \geq A^*_{t_i} \geq k D_{t_i} \\ q_l D_{t_i} & \text{otherwise} \end{cases} \tag{9}$$

where

$$A^*_{t_i} = A_{t_{i-1}} + \int_{t_{i-1}}^{t_i} (\mu_A A_s + \eta D_s) ds + \int_{t_{i-1}}^{t_i} \phi_A A_s \, dr_s + \int_{t_{i-1}}^{t_i} \sigma_A A_s) dW_{A,s}$$

By (9), q_u and q_l respectively set the upper and lower bounds for the bank's asset value.

3.2.2. Forbearance and Moral Hazard

We assume that the bank's risk-taking behavior (or moral hazard) is governed by the bank's asset value. If the new asset value is greater than the level required by the capital standard, then the bank functions normally and its asset risk characteristics remain unchanged. If the bank's asset value breaches the capital standard (that is, becomes lower than q_l times the bank's deposits) but is tolerated by the regulatory authority, then moral hazard behavior occurs – that is, the bank will take more risk in its assets. One simple way to model this effect is to force an increase in the standard deviation of a bank's asset value. Specifically, this action increases the volatility of its assets by $100w\%$. This adjustment process can be described as follows:

$$A_{t_i} = \begin{cases} (1+\omega)\sigma_A(t_i - 1) & \text{if } q_l D_{t_i} \geq A^*_{t_i} \geq \rho D_{t_i} \\ \sigma_A(t_i) & \text{otherwise} \end{cases} \tag{10}$$

where $\sigma_A(\cdot)$ is indexed by time to reflect its time-varying nature. This completes the specification of our analytical framework. We will carry out a numerical analysis to study the model's implications in the next section.

4. NUMERICAL ANALYSIS

This section estimates the subdebt prices and yield spreads in alternative scenarios using the Monte Carlo method. The simulation is conducted on a weekly basis with 50,000 sample paths. We follow Duan and Yu (2005) to perform the simulation, and the details of our procedures are described in the appendix.

4.1. Parameter Values

As a reference point for the numerical analysis, a base set of parameters is established and summarized in Table 1. Deviations from the base values provide insights into how changes in the characteristics of asset-liability structure, debt structure, interest rate process, net growth rate of deposits, moral hazard behavior, and regulatory responses affect subdebt values. The maturities of subdebt are set from 1 to 20 years, and the auditing is assumed to take place at the end of every year. The parameters q_u and q_l are set to be 1.3 and 1.087, respectively. The asset value will be reset periodically at the auditing times to reflect that the bank will not hold more capital than the amount that is deemed sufficient. Recall that the parameter value of q_l is consistent with the 83 capital standard established under the Basel Accord. To study the impact of a looser capital standard, we also consider the case that $q_l = 1.05$, 1.03, and 1. The initial capital positions of the asset-liability (A/D) ratios of 1.1, 1.15, 1.2, and 1.25 are examined. These asset-liability ratios fall inside the range established by q_u and q_l. We do not consider the cases where the bank's capital positions are higher

Table 1. Parameters Definition and Base Values.

Asset Parameters		Values
A	Bank's assets	
A/D	Asset-Deposit ratios	1.1 ~ 1.25
μ_A	Drift due to credit risk	
φ	Interest rate elasticity of asset	0, -3, -5
σ_A	Volatility of credit risk	5%
W_A	Weiner process for credit shock	
Deposit Parameters		
D	Total interest-bearing deposits	
η	Net growth rate of deposits	0%
T_D	Average deposit maturity	0, 3, 5
Interest Rate Parameters		
r	Initial instantaneous interest rate	5%
k	Magnitude of mean-reverting force	0.2
m	Long-run mean of interest rate	5%
υ	Volatility of interest rate	10%
λ	Market price of interest rate risk	-0.01
Z	Weiner process for interest rate shock	
Other Parameters		
SD	Face amount of subdebt	
E	Bank's equity	
q_u	Ceiling trigger for withdrawing excess capital	1.3
q_l	Capital standard	1.087
ρ	Capital forbearance level	0.97
ω	Moral hazard intensity	0.2

than 1.25. Limiting the analysis to these cases amounts to considering only weakly capitalized banks.

The parameter governing net annual growth rate on deposits, i.e.,η, is set at 0% and -3% and 3% which will be used for comparison. This study models the fact that the bank has a fairly constant turnover of deposits and assumes the bank's average deposit maturities (T_D) are 0, 3, and 5 years. The assumption lets the bank keep the interest rate elasticity of its deposits ($-B(T_D)$) at 0, -2.12, and -2.85, respectively, over time. The interest rate elasticity of the bank's assets, i.e.,ϕ_A, are set at 0, -3, and -5. The difference in the interest rate elasticity of the bank's assets and deposits measures the degree of mismatch in the interest rate risk exposure of assets and deposits.

The volatility of the asset return that is caused by the credit risk is set to be 5%.[6] The ratios of the face amount of subdebt to the bank's equity value are set at 10%, and other values will be used to measure the effect of debt structure on subdebt valuation. The initial spot interest rate and the long-run interest rate are both set at 5%. The mean-reverting force is set to be 0.2, while the volatility of the interest rate is set at 10%. The market price of interest rate risk is set at −0.01. The term structure parameters are all within the ranges typically used in the previous literature.[7]

5. RESULTS AND DISCUSSIONS

Tables 2 and 3 report the subdebt prices and yield spreads under alternative combinations of the interest rate elasticity of bank assets and the average deposit maturity. Panels A, B, and C represent the estimates in the case where the combination of the interest rate elasticity of the bank's asset and the average deposit maturity, i.e., (ϕ_A, T_D), is set to be (−5, 3), (−3, 5), and (0, 0), respectively. For the case of (0, 0), we eliminate the interest rate risk on both sides of the bank's balance sheet.

5.1. Subdebt Prices under PCA

Table 2 reports the estimates in which regulators audit the bank annually and reorganize the bank whenever the bank's capital level breaches the capital standard,q_l= 1.087. The study assumes that undercapitalized banks will be reorganized through either the purchase-and-assumption or the government-assisted merger method as in the U.S. experience.[8] Table 2 shows that the subdebt prices (yield spreads) increase (decrease) with the bank's initial capital position, and the changes of prices and spreads are more sensitive for low capital positions and short maturities than for high capital positions and long maturities.

Comparing the corresponding cells in Panels A, B, and C, the subdebt price in Panel A is the lowest and the yield spread is the highest among the three panels. This is because the degree of mismatch in the interest rate risk exposure of the bank's assets and deposits in the case of Panel A is the largest among the three cases. On the contrary, in case of no interest rate risk (i.e., Panel C), or a perfect match of interest rate elasticity in assets and deposits, the subdebt price is the highest and the yield spread is the lowest. It indicates that good interest rate risk management that eliminates the interest-rate-risk mismatch of assets and deposits can raise the subdebt price and lower the yield spread required by investors.

We also measure the effect of the capital standard on subdebt prices and yield spreads. Figs. 1 and 2 show the debt prices and yield spreads while setting the capital standard (q_l) to be 1.087, 1.05, and 1. According to Figs. 1 and 2, the higher the capital standard, the higher the subdebt prices and the lower the yield spreads. This result is intuitive: the higher is the capital standard, the less

Table 2. Subdebt Prices (Yield Spreads) under Prompt Corrective Actions.

Maturity	A/D = 1.1	1.15	1.2	1.25
Panel A: $(\varphi_A, T_D) = (-5, 3)$				
1	0.9078	0.9437	0.9490	0.9494
	(4.4752)	(0.5994)	(0.0416)	(0.0010)
3	0.7592	0.8125	0.8370	0.8486
	(3.9792)	(1.7187)	(0.7287)	(0.2697)
5	0.6465	0.6977	0.7284	0.7484
	(3.5179)	(1.9927)	(1.1311)	(0.5917)
10	0.4660	0.4851	0.5123	0.5324
	(2.8669)	(2.0271)	(1.4821)	(1.0974)
20	0.2231	0.2420	0.2560	0.2663
	(2.2925)	(1.8872)	(1.6059)	(1.4088)
Panel B: $(\varphi_A, T_D) = (-3, 5)$				
1	0.9089	0.9449	0.9490	0.9494
	(4.3546)	(0.4760)	(0.0386)	(0.0010)
3	0.7630	0.8160	0.8384	0.8493
	(3.8127)	(1.5759)	(0.6711)	(0.2404)
5	0.6510	0.7030	0.7318	0.7487
	(3.3804)	(1.8411)	(1.0385)	(0.5820)
10	0.4532	0.4932	0.5189	0.5367
	(2.7071)	(1.8609)	(1.3537)	(1.0153)
20	0.2293	0.2492	0.2629	0.2718
	(2.1563)	(1.7400)	(1.4718)	(1.3067)
Panel C: $(\varphi_A, T_D) = (0, 0)$				
1	0.9133	0.9450	0.9491	0.9494
	(3.8774)	(0.4656)	(0.0275)	(0.0001)
3	0.7721	0.8212	0.8411	0.8501
	(3.4185)	(1.3608)	(0.5631)	(0.2091)
5	0.6647	0.7119	0.7384	0.7533
	(2.9624)	(1.5895)	(0.8611)	(0.4595)
10	0.4703	0.5074	0.5303	0.5466
	(2.3372)	(1.5783)	(1.1361)	(0.8343)
20	0.2449	0.2647	0.2762	0.2849
	(1.8282)	(1.4383)	(1.2255)	(1.0713)

Notes: This table reports the prices (in per dollar of face value) and yield spreads (in percentage) of subdebt for alternative combinations of interest rate elasticities of bank's assets and deposits (φ_A, T_D) while fixing the capital standard (q_l) at 1.087, and other parameter values as in Table 1.
A/D represents the initial asset-liability or capital position of the bank.
All estimates are computed using 50,000 simulation runs.

Table 3. Subdebt Prices (Yield Spreads) under Capital Forbearance.

Maturity	A/D = 1.1	1.15	1.2	1.25
Panel A: $(\varphi_A, T_D) = (-5, 3)$				
1	0.9055	0.9434	0.9490	0.9493
	(4.7350)	(0.6323)	(0.0369)	(0.0023)
3	0.6661	0.7683	0.8227	0.8450
	(8.3408)	(3.5802)	(1.3012)	(0.4101)
5	0.5020	0.6138	0.6896	0.7276
	(8.5790)	(4.5566)	(2.2281)	(1.1545)
10	0.2640	0.3521	0.4251	0.4702
	(8.1100)	(5.2319)	(3.3468)	(2.3397)
20	0.0793	0.1167	0.1487	0.1724
	(7.4672)	(5.5318)	(4.3216)	(3.5822)
Panel B: $(\varphi_A, T_D) = (-3, 5)$				
1	0.9099	0.9442	0.9491	0.9494
	(4.2506)	(0.5486)	(0.0257)	(0.0001)
3	0.6751	0.7760	0.8248	0.8457
	(7.8908)	(3.2482)	(1.2152)	(0.3822)
5	0.5123	0.6259	0.6935	0.7326
	(8.1730)	(4.1661)	(2.1140)	(1.0184)
10	0.2789	0.3672	0.4365	0.4793
	(7.5637)	(4.8115)	(3.0831)	(2.1481)
20	0.0882	0.1282	0.1617	0.1840
	(6.9358)	(5.0652)	(3.9026)	(3.2574)
Panel C: $(\varphi_A, T_D) = (0, 0)$				
1	0.9133	0.9447	0.9491	0.9494
	(3.8763)	(0.4939)	(0.0305)	(0.0001)
3	0.6922	0.7839	0.8304	0.8476
	(7.0586)	(2.9131)	(0.9910)	(0.3087)
5	0.5388	0.6398	0.7063	0.7400
	(7.1637)	(3.7269)	(1.7482)	(0.8172)
10	0.3098	0.3929	0.4605	0.5001
	(6.5098)	(4.1345)	(2.5471)	(1.7232)
20	0.1086	0.1504	0.1852	0.2070
	(5.8911)	(4.2642)	(3.2228)	(2.6681)

Notes: This table reports the prices (in per dollar of face value) and yield spreads (in percentage) of subdebt for alternative combinations of interest rate elasticities of bank's assets and deposits (φ_A, T_D) while fixing capital forbearance at $(\rho=)$ 0.97, moral hazard at $(\omega =)$ 0.2, and other parameter values as in Table 1.
A/D represents the initial asset-liability or capital position of the bank.
All estimates are computed using 50,000 simulation runs.

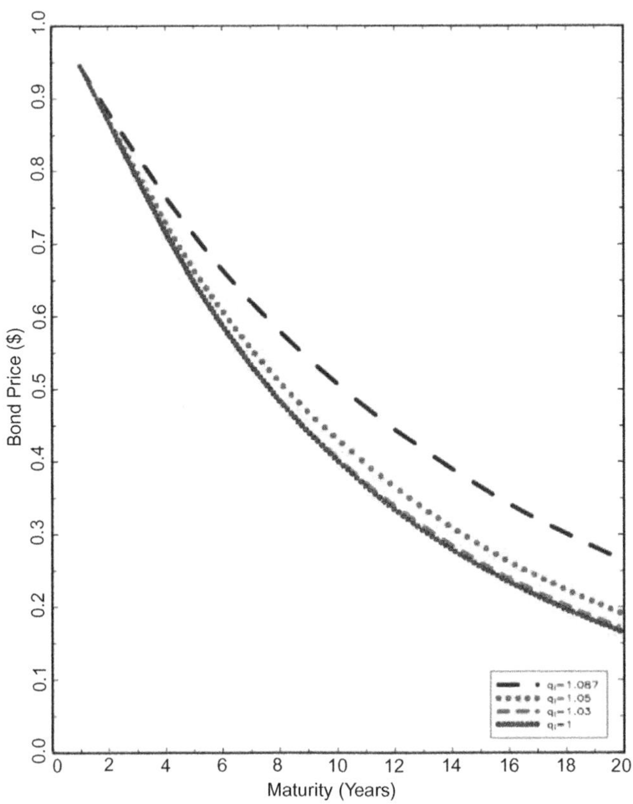

Fig. 1. Bond Prices for Alternative Capital Standards without Capital Forbearance and Moral Hazard (η, ϕ_A, T_D) = (0,0,0), A/D = 1.15, SD/E = 0.1, q_1 = 1, 1.03, 1.05, 1.087.

likely that subdebt holders will suffer losses when the bank is reorganized. Both figures show that the magnitude of the decrement in debt prices and the increment in yield spreads are more substantial at the shorter ends of maturities than those at the longer ends of maturities.

5.2. Subdebt Prices under Forbearance

Table 3 reports the subdebt prices and yield spreads when forbearance and moral hazard behavior are possible. The moral hazard behavior refers to

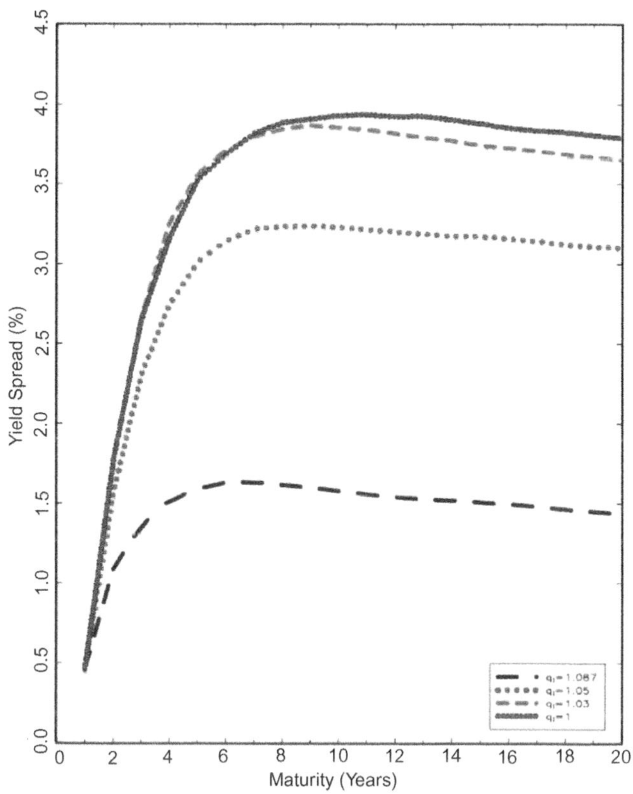

Fig. 2. Yield Spreads for Alternative Capital Standards without Capital Forbearance and Moral Hazard (η, ϕ_A, T_D) = (0,0,0), A/D = 1.15, SD/E = 0.1, q_1 = 1, 1.03, 1.05, 1.087.

forbearance-induced risk-taking activities. This study assumes that troubled banks will increase their portfolio risk by 20% (i.e.,ω= 0.2) when their asset values fall below their deposit liabilities. Table 3 shows that the possibility of forbearance and moral hazard drives the subdebt prices lower and raises the yield spreads, because forbearance and moral hazard increase the default risk of subdebt. It also shows that the effect of the forbearance is more significant for banks with low initial capital and subdebts with long term to maturity. As in Table 2, Table 3 also shows that the interest rate risk lowers the prices of subdebt and widens the yield spreads. The impact is more profound in the presence of capital forbearance than PCA.

Figs. 3 and 4 illustrate the effects of capital standards across maturity on the subdebt prices using the case that (η, ϕ_A, T_D) = (0,0,0) and A/D =1.15. The

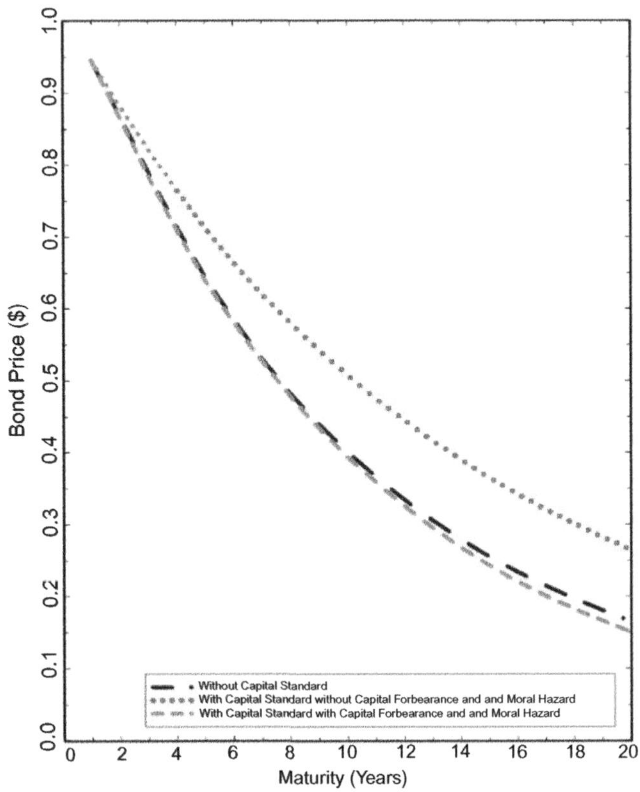

Fig. 3. Bond Prices for Alternative Conditions $q1 = 1.087$ $(\eta, \phi_A, T_D) = (0,0,0)$ $A/D = 1.15$, $SD/E = 0.1$.

upper (lower) curve of Fig. 3 (4) represents the subdebt price (yield spread) when regulators enforce the prompt corrective actions at a minimum capital standard of 1.087, respectively. The lower (upper) two curves of subdebt prices (yield spreads) in Fig. 3 (4) allow for capital forbearance and no capital standard. Note that capital forbearance decreases (increases) the debt price (yield spread) across all maturities and its effect increases with the time to maturity. For instance, a 20-year subdebt may command a higher yield spread of about 13 basis points than a 10-year bond.

The results that a higher capital standard in the PCA case raises subdebt prices and reduces subdebt yield spreads and that capital forbearance reduces subdebt prices and raises subdebt spreads have policy implications. They imply that enhancing market discipline in the bank industry may reduce the subdebt spreads required by investors. To preserve the value of their investments, subdebt holders have strong incentives to push the regulatory authority to handle

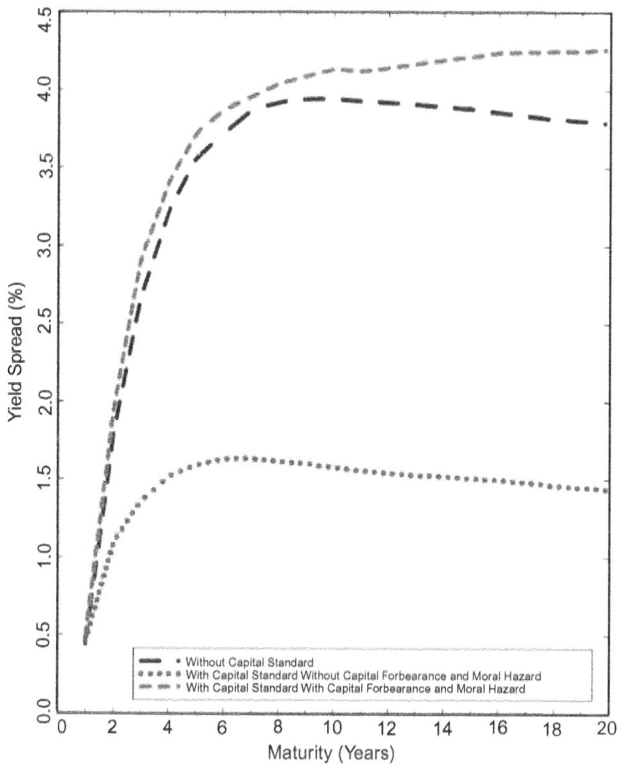

Fig. 4. Yield Spreads for Alternative Conditions $q_1 =$ 1.087 $(\eta, \phi_A, T_D) = (0,0,0)$ A/D = 1.15, SD/E = 0.1.

problem banks earlier.[9] Therefore, one way to enhance market discipline of banks is to give subdebt investors the rights to force timely reorganization of banks whose asset values breach the capital standard. The rights can be written in the covenants of subdebt. This will increase k (that is,q_l in the PCA case and ρ in the forbearance case) in our model. As illustrated by our results, this arrangement will not only reduce the risk-taking problem by banks, but also make issuing subdebt less costly for banks because subdebt spreads become lower when k increases.

5.3. Debt Structure and Deposit Growth

This study also simulates how the growth rate of deposits (η) and the subdebt-to-equity ratio affect the yield spreads.[10] For a subdebt of 10-year maturity under capital regulation of PCA, Table 4 shows that a positive deposit growth

Table 4. Yield Spreads under Alternative Combinations of Deposit Growth Rates and Debt Structure.

SD/E	$\eta = -3\%$	-2%	-1%	0%	1%	2%	3%
Panel A: $A/D = 1.1$							
0.05	9.6219	6.1596	3.7478	2.1283	1.1810	0.6281	0.3401
0.1	10.1918	6.6073	4.0052	2.3410	1.3062	0.7130	0.3659
0.2	11.4817	7.4986	4.6838	2.7500	1.5737	0.8472	0.4595
0.3	12.8107	8.4119	5.3458	3.2199	1.8746	1.0197	0.5641
0.4	14.1677	9.3812	6.0571	3.7110	2.1699	1.2649	0.7054
0.5	15.3735	10.3425	6.7922	4.1988	2.5924	1.4961	0.8712
Panel B: $A/D = 1.15$							
0.05	7.9549	4.7520	2.7430	1.4104	0.7053	0.3162	0.1463
0.1	8.5439	5.2279	2.9786	1.5824	0.7941	0.3763	0.1640
0.2	9.9903	6.1536	3.6575	2.0013	1.0257	0.5040	0.2241
0.3	11.4387	7.2975	4.3159	2.4377	1.2980	0.6377	0.3290
0.4	12.8986	8.2619	5.1245	2.9626	1.6060	0.8644	0.1454
0.5	14.1239	9.4014	5.8271	3.5254	1.9722	1.0607	0.5619
Panel C: $A/D = 1.2$							
0.05	6.4148	3.6459	1.9796	0.9707	0.4525	0.1873	0.0767
0.1	7.1837	4.1133	2.2377	1.1224	0.5205	0.2286	0.0883
0.2	8.6059	5.0924	2.8517	1.4612	0.7094	0.3175	0.1335
0.3	10.0918	6.2442	3.5169	1.8847	0.9551	0.4405	0.1971
0.4	11.4043	7.1906	4.2365	2.3744	1.2213	0.6027	0.2762
0.5	12.6948	8.0932	4.9518	2.8482	1.5273	0.7647	0.3865
Panel D: $A/D = 1.25$							
0.05	5.1860	2.9107	1.4904	0.7062	0.2998	0.1114	0.0444
0.1	5.5197	3.2939	1.6974	0.8140	0.3603	0.1450	0.0536
0.2	7.3235	4.2955	2.2965	1.1307	0.5234	0.2177	0.0913
0.3	8.7429	5.2442	2.9496	1.4903	0.7078	0.3069	0.1313
0.4	10.0595	6.2264	3.5669	1.9239	0.9554	0.4548	0.1982
0.5	11.3012	7.0403	4.1423	2.3289	1.2102	0.5934	0.2731

Notes: This table reports the yield spreads (in percentage) of subdebt for alternative combinations of the bank's capital position (A/D), deposit growth rates (η), and the ratio of the amount of subdebt issued to equity (SD/E) while fixing the capital standard (q_l) at 1.087 and no interest rate risk.
A/D represents the initial asset-liability or capital position of the bank.
All estimates are computed using 50,000 simulation runs.

rate reduces the yield spreads substantially. Since deposit growth increases a bank's total assets and improves its capital position for the same amount of subdebt, default risk is reduced. For instance, in our simulation case, the yield spread decreases by 785 basis points when the deposit growth rate increases from -3% to 0%.

More subdebts which are issued relatively to the same amount of assets raise the default risk of subdebts. Thus, Table 4 shows that the yield spread decreases with the deposit growth rate and increases with the ratio of subdebt to equity. The impact on the yield spread due to changes in the deposit growth rate dominates that of the subdebt-to-equity ratio.

Fig. 5 further illustrates the effect of the deposit growth rate on the yield spreads of subdebts when capital forbearance is possible. It indicates that when the bank has a large positive deposit growth rate, say 3%, the yield spread is very small and the maturity of the subdebt does not matter. However, when the bank has a large negative growth of deposits, it enhances the impact of forbearance and the yield spread becomes substantial and rises sharply for short maturities.

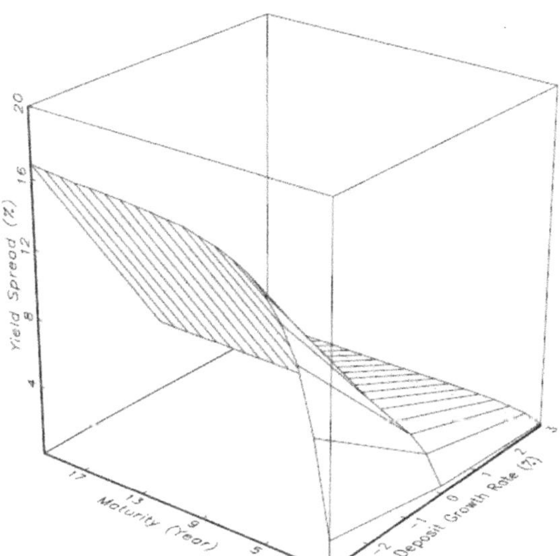

Fig. 5. Yield Spreads for Alternative Combinations of Net Deposit Growth Rates and Maturities with Forbearance and Moral Hazard A/D = 1.15 $(\phi_A, T_D) = (0,0)$, $q_1 = 1.087$.

6. CONCLUSION

This study develops a structural model to price subdebt by taking into account capital standards, regulatory responses, a bank's risk-taking behavior, interest rate risk, and other financial characteristics of the bank and the subdebt. The numerical estimates show how subdebt prices and spreads are determined by the model variables and capital regulations. The results also measure the impacts of the model's key variables on subdebt prices and spreads and show how the relationship between bank risk and subdebt yield spreads may be affected.

Our valuation model has interesting policy implications. It points out that subdebt prices and yield spreads are different under different regulatory policies. The PCA drives up subdebt prices and reduces yield spreads, while forbearance has the reverse effect. Moreover, the higher the capital standard is under PCA, the higher the prices of subdebt will be.

This subdebt valuation model also provides useful implications for empirical studies of the relationship between bank risk and subdebt yield spread since it can perform a comprehensive comparative static analysis for all variables in the model. Empirical studies based on a simplified risk-spread relationship could mislead the inferences and implications. The impact of how each variable affects the prices and spreads may be different in magnitude and direction under PCA and under forbearance. For example, the impact of the subdebt-to-equity ratio is more substantial in the presence of capital forbearance than for PCA. Also, the risk-spread relation becomes less significant under the PCA case than under the forbearance case. In addition, the significance and sign of the risk-spread relation may also change when one of the model variables, such as the net deposit growth rate, is not controlled.

This multi-period valuation model for subdebt offers a useful platform for future research on both theoretical and empirical dimensions. The model can be extended to incorporate other types of regulatory interventions and bank behavior in order to derive theoretical debt prices, and the exact relation between a variable of interest and the subdebt prices measured from the model serves as a benchmark for empirical studies.

NOTES

1. See Basel Committee on Banking Supervision (2004).

2. This contrasts to the reduced-form approach that models the default/recovery probability directly as an exogenous process in valuing risky debt. Examples include Jarrow and Turnbull (1995), Duffie and Singleton (1999), Fan et al. (2003), etc.

3. For example, see Merton (1974), Brenann and Schwartz (1980), and Ronn and Verma (1986).

4. The incentive problems among regulators, insured banks, and other market participants are well documented in Kane (1995).

5. Kane (2001) explains why capital forbearance is pervasive in the regulated financial industry.
6. The value is consistent with the 5.33 level found by Mehran and Rosenberg (2008).
7. See the estimates reported in Table 2A of Duan and Simonato (1999).
8. Bartholomew (1991) reports data for 1,730 thrifts that were resolved during the period from 1980 to 1990. Of these 1,730 thrifts, 1478 institutions (or 85.43) were resolved through these two forms of reorganization.
9. This point is also discussed in Federal Reserve System (2000).
10. We have simulated scenarios under alternative debt structures, capital positions, and term structure of interest rates, but for ease of presentation we report only part of the results either in tables or in figures. All other results are available upon request from the authors.

REFERENCES

Avery, R. B., Belton, T. M., & Goldberg, M. (1988). Market discipline in regulating bank risk: New evidence from the capital markets. *Journal of Money, Credit, and Banking*, *20*, 597–610.

Bartholomew, P. (1991). The cost of forbearance during the thrift crisis, U.S. Congressional Budget Offices Staff Memorandum, Washington DC.

Basel Committee on Banking Supervision. (2003). Markets for bank subordinated debt and equity in Basel Committee Member Countries, Working Paper No. 12.

Basel Committee on Banking Supervision. (2004). International convergence of capital measurement and capital standards. A revised framework.

Black, L., Correa, R., Huang, X., & Zhou, H. (2016). The systemic risk of European banks during the financial and sovereign debt crises. *Journal of Banking & Finance*, *63*, 107–125.

Brenann, M. J., & Schwartz, E. S. (1980). Analyzing convertible bonds. *Journal of Financial and Quantitative Analysis*, *15*, 907–929.

Chang, C. C., & Yu, M.-T. (2017). Bank contingent capital: Valuation and the role of market discipline. *Journal of Financial Services Research*, doi:10.1007/s10693-016-0259-9

Chen, A. H., Robinson, K. J., & Siems, T. F. (2004). The wealth effects from a subordinated debt policy: Evidence from passage of the Gramm-Leach-Bliley Act. *Review of Financial Economics*, *13*, 103–119.

Cox, J., Ingersoll, J., & Ross, S. (1985). The term structure of interest rates. *Econometrica*, *53*, 363–384.

DeYoung, R., Flannery, M. J., Lang, W. W., & Sorescu, S. (2001). The information content of bank exam ratings and subordinated debt prices. *Journal of Money, Credit and Banking*, *33*, 900–925.

Duan, J., & Simonato, J. (1999). Estimating and testing exponential-affine term structure models by Kalman Filter. *Review of Quantitative Finance and Accounting*, *13*, 111–135.

Duan, J.-C., Moreau, A., & Sealey, C. W. (1995) Deposit insurance and bank interest rate risk: Pricing and regulatory implications. *Journal of Banking and Finance*, *19*, 1091–1108.

Duffie, D., & Singleton, K. (1999). Modeling term structures of defaultable bonds. *Review of Financial Studies*, *12*, 687–720.

Duan, J.-C., & Yu, M.-T. (2005). Fair insurance guaranty premia in the presence of risk-based capital regulations, stochastic interest rate and catastrophe risk. *Journal of Banking and Finance*, *29*, 2435–2454.

Evanoff, D. D., & Wall, L. D. (2001). SND yield spreads as bank risk measures. *Journal of Financial Services Research*, *19*, 121–146.

Evanoff, D. D., & Wall, L. D. (2002). Measures of the riskiness of banking organizations: Subordinated debt yields, risk-based capital, and examination ratings. *Journal of Banking and Finance*, *26*, 989–1009.

Fan, R., Haubrich, J. G., Ritchken, P., & Thomson, J. B. (2003). Getting the most out of a mandatory subordinated debt requirement. *Journal of Financial Services Research*, *24*, 149–179.

Federal Reserve System. (2000). The feasibility and desirability of mandatory subordinated debt, report.

Flannery, M. J. (2016). Stabilizing large financial institutions with contingent capital certificates. *Quarterly Journal of Finance*, *6*(02).

Flannery, M. J., & Sorescu, S. M. (1996). Evidence of bank market discipline in subordinated debenture yields. *Journal of Finance*, *51*, 1347–1377.

Gorton, G., & Santomero, A. M. (1990). Market discipline and bank subordinated debt. *Journal of Money, Credit and Banking*, *22*, 119–128.

Goyal, V. K. (2005). Market discipline of bank risk: Evidence from subordinated debt contracts. *Journal of Financial Intermediation*, *14*, 318–350.

Hanweck, G. A., & Spellman, L. J. (2003). Forbearance expectation and the subordinated debt signal of bank insolvency, paper presented at FMA Annual Meeting, October 10, 2003.

Harrison, J. M., & Pliska, S. R. (1981). Martingales and stochastic integrals in the theory of continuous trading. *Stochastic processes and their applications*, *11*, 215–260.

Jarrow, R. A., & Turnbull, S. (1995). Pricing derivatives on financial securities subject to default risk. *Journal of Finance*, *50*, 53–86.

Kane, E. J. (1995). Three paradigms for the role of capitalization requirements in insured financial institutions. *Journal of Banking and Finance*, *19*, 431–459.

Kane, E. J. (2001). Dynamic inconsistency of capital forbearance: Long-run vs. short-run effects of too-big-to-fail policymaking. *Pacific Basin Finance Journal*, *9*, 281–300.

Krishnan, C. N. V., Ritchken, P. H., & Thomson, J. B. (2005). Monitoring and controlling bank risk: Does risky debt help. *Journal of Finance*, *60*, 343–378.

Lee, J.-P., & Yu, M.-T. (2002). Pricing default-risky CAT bonds with moral hazard and basis risk. *Journal of Risk and Insurance*, *69*, 25–44.

Levonian, M. (2001). Subordinated debt and the quality of market discipline in banking, Federal Reserve Bank of San Francisco.

Mehran, H., & Rosenberg, J. (2008). *The effect of CEO stock options on. Bank investment choice, borrowing, and capital*, Federal Reserve Bank of New York, Staff Reports no. 305.

Merton, R. (1974). On the pricing of corporate debt: The risk structure of interest rates. *Journal of Finance*, *29*(May).

Miller, S., Olson, E., & Yeager, T. J. (2015). The relative contributions of equity and subordinated debt signals as predictors of bank distress during the financial crisis. *Journal of Financial Stability*, *16*, 118–137.

Nguyen, T. (2013). The disciplinary effect of subordinated debt on bank risk taking. *Journal of Empirical Finance*, *23*, 117–141.

Osterberg, W. P., & Thomson, J. B. (1991). The effect of subordinated debt and surety bonds on the cost of capital for banks and the value of federal deposit insurance. *Journal of Banking and Finance*, *15*, 939–953.

Pennacchi, G. (1987). Alternative forms of deposit insurance: Pricing and bank incentive issues. *Journal of Banking and Finance*, *11*, 291–312.

Pennacchi, G. (2010). A structural model of contingent bank capital, working paper.

Ronn, E., & Verma, A. (1986). Pricing risk-adjusted deposit insurance: An option-based model. *Journal of Finance*, *41*, 871–895.

Schellhorn, C. D., & Spellman, L. J. (1996). Subordinated debt prices and forward looking estimates of bank asset volatility. *Journal of Economics and Business*, *48*, 337–347.

Sironi, A. (2003). Testing for market discipline in the European banking industry: Evidence from subordinated debt issues. *Journal of Money, Credit and Banking*, *35*(3), 443–472.

Vasicek, O. A. (1977). An equilibrium characterization of the term structure. *Journal of Financial Economics*, *5*, 177–188.

APPENDIX: SIMULATION METHOD AND PROCEDURES

Applying Ito's lemma to the logarithm of the bank's assets value, Equation (5) becomes the following system:

$$\ln(A_t) = \left(r_t A_t + \eta \frac{D_t}{A_t} - \frac{1}{2}\phi_A^2 \upsilon^2 r_t - \frac{1}{2}\sigma_A^2\right)dt + \phi_A \upsilon \sqrt{r_t} dZ_t^* + \sigma_A dW_{A,t}^* \qquad \text{(A1)}$$

Its solution, for any $\tau \geq 0$, is:

$$A_{t+\tau} = A_t \exp\left(\sigma_A(W_{A,t+\tau}^* - W_{A,t}^*) - \frac{1}{2}\sigma_A^2 \tau\right)$$

$$+\exp\left[\eta \int_t^{t+\tau} \frac{D_s}{A_s} ds + \left(1 - \frac{1}{2}\phi_A^2 \upsilon^2\right) \int_t^{t+\tau} r_s\, ds + \phi_A \upsilon \int_t^{t+\tau} \sqrt{r_s}\, dZ_s^*\right] \qquad \text{(A2)}$$

The solution suggests a simple way of simulating the asset value at the auditing time points. First, we simulate the risk-neutralized interest rate process as in equation (4) to approximate the whole sample path. This in turn allows us to compute the quantity of interest: $\int_t^{t+1} r_s\, ds$ and $\int_t^{t+1} \sqrt{r_s}\, dZ_s^*$. Second, we simulate $(W_{A,t+1}^* - W_{A,t}^*)$ using the fact that they are independent of the path of r_t.

Combining $(W_{A,t+1}^* - W_{A,t}^*)$ with the simulated $\int_t^{t+1} r_s\, ds$ and $\int_t^{t+1} \sqrt{r_s}\, dZ_s^*$ yields a value for A_{t+1} as described in equation (A2). For a specific average deposit maturity and the net rate of increment in deposits, using equation (6) in conjunction with the simulated interest rate obtains the simulated value of deposits. After simulating these processes, the value of subdebt can be easily calculated via averaging over the contingent payoffs corresponding to the simulated values.

ACCOUNTING FRAUD, AUDIT FEES, AND GOVERNMENT INTERVENTION IN CHINA

Jingjing Yang and Hao-Chang Sung

ABSTRACT

We analyze the economic consequence of government intervention on the incidence of accounting fraud and audit fees of both Big 4 and local big auditors on Chinese audit market in the period 2006–2013. In 2009, Chinese government issued favorable polices to local big auditors and required certain Chinese companies to give priority to these auditors. We find that market share of Big 4 auditors is quite stable before and after government intervention, but market share of local big auditors increases at the cost of local small auditors after intervention. Although audit fee premiums of both local big and Big 4 auditors have increased after intervention, the positive effect of local big auditors on audit fee premiums has significantly decreased. Further, both Big 4 and local big auditors are not likely to reduce the incidence of accounting fraud in pre- and post-intervention period. Our results suggest that Chinese government support to local auditors does not significantly enhance these auditors' competitiveness in terms of audit fee and audit quality.

Keywords: Government intervention; auditors; audit fees; accounting fraud; market

Advances in Pacific Basin Business, Economics and Finance, Volume 5, 101–120
Copyright © 2017 by Emerald Publishing Limited
All rights of reproduction in any form reserved
ISSN: 2514-4650/doi:10.1108/S2514-465020170000001005

1. INTRODUCTION

The audit market is less concentrated in China when compared with the oligopolistic audit market structure in the United States (Sarath and Xin, 2014). Local big and international Big 4 audit firms constitute the major providers of audit services in China. From 2006 to 2009, the Big 4's average market share in China by number of clients and by fee revenues was 7% and 29%, respectively. On the other hand, the average market share of the local big auditors in China by number of clients and by fee revenues was approximately 37% and 32%, respectively. This indicates that the supply of audit services in China is more competitive than that in the United States. However, the average audit fees of Big 4 are still higher than those of local big audit firms. To help local auditors compete with international auditors, State Council of China released the "Circular of Some Opinions on Enhancing Development of China's CPA Industry" (State Council of the People's Republic of China, Guo Ban Fa [2009] No. 56; hereafter Circular) on October 3, 2009. The Circular requires certain Chinese companies to give priority to large local auditors and increase monitoring and discipline with respect to the quality of audit services.

This study examines the economic consequence of government intervention on audit market in China. We aim to find out: (1) the impact of government intervention on the pricing ability of both international and local big auditors; (2) the impact of government intervention on the incidence of financial statement fraud for local big auditors. Answering these questions allows us to better understand whether government intervention leads to unfair competition (i.e., local big auditors charge relatively higher audit fee but do not enhance audit quality after government intervention) or enhances local big auditors' competitiveness in the audit market (i.e., local big auditors charge higher audit fee and also enhance audit quality after government intervention). Moreover, from the perspective of government intervention, this study re-examines whether a large audit firm is an effective mechanism to reduce the incidence of fraud for a country with strong government sanctions (Chen, Firth, Gao, & Rui, 2006; Lisic, Silveri, Song, & Wang, 2015).Our analyses are based on a sample of 12,221 observations of Chinese listed firms and their auditors from 2006 to 2013. We classify local auditors into two groups: local big auditors and local small (remained) auditors. Local big auditors are consisted of eight local auditors nominated by the Ministry of Finance (MOF) to compete with Big 4 auditors. These eight top local audit firms are: Li Xin, Tian Jian, Li Xin Da Hua, Xin Yong Zhong He, Guo Fu Hao Hua, Jing Du Tian Hua, Zhong Rui Yue Hua, and Da Xin. The remaining are classified as "local small auditors."

Existing studies have examined economic consequence of government policies on audit markets in China. For instance, Chan and Wu (2011) examine the effect of the mergers and acquisitions of Chinese audit firms induced by government policies on audit quality. They suggest that an increase in audit firm size does not necessarily lead to improvement in audit quality. Chen, Chen, Lobo, and Wang (2011) examine the audit quality (which is measured by audit firm size) on earnings management and cost of equity capital for State-Owned Enterprises (SOEs) and Non-State Owned Enterprises (NSOEs) after financial independence of audit firms from the local government agencies. They find that a large audit firm size could reduce earnings management in NSOEs than in SOEs. Lisic et al. (2015) examine whether government sanctions in China motivate audit firms to provide high audit quality and reduce the incidence of financial statement fraud. They find that companies audited by large audit firms are less likely to commit financial statement fraud. Our study is most related to Lisic et al. (2015): both studies examine the impact of audit firms on the incidence of financial statement fraud. Lisic et al. (2015) conduct this issue in a regression testing with a sample of entire observations. Different from Lisic et al. (2015), our study employs logistic regression testing with a sample of fraudulent firms and their matched non-fraudulent firms. This helps avoid testing error due to too small fraud samples within the whole sample (the proportion of fraudulent firm-year observations on the whole sample is only 2.67% in our study).

The main results of our study are as following. While market share of Big 4 auditors is relatively stable in both pre- and post-intervention periods, market share of local big auditors increases at the cost of local small auditors post-intervention. The audit fee of both local big and Big 4 auditors has increased after government intervention. Big 4 auditors still charge the highest audit fees among all types of auditors in the post-intervention period. However, the positive effect of local big auditors on audit fee premium has decreased after government intervention. Local big auditors are not likely to reduce the incidence of financial fraud in the post-intervention period. Consistent with Chen et al. (2006),[1] we find that Big 4 auditors have no effect on the incidence of corporate fraud either. Moreover, we show that the percentage ownership of the largest shareholder has no effect on the incidence of financial fraud in pre-intervention period, but this is significantly positive in post-intervention period. This indicates that the block shareholder may have incentives to encourage fraud after intervention.

Our empirical evidence shows that large auditors do not necessarily reduce the incidence of accounting fraud with government sanction in China, which contradicts the results of Lisic et al. (2015). Our results indicate that local big auditors do not charge higher audit fee premiums and do not provide higher audit quality after government intervention. As such, government intervention may not enhance these auditors' competiveness in audit market in China.

Our research results also imply that, in order to maintain high audit fees from clients, Big 4 auditors may be less likely to deliver the auditing resources required to uncover fraud, since these devoted resources do not best serve the clients' needs. This is consistent with Ke, Lennox, and Xin (2014) in which Big

4 auditors provide low quality audits to companies that are listed only in China.

Our study is related to the literature of Kinney (2005) and Maijoor and Vanstraelen (2012) who call for more research into the economic consequences of government interventions. The government intervention for particular type of auditors allows us to investigate the impact of such direct government intervention on audit market structure, audit fee premium, and the incidence of financial fraud. This may receive more attention from regulator, local auditors, and international auditors who pay special attention to the consequences of government direct intervention on the audit market.

Our policy implication is that sole government intervention on local big auditors may not increase both their audit fee premiums per se and audit quality. To further foster local big auditors' competitiveness, it would be useful for Chinese regulators to consider more other effective mechanisms, such as private litigation against auditors and improved disclosures on audit service.

The remainder of this study proceeds as follows. We discuss the institutional background of the audit market in China in Section 2. We develop our main hypothesis in Section 3, and present the sample selection process and research design in Section 4. The empirical results and additional analyses are reported in Section 5. Section 6 concludes above remarks.

2. INSTITUTIONAL BACKGROUND

Since economic reform in 1979, the Chinese government has embarked upon various reforms to improve the economic efficiency and change the ownership structure of corporations. In 1980, Chinese government allowed for joint ventures between domestic and foreign companies. The foundation of Chinese Institute of Certified Public Accountants (CPA) was established in the same year. In the early 1990s, Shanghai and Shenzhen stock exchanges were established. This opens the demand for auditing services to the companies listed on these exchanges. To perform the services, CPA firms must obtain a license from the China Securities Regulatory Commission (CSRC) and the MOF. In 1992, international accounting firms were allowed to joint ventures with domestic CPA firms. Further, they have also been permitted to invest in and control domestic audit firms since 1999. Since 1999, China has granted foreign investment enterprises, including Sino-foreign joint ventures, a period of up to five years of income tax exemptions and reductions.

Although the accounting profession in China has undergone rapid expansion, most local auditors remain small in terms of the number of listed clients (Chan & Wu, 2011). To satisfy the audit services needs from capital market and SOEs and help local auditors compete with large international accounting firms when the latter are allowed to operate directly in China after the country's accession to the WTO, MOF encouraged local auditors to increase their size via mergers and acquisitions in 1999. To further facilitate local auditors' competitiveness, the State Council of China released the Circular which encourages firms (especially for firms listed overseas, firms in finance, energy, and communication industries, and SOEs involved in national welfare and the people's livelihood) to give priority to local big auditors in 2009.

3. HYPOTHESIS DEVELOPMENT

Gerakos and Syverson (2015) point out that firms seeking audit services choose among several auditors, and each potential auditor provides varying aspects of service that are potentially valued differentially by each client firm. On the other hand, each client firm considers how well the attributes of each audit firm's service match its needs (these attributes include the audit fees) and hires the audit firm that offers the best net value. Moreover, literature has investigated the consequences of government intervention over the appointment of auditor on audit market, such as joint-audit (e.g., Andre, Broye, Pong, & Schatt, 2014) as well as the impact of mandatory rotation (e.g., Chi, Huang, Liao, & Xie, 2009; Ruiz-Barbadillo, Gó mez-Aguilar, & Carrera, 2009) and finds out that government intervention may affect companies' auditors appointment but not necessarily enhance audit quality. Based on these studies, we expect that Chinese government's favorable policies toward local big auditors affect market shares and audit fees in audit market.

3.1. The Impact of Government Intervention on Audit Market Structure

The government intervention, "Circular," has two important features. First, it favors particular type of local auditors, eight top local auditors, and distinguishes them from other local small auditors. Consequently, Circular may put local small and Big 4 auditors in a disadvantaged position. More specifically, it encourages firms in certain industries and certain types of SOEs to give priority to local big auditors. Since these firms consist of a great proportion in Chinese stock markets, the government intervention could exert significant influence on the demands of audit market. Moreover, Circular also specifies a more rigorous monitoring and discipline with respect to the quality of audit services, especially for underqualified small auditors and their client firms. These firms may thus receive an increasing scrutiny from regulators after the issuance of the Circular. Consequently, client firms who choose underqualified small auditors may switch to local big auditors when small auditors are under increased regulatory scrutiny. Besides, local big auditors have increased their service capacity via acquisitions of small local auditors. These would further increase market demand in local big auditors, and enhance their market share. Moreover, market shares of local small auditors will thus decrease.

Literature shows that among corporations with Big 4 auditors, those that are larger and more complex operationally are less likely to dismiss their auditors (Hennes, Leone, & Miller, 2014). Since clients of Big 4 auditors in China are usually the leading firms in terms of firm size in their respective industries and are also very large and complex firms, we expect that those clients are less likely to replace their Big 4 auditors.

Based on above discussion, we hypothesize that:

H1a: Local big auditors' market share increases after government intervention.

H1b: Small local auditors' market share decreases after government intervention.

H1c: Big 4 auditors' market share does not decrease after government intervention.

3.2. The Impact of Government Intervention on Audit Fees

Prior studies have examined the audit fee discrepancy between Big 4 and non-Big 4 auditors in China. For instance, Wang and Iqbal (2009) find evidence of Big 4 auditors' premiums for brand name as well as industry specialization in both the statutory and supplementary markets. Big 4 auditors who are industry specialists earn additional premiums in the statutory market as compared to non-industry specialists. We expect that government intervention will affect both local big auditors and Big 4 auditors' audit fees. Since government intervention favors local big auditors, this will increase the demand for local big auditors and in turn lead to an increase in local big auditors' audit fees. In contrast, if clients of Big 4 auditors have not yet switched to local auditors after government intervention as discussed above, then Big 4 auditors may not necessarily decrease their audit fees to attract more clients. Accordingly, we hypothesize that:

H2a: Local big auditors' audit fees increase after government intervention.

H2b: Big 4 auditors' audit fees do not decrease after government intervention.

3.3. The Impact of Government Intervention on the Incidence of Accounting Fraud

In China, the threat of civil litigation is very weak and so the actions of the Chinese Security Regulatory Committee (CSRC) assume more importance as a deterrent to accounting fraud (Chen et al. 2006). The CSRC and the MOA believe that auditors have the responsibility to detect and report frauds and impose sanction on auditors that fail to detect and report fraud in clients' financial statements (Firth, Mo, & Wong, 2005).

Although government intervention may increase auditors' size, this may not be an effective mechanism to discipline fraudulent behaviors (Aggarwal, Hu, & Yang, 2014; Chen et al., 2006). However, Lisic et al. (2015) examine whether government sanctions can substitute for claimholder litigation to ensure audit quality and find that auditors in general and large auditors in particular reduce the incidence of financial statement fraud in China. It is noteworthy that Lisic et al.'s (2015) empirical study relies on full sample regression testing which is sensitive to proportion of fraud observations. In this study, we expect that auditors may have no effect on the incidence of fraud after government intervention. Accordingly, we hypothesize that:

> **H3a:** Local big auditors cannot reduce the incidence of fraud after government intervention.
>
> **H3b:** Big 4 auditors cannot reduce the incidence of fraud after government intervention.

4. SAMPLE SELECTION PROCESS AND RESEARCH DESIGN

4.1. Sample Selection and Matching Criteria

To form the sample, we start from collecting data of all listed firms and their auditors covering the period from 2006 to 2013. The initial sample consists of 15,774 observations. There are 74 and 2,017 observations with missing values for auditors and audit fees, respectively. As such, the samples used to count market share of different types of auditors are 15,700 (market share by number of clients) and 13,757 (market share by audit fees). We further exclude 265 observations of listed firms in financial sector, and 1,271 observations with missing values for control variables from our sample. Consequently, the sample used to examine the audit fee premiums of Big 4 auditors includes 12,221 observations.

There are 326 fraud cases over the 8-year period. Each fraud firm is matched with a non-fraud firm according to the following criteria: the matched non-fraud firm must be listed on the same stock exchange (i.e., Shanghai Stock Exchange and Shenzhen Stock exchange), be of similar size with total assets being within ±30%, and must be in the same 13-industry CSRC code. Any control is matched with only one fraud firm in a year, that is, matching without replacement. Hence, we obtain a unique match for each fraud firm.[2] The data of auditors (including tenure and audit fees) are obtained from the *Taiwan Economic Journal* (TEJ) Database. All other data are collected from the Sinofin Economic and Financial Databases.

4.2. Methodology

To investigate the impact of the intervention on audit fee premiums of Big 4 (local big) auditors, we estimate the following Ordinary Least Square (OLS) regression:

$$\begin{aligned}\mathrm{AUDIT\_FEE}_{i,t} = {} & \alpha_0 + \alpha_1\mathrm{BIG4}_{i,t} + \alpha_2\mathrm{TENURE}_{i,t} + \alpha_3\mathrm{GC}_{i,t} + \alpha_4\mathrm{ROA}_{i,t} \\ & + \alpha_5\mathrm{CASH}_{i,t} + \alpha_6\mathrm{LEV}_{i,t} + \alpha_7\mathrm{GROWTH}_{i,t} + \alpha_8\mathrm{CURRENT}_{i,t} \\ & + \alpha_9\mathrm{CA\_TA}_{i,t} + \alpha_{10}\mathrm{ARINV}_{i,t} + \alpha_{11}\mathrm{LOSS}_{i,t} + \alpha_{12}\mathrm{SOE}_{i,t} \\ & + \alpha_{13}\mathrm{SEO}_{i,t} + \alpha_{14}\mathrm{AGE}_{i,t} + \alpha_{15}\mathrm{CROSS\_LIST}_{i,t} \\ & + \mathrm{INDUSTRY\_DUMMIES}_{i,t} + \varepsilon\end{aligned} \tag{1}$$

$$\begin{aligned}\mathrm{AUDIT\_FEE}_{i,t} = {} & \alpha_0 + \alpha_1\mathrm{LOCAL\_BIG4}_{i,t} + \alpha_2\mathrm{TENURE}_{i,t} + \alpha_3\mathrm{GC}_{i,t} + \alpha_4\mathrm{ROA}_{i,t} \\ & + \alpha_5\mathrm{CASH}_{\mathrm{i,t}} + \alpha_6\mathrm{LEV}_{i,t} + \alpha_7\mathrm{GROWTH}_{i,t} + \alpha_8\mathrm{CURRENT}_{i,t} \\ & + \alpha_9\mathrm{CA\_TA}_{i,t} + \alpha_{10}\mathrm{ARINV}_{i,t} + \alpha_{11}\mathrm{LOSS}_{i,t} + \alpha_{12}\mathrm{SOE}_{i,t} \\ & + \alpha_{13}\mathrm{SEO}_{i,t} + \alpha_{14}\mathrm{AGE}_{i,t} + \alpha_{15}\mathrm{CROSS\_LIST}_{i,t} \\ & + \mathrm{INDUSTRY\_DUMMIES}_{i,t} + \varepsilon\end{aligned} \tag{2}$$

where AUDIT_FEE is the natural log of audit fees. BIG4 is a dummy variable, which takes the value of 1 if the audit firm is one of Big 4 auditors, and 0 otherwise. LOCAL_BIG is a dummy variable, which takes the value of 1 if the audit firm is one of the eight local top auditors. TENURE is the audit tenure. GC is a dummy variable, which takes the value of 1 if the auditor issues a going concern opinion, and 0 otherwise; ROA stands for the return on total assets; CASH is the operating cash flow scaled by total assets; LEV is total liabilities scaled by total assets; GROWTH is sales growth ratio; CURRENT is current liabilities scaled by current assets; CA_TA is current assets scaled by total assets; ARINV is the sum of accounting receivable and inventories scaled by total assets; LOSS is another dummy variable, which takes the value of 1 if the firm's net income is negative, and 0 otherwise; SOE takes the value of 1 if the firm is controlled by government or its agencies, and 0 otherwise; SEO takes the value of 1 if the firm has seasoned equity offering in the current year, and 0 otherwise; AGE stands for the number of years between the IPO and current year; CROSS_LIST takes the value of 1 if the firm is also listed on Hong Kong Stock Exchange or issues B-shares. We also include industry fixed effects in our regression.

To investigate the impact of intervention on the monitoring effect of Big 4 (local big) auditors, we estimate the following logistic model:

$$\begin{aligned}\text{FRAUD(Fraud} = 1) = {} & \alpha_0 + \alpha_1\text{BIG4}_{i,t} + \alpha_2\text{TENURE}_{i,t} + \alpha_3\text{TOP}_{i,t} + \alpha_4\text{ROA}_{i,t} \\ & + \alpha_5\text{CASH}_{i,t} + \alpha_6\text{LEV}_{i,t} + \alpha_7\text{GROWTH}_{i,t} \\ & + \alpha_8\text{CURRENT}_{i,t} + \alpha_9\text{CA\_TA}_{i,t} + \alpha_{10}\text{ARINV}_{i,t} \\ & + \alpha_{11}\text{LOSS}_{i,t} + \alpha_{12}\text{SIZE}_{i,t} + \alpha_{13}\text{SOE}_{i,t} + \alpha_{14}\text{SEO}_{i,t} \\ & + \alpha_{15}\text{AGE}_{i,t} + \alpha_{16}\text{CROSS\_LIST}_{i,t} + \varepsilon\end{aligned} \tag{3}$$

$$\begin{aligned}\text{FRAUD(Fraud} = 1) = {} & \alpha_0 + \alpha_1\text{LOCAL\_BIG4}_{i,t} + \alpha_2\text{TENURE}_{i,t} + \alpha_3\text{TOP}_{i,t} \\ & + \alpha_4\text{ROA}_{i,t} + \alpha_5\text{CASH}_{i,t} + \alpha_6\text{LEV}_{i,t} + \alpha_7\text{GROWTH}_{i,t} \\ & + \alpha_8\text{CURRENT}_{i,t} + \alpha_9\text{CA\_TA}_{i,t} + \alpha_{10}\text{ARINV}_{i,t} \\ & + \alpha_{11}\text{LOSS}_{i,t} + \alpha_{12}\text{SIZE}_{i,t} + \alpha_{13}\text{SOE}_{i,t} + \alpha_{14}\text{SEO}_{i,t} \\ & + \alpha_{15}\text{AGE}_{i,t} + \alpha_{16}\text{CROSS\_LIST}_{i,t} + \varepsilon\end{aligned} \tag{4}$$

where FRAUD is a dummy variable, which takes the value of 1 if fraud has occurred at the firm, and 0 otherwise. TOP is the percentage of shares held by the single-largest shareholder. We include TOP in the logistic regression to control for the effect of the largest shareholder on the incidence of fraud. The other variables used in the logistic regression are the same as those used in regression (1) and (2). However, the sample used to estimate the logistic regression only includes fraudulent firms and the matched non-financial firms. We further use the entire sample to re-estimate the logistic regression for the robustness check.

5. EMPIRICAL RESULTS

5.1. Main Result

We firstly examine market shares of both Big 4 and local auditors from 2006 to 2013. Since the government released a circular to support around eight top local auditors in 2009, we further classify local auditors into two groups: local big and local small auditors. Local big auditors include eight local auditors nominated by the MOF to compete with Big 4 international auditors. The rest of local auditors are classified as local small auditors. As shown in Panel A of Table 1, market share measured by the number of clients of local big auditors significantly increases from 37.82% to 50.70%, and their market share measured by audit fees also substantially increases from 32.08% to 43.42%. This supports the hypothesis H1a. On the other hand, market share of Big 4 auditors in terms of both the number of clients and the amount of audit fees slightly drops after the government intervention. Market share of local small auditors drops. As such, H1b is supported, but H1c is not. It is noteworthy that local big auditors have acquired or merged with many small auditors after 2009. This helps them obtain many clients used to belong to local small auditors. Considering that market share of Big 4 auditors has been relatively stable, market share of local big auditors increases, to a certain extent, at the cost of local small auditors.

Panel B of Table 1 shows the statistics of companies that change auditor type from 2006 to 2013.[3] There are only a few companies that switch from local auditors to Big 4 auditors and also the other way around. Before the intervention, 255 companies change auditor type from local small to local big auditors, and 189 companies change in the opposite way. However, during the post-intervention period, 557 companies switch auditor from local small to local big auditors, and only 164 companies change auditor type in the opposite way.

Panel C of Table 1 shows market share of Big 4 auditors in different industries. Big 4 auditors have the highest market share in transportation industry during the entire sample period, and their market share increases substantially in construction industry during the post-intervention period. None of firms in agriculture or communication and culture industries have employed Big 4 auditing forms during the entire sample period.

Table 2 shows the statistics of audit fees of different types of auditors. The audit fees of all types of auditors have significantly increased after government intervention. As of the amount of audit fees, the highest fees charged by the Big 4 auditors can be as high as 183,000,000 from 2006 to 2009 and 207,000,000 from 2010 to 2013. In comparison, the highest audit fees charged by local auditors are less than 10% of that charged by Big 4 auditors. Therefore, both H2a and H2b are supported.

Table 1. Market Share Big 4 vs. Non-Big 4.

Panel A: Market Share

Period	Auditor	*N*	Market Share by Clients	*N* (Fee Available)	Market Share by Audit Fees
2006–2009	Big_4	436	6.95%	273	29.11%
	Local_Big	2373	37.82%	1965	32.08%
	Small	3463	55.21%	2895	37.95%
	Total	6272		5133	
2010–2013	Big_4	581	6.16%	451	25.76%
	Local_Big	4779	50.70%	4446	43.42%
	Small	4068	43.16%	3728	30.66%
	Total	9428		8625	

Panel B: Auditor Switch

Period	SWITCH	*N*
2006–2009	From Small to Big_4	11
	From Small to Local_Big	255
	From Local Big to Big_4	12
	From Big_4 to Local_Big	26
	From Big_4 to Small	21
	From Local_Big to Small	189
	Remain Big_4	371
	Remain Local_Big	1922
	Remain Small	3038
2010–2013	From Small to Big_4	19
	From Small to Local_Big	557
	From Local Big to Big_4	18
	From Big_4 to Local_Big	20
	From Big_4 to Small	2
	From Local_Big to Small	164
	Remain Big_4	419
	Remain Local_Big	3810
	Remain Small	3541

Panel C: Market Share by Industry

Market Share Rank	06–13 Industry	06–09 Industry	10–13 Industry
1	Transportation	Transportation	Transportation
2	Mining	Mining	Construction

Table 1. (*Continued*)

Panel C: Market Share by Industry

Market Share Rank	06–13 Industry	06–09 Industry	10–13 Industry
3	Construction	Real estate	Mining
4	Real estate	Social Services	Real estate
5	Utilities	Utilities	Utilities
6	Social Services	Construction	Social Services
7	Industrial and manufacturing	Information Technology	Wholesale and retail trade
8	Wholesale and retail trade	Industrial and manufacturing	Industrial and manufacturing
9	Information Technology	Wholesale and retail trade	Conglomerates
10	Conglomerates	Conglomerates	Information Technology
11	Agriculture, Communication and Culture	Agriculture, Communication and Culture	Agriculture, Communication and Culture

Table 3 shows the descriptive statistics of all variables used in this study. The longest tenure of auditors is 13 years. 50.7% of listed firms are ultimately controlled by government or its agencies. 6.3% of listed firms are also listed in Hong Kong or issuing B-shares. 1.4% of listed firms receive going concern opinion from their auditors.

Table 4 reports the result of OLS regressions used to examine the audit fee premiums of auditor type. In Panel A of Table 4, the coefficient of BIG4 is significantly positive at the 1% level across all regressions. The difference between the coefficient of BIG4 in regression 2 and that in regression 3 does not decrease significantly, which suggests that government intervention does not reduce the positive effect of Big 4 auditors on audit fee premium. In Panel B of Table 4, the coefficient of LOCAL_BIG is significantly positive as well. However, the positive effect of local big auditors on audit fee premium decreases after government intervention. This implies that Chinese government's favorable policies do not facilitate local big auditors' audit fee pricing power. The results on control variables are overall consistent with the literature (e.g., Xin and Sarath, 2014).For example, auditors with longer tenure charge higher audit fees; cross-listed and larger size companies and companies with negative net income are charged for higher audit fees.

The result of the effect of auditor type on the incidence of fraud is reported in Tables 5 and 6. The sample used to estimate logistic regressions includes all fraudulent firms and their matched non-fraud firms. As shown in Table 5, the coefficients of BIG4 is not statistically significant across all regressions, which

Table 2. Audit Fees of Different Types of Auditors.

Panel A: Differences in Audit Fees (Natural Log) between 2006 and 2009 and 2010 and 2013

AUDITOR	2006–2009			2010–2013			Mean diff *t*-value	Median diff *z*-value
	N	Mean	Median	*N*	Mean	Median		
BIG4	273	14.492	14.403	451	14.692	14.557	−0.200***	−0.154***
							−2.770	−2.939
LOCAL_BIG	1964	13.181	13.122	4446	13.373	13.305	−0.191***	−0.182***
							−12.570	−12.390
SMALL	2895	13.007	12.983	3728	13.239	13.218	−0.232***	−0.235***
							−19.260	−19.240

Panel B: Descriptive Statistics of Audit Fees of Different Types of Auditors

	AUDITOR	*N*	Mean	Median	Std. Dev.	Min	Max
2006–2009	BIG4	273	4144311	1800000	13967915	170000	183000000
	LOCAL_BIG	1964	634771	500000	546638	45000	11810000
	LOCAL_SMALL	2895	509366	435000	458262	70000	15000000
2010–2013	BIG4	451	4558967	2100000	11704168	360000	207000000
	LOCAL_BIG	4446	779400	600000	785387	10000	15240000
	LOCAL_SMALL	3728	656450	550000	539086	100000	9480000

Note: ***, **, and * represent statistically significant at the 0.01, 0.05, and 0.10 levels, respectively.

suggests that Big 4 auditors are not able to reduce the propensity of corporate fraud in listed firms in China before and after government intervention in the audit market. As such, Big 4 auditors are not able to serve as effective monitors in China. This is consistent with Chen et al. (2006). Table 6 reports the effect of local big auditors on the incidence of corporate fraud. The coefficients of LOCAL_BIG are not statistically significant across all regressions either. This indicates that local big auditors are not able to provide monitoring effects in listed firms after they get more market share by receiving the support from government. As such, both H3a and H3b are supported. Moreover, the coefficient of TOP in Tables 5 and 6 are not statistically significant in pre-intervention period. However, these coefficients are significantly positive in post-intervention period. This suggests that the percentage of ownership of the largest shareholder has an impact on a firm's propensity to commit fraud after intervention.

5.2. Sensitivity Analysis

To confirm the robustness of our empirical results, we further use the whole sample to estimate the effect of Big 4 and local big auditors on the incidence of

Table 3. Descriptive Statistics.

	Mean	Median	Std. Dev.	Min	Max
FEE	13.312	13.218	0.628	9.210	17.517
TENURE	4.107	3.000	3.003	1.000	13.000
ROA	0.038	0.035	0.063	−0.984	0.864
CASH	0.045	0.045	0.084	−0.585	0.892
LEV	0.467	0.479	0.211	0.007	0.999
GROWTH	0.179	0.126	0.402	−0.895	3.963
CURRENT	2.281	1.395	3.257	0.038	49.440
CA_TA	0.553	0.567	0.216	0.011	1.000
ARINV	0.271	0.247	0.175	0.000	0.897
LOSS	0.092	0.000	0.290	0.000	1.000
SIZE	21.733	21.598	1.216	17.769	27.387
SOE	0.507	1.000	0.500	0.000	1.000
SEO	0.084	0.000	0.277	0.000	1.000
AGE	9.071	9.000	5.472	0.000	23.000
CROSS_LIST	0.063	0.000	0.242	0.000	1.000
IND	3.284	3.000	0.678	1.000	8.000
GC	0.014	0.000	0.115	0.000	1.000

corporate fraud. As shown in Table 7, the coefficients of BIG4 are even positively significant at the 10% level in regressions 1 and 3, and insignificant in regression 2. This suggests that Big 4 auditors do not play a monitoring role during our sample period. The coefficients of LOCAL_BIG are not statistically significant across all regressions. Overall, the results reported in Table 7 support the empirical findings derived from Table 6. Moreover, we further exclude the fraud type of postponement or delay in disclosure from our sample to focus on the financial fraud only. The empirical results remain unchanged.[4]

6. CONCLUSION

We investigate the consequence of Chinese government's favorable policies toward local big auditors on audit market. Our study examines whether government intervention leads to unfair competition or enhances local big firms' competitiveness. We identify a sample of firms in both pre- and post-intervention periods. Our empirical evidence shows that market share of Big 4 auditors is quite stable in both pre- and post-intervention periods, but market share of local big auditors increases at the cost of local small auditors after government

Table 4. Regression Results.

Panel A: Big 4 Audit Fee Premiums

$$\begin{aligned}AUDIT\_FEE_{i,t} = {} & \alpha_0 + \alpha_1 BIG4_{i,t} + \alpha_2 TENURE_{i,t} + \alpha_3 GC_{i,t} + \alpha_4 ROA_{i,t} \\ & + \alpha_5 CASH_{i,t} + \alpha_6 LEV_{i,t} + \alpha_7 GROWTH_{i,t} + \alpha_8 CURRENT_{i,t} \\ & + \alpha_9 CA\_TA_{i,t} + \alpha_{10} ARINV_{i,t} + \alpha_{11} LOSS_{i,t} + \alpha_{12} SOE_{i,t} + \alpha_{13} SEO_{i,t} \\ & + \alpha_{14} AGE_{i,t} + \alpha_{15} CROSS\_LIST_{i,t} + INDUSTRY\_DUMMIES_{i,t} + \varepsilon\end{aligned}$$

Variable	Whole Sample		2006–2009		2010–2013	
	Regression 1		Regression 2		Regression 3	
	Coefficient	*p*-value	Coefficient	*p*-value	Coefficient	*p*-value
Intercept	5.699***	*<.0001*	6.124***	*<.0001*	5.891***	*<.0001*
BIG4	0.613***	*<.0001*	0.691***	*<.0001*	0.583***	*<.0001*
TENURE	0.007***	*<.0001*	0.003	*0.177*	0.008***	*<.0001*
GC	0.130***	*<.0001*	0.106***	*0.001*	0.145***	*<.0001*
ROA	−0.077	*0.332*	0.029	*0.799*	−0.088	*0.412*
CASH	0.056	*0.242*	0.181**	*0.012*	0.118*	*0.069*
LEV	−0.081***	*0.001*	−0.005	*0.912*	−0.048	*0.134*
GROWTH	−0.034***	*0.000*	−0.054***	*<.0001*	−0.022*	*0.072*
CURRENT	−0.010***	*<.0001*	−0.014***	*0.000*	−0.010***	*<.0001*
CA_TA	0.270***	*<.0001*	0.294***	*<.0001*	0.173***	*<.0001*
ARINV	−0.169***	*<.0001*	−0.180***	*0.002*	−0.093**	*0.024*
LOSS	0.056***	*0.000*	0.076***	*0.002*	0.042**	*0.035*
SIZE	0.348***	*<.0001*	0.321***	*<.0001*	0.342***	*<.0001*
SOE	−0.138***	*<.0001*	−0.105***	*<.0001*	−0.128***	*<.0001*
SEO	−0.027**	*0.038*	−0.003	*0.873*	−0.020	*0.276*
AGE	0.001	*0.376*	0.004***	*0.004*	−0.003***	*0.005*
CROSS_LIST	0.308***	*<.0001*	0.233***	*<.0001*	0.364***	*<.0001*
INDUSTRY	YES		YES		YES	
R-square	0.604		0.573		0.614	
N	12221		4526		7695	

Coefficients of Big 4 in Regressions 2 and 3 Coefficient diff 0.108, *p*-value 0.373

Panel B: Local Big Auditors' Audit Fee Premiums

Variable	Whole Sample		2006–2009		2010–2013	
	Regression 1		Regression 2		Regression 3	
	Coefficient	*p*-value	Coefficient	*p*-value	Coefficient	*p*-value
Intercept	5.076***	<.0001	5.292***	<.0001	5.314***	<.0001
LOCAL_BIG	0.058***	<.0001	0.065***	<.0001	0.035***	0.000
TENURE	0.009***	<.0001	0.002	0.337	0.009***	<.0001

Table 4. *(Continued)*

Panel B: Local Big Auditors' Audit Fee Premiums

Variable	Whole Sample		2006–2009		2010–2013	
	Regression 1		Regression 2		Regression 3	
	Coefficient	*p*-value	Coefficient	*p*-value	Coefficient	*p*-value
GC	−0.025	0.335	0.033	0.443	−0.052	0.109
ROA	−0.065	0.429	0.029	0.810	−0.070	0.529
CASH	0.119**	0.018	0.266***	0.001	0.143**	0.033
LEV	−0.111***	<.0001	−0.062	0.151	−0.079**	0.018
GROWTH	−0.037***	0.001	−0.057***	<.0001	−0.027**	0.039
CURRENT	−0.010***	<.0001	−0.014***	0.001	−0.011***	<.0001
CA_TA	0.219***	<.0001	0.235***	<.0001	0.139***	<.0001
ARINV	−0.140***	<.0001	−0.146**	0.017	−0.074*	0.084
LOSS	0.079***	<.0001	0.106***	<.0001	0.062***	0.003
SIZE	0.378***	<.0001	0.362***	<.0001	0.371***	<.0001
SOE	−0.141***	<.0001	−0.127***	<.0001	−0.126***	<.0001
SEO	−0.026*	0.052	−0.004	0.838	−0.023	0.214
AGE	−0.001	0.305	0.003*	0.078	−0.004***	<.0001
CROSS_LIST	0.492***	<.0001	0.407***	<.0001	0.549***	<.0001
R-square	0.568		0.520		0.581	
No. of Obs.	12221		4526		7695	
Coefficients of LOCAL_BIG in Regressions 2 and 3						
Coefficient diff 0.030, *p*-value 0.015						

Note: ***, **, and * represent statistically significant at the 0.01, 0.05, and 0.10 levels, respectively.

Table 5. Logistic Regression Results (Using Matched Sample).

$$\begin{aligned} \text{FRAUD(Fraud} = 1) = {} & \alpha_0 + \alpha_1\text{BIG4}_{i,t} + \alpha_2\text{TENURE}_{i,t} + \alpha_3\text{TOP}_{i,t} + \alpha_4\text{ROA}_{i,t} \\ & + \alpha_5\text{CASH}_{i,t} + \alpha_6\text{LEV}_{i,t} + \alpha_7\text{GROWTH}_{i,t} + \alpha_8\text{CURRENT}_{i,t} \\ & + \alpha_9\text{CA\_TA}_{i,t} + \alpha_{10}\text{ARINV}_{i,t} + \alpha_{11}\text{LOSS}_{i,t} + \alpha_{12}\text{SIZE}_{i,t} \\ & + \alpha_{13}\text{SOE}_{i,t} + \alpha_{14}\text{SEO}_{i,t} + \alpha_{15}\text{AGE}_{i,t} + \alpha_{16}\text{CROSS\_LIST}_{i,t} + \varepsilon \end{aligned}$$

Variable	Whole Sample		2006–2009		2010–2013	
	Regression 1		Regression 2		Regression 3	
	Coefficient	*p*-value	Coefficient	*p*-value	Coefficient	*p*-value
Intercept	−1.112	0.514	−3.348	0.325	0.646	0.768
BIG4	0.078	0.833	−0.243	0.715	0.206	0.662

Table 5. *(Continued)*

$$\begin{aligned}\text{FRAUD(Fraud} = 1) = {} & \alpha_0 + \alpha_1 \text{BIG4}_{i,t} + \alpha_2 \text{TENURE}_{i,t} + \alpha_3 \text{TOP}_{i,t} + \alpha_4 \text{ROA}_{i,t} \\ & + \alpha_5 \text{CASH}_{i,t} + \alpha_6 \text{LEV}_{i,t} + \alpha_7 \text{GROWTH}_{i,t} + \alpha_8 \text{CURRENT}_{i,t} \\ & + \alpha_9 \text{CA\_TA}_{i,t} + \alpha_{10} \text{ARINV}_{i,t} + \alpha_{11} \text{LOSS}_{i,t} + \alpha_{12} \text{SIZE}_{i,t} \\ & + \alpha_{13} \text{SOE}_{i,t} + \alpha_{14} \text{SEO}_{i,t} + \alpha_{15} \text{AGE}_{i,t} + \alpha_{16} \text{CROSS\_LIST}_{i,t} + \varepsilon\end{aligned}$$

Variable	Whole Sample		2006–2009		2010–2013	
	Regression 1		Regression 2		Regression 3	
	Coefficient	*p*-value	Coefficient	*p*-value	Coefficient	*p*-value
TENURE	0.021	0.469	0.022	0.715	0.032	0.352
TOP	0.950*	0.088	0.857	0.375	1.324*	0.075
ROA	−0.945	0.479	−1.536	0.519	−1.357	0.419
CASH	−0.374	0.739	0.165	0.938	−0.268	0.851
LEV	0.537	0.316	−0.059	0.958	1.812**	0.014
GROWTH	−0.384*	0.085	−0.334	0.332	−0.268	0.408
CURRENT	0.065*	0.071	0.435*	0.063	0.089**	0.027
CA_TA	−1.139*	0.096	−1.455	0.253	−0.886	0.331
ARINV	1.517*	0.059	−0.381	0.798	2.307**	0.023
LOSS	−0.258	0.457	−0.176	0.764	−0.237	0.604
SIZE	0.031	0.706	0.198	0.213	−0.110	0.300
SOE	−0.434**	0.017	−0.778**	0.012	−0.383	0.118
SEO	0.359	0.220	0.902*	0.057	0.040	0.924
AGE	0.013	0.463	−0.052	0.205	0.201	0.365
CROSS_LIST	0.364	0.307	1.017*	0.082	0.304	0.600
INDUSTRY	YES		YES		YES	
Pseudo R-square	0.022		0.0725		0.0414	
N	652		252		400	

Note: ***, **, and * represent statistically significant at the 0.01, 0.05, and 0.10 levels, respectively.

intervention. Although audit fees in both local big and Big 4 auditors have increased after intervention, the positive effect of local big auditors on audit fee premium has decreased. Using a matched sample, we show that both Big 4 and local big auditors had no effect on the incidence of accounting fraud in both pre- and post-intervention periods. Our empirical result is robust when accounting for the entire sample. Our empirical results suggest that Chinese government intervention may not enhance local big auditors' competitiveness. Moreover, we find that the block shareholder has a positive impact on the incidence of financial fraud in post-intervention period.

Our results have important policy implications. Since both local big and Big 4 auditors may cater for clients' needs and limit the resources they devote to

Table 6. Logistic Regression Results (Using Matched Sample).

$$\text{FRAUD(Fraud} = 1) = \alpha_0 + \alpha_1\text{LOCAL\_BIG}_{i,t} + \alpha_2\text{TENURE}_{i,t} + \alpha_3\text{TOP}_{i,t} + \alpha_4\text{ROA}_{i,t} + \alpha_5\text{CASH}_{i,t} + \alpha_6\text{LEV}_{i,t} + \alpha_7\text{GROWTH}_{i,t} + \alpha_8\text{CURRENT}_{i,t} + \alpha_9\text{CA\_TA}_{i,t} + \alpha_{10}\text{ARINV}_{i,t} + \alpha_{11}\text{LOSS}_{i,t} + \alpha_{12}\text{SIZE}_{i,t} + \alpha_{13}\text{SOE}_{i,t} + \alpha_{14}\text{SEO}_{i,t} + \alpha_{15}\text{AGE}_{i,t} + \alpha_{16}\text{CROSS\_LIST}_{i,t} + \varepsilon$$

Variable	Whole Sample		2006–2009		2010–2013	
	Regression 1		Regression 2		Regression 3	
	Coefficient	*p*-value	Coefficient	*p*-value	Coefficient	*p*-value
Intercept	−1.131	0.491	−3.059	0.345	0.533	0.803
LOCAL_BIG	−0.127	0.453	0.101	0.732	−0.173	0.443
TENURE	0.016	0.592	0.025	0.681	0.025	0.482
TOP	0.968*	0.082	0.852	0.378	1.364*	0.065
ROA	−1.005	0.455	−1.403	0.559	−1.346	0.422
CASH	−0.361	0.747	0.112	0.957	−0.159	0.911
LEV	0.537	0.315	−0.065	0.953	1.807**	0.014
GROWTH	−0.395*	0.077	−0.337	0.329	−0.304	0.354
CURRENT	0.066*	0.067	0.443*	0.059	0.090**	0.026
CA_TA	−1.121	0.101	−1.459	0.253	−0.890	0.329
ARINV	1.517*	0.059	−0.357	0.811	2.343**	0.021
LOSS	−0.266	0.442	−0.157	0.789	−0.257	0.575
SIZE	0.035	0.651	0.180	0.224	−0.098	0.341
SOE	−0.433**	0.017	−0.771**	0.012	−0.381	0.120
SEO	0.361	0.218	0.913*	0.053	0.054	0.899
AGE	0.013	0.471	−0.051	0.212	0.019	0.386
CROSS_LIST	0.359	0.283	0.935*	0.075	0.309	0.532
INDUSTRY	YES		YES		YES	
Pseudo R-square	0.0225		0.0725		0.0421	
N	652		252		400	

Note: ***, **, and * represent statistically significant at the 0.01, 0.05, and 0.10 levels, respectively.

detecting and eliminating fraud, regardless of government intervention, effective disciplinary mechanisms are required.

NOTES

1. Using the fraud data from 1999 to 2003, Chen et al. (2006) investigate the effect of corporate governance on the incidence of fraud in China, and find that Big 4 auditors are unlikely to reduce the incidence of fraud in China.

Table 7. Logistic Regression Result (Using Whole Sample).

Variable	Whole Sample		2006–2009		2010–2013	
	Regression 1		Regression 2		Regression 3	
	Coefficient	*p*-value	Coefficient	*p*-value	Coefficient	*p*-value
Intercept	−4.165***	*0.001*	−6.940***	*0.001*	−2.400	*0.140*
BIG4	0.415*	*0.094*	0.017	*0.965*	0.630*	*0.059*
CONTROL VARS	YES		YES		YES	
Pseudo R-square	0.017		0.029		0.026	
N	12221		4526		7695	
Intercept	−4.710***	*<.0001*	−7.080***	*0.000*	−3.064*	*0.054*
LOCAL_BIG	−0.004	*0.971*	0.171	*0.363*	−0.056	*0.709*
CONTROL VARS	YES		YES		YES	
Pseudo R-square	0.016		0.030		0.024	
N	12221		4526		7695	

Note: ***, **, and * represent statistically significant at the 0.01, 0.05, and 0.10 levels, respectively.

2. Chen et al. (2006) also employ similar method to construct their sample to investigate the effect of corporate governance mechanisms on corporate fraud in China.
3. In our observations, each company changes auditor type at most one time in the periods 2006–2009 and 2010–2013.
4. Postponement/delay in disclosure accounts for almost 30% of all fraud cases. Therefore, we include this type of fraud to maintain the sample size, as there are only 376 fraud cases during the entire sample period. Due to the size limit, the result is not reported, but is available upon request.

ACKNOWLEDGMENT

Jingjing Yang thanks for the support from the sponsorship of the National Nature Science Foundation of China (Project No. 71563020); Hao-Chang Sung appreciates the support from the sponsorship of the National Planning Office of Philosophy and Social Science of China (Project No. 15BJY011).

REFERENCES

Aggarwal, R., Hu, M., & Yang, J. (2014). Fraud, market reaction, and the role of institutional investors in Chinese listed firms. *The Journal of Portfolio Management*, *41*(2), 92–109.

Andre, P., Broye, G., Pong, C., & Schatt, A. (2014). Are joint audits associated with higher audit fees? Available at SSRN 2039001.

Chan, H., & Wu, D. (2011). Aggregate quasi rents and auditor independence: Evidence from audit firm mergers in China. *Contemporary Accounting Research*, *28*(1), 175–213.

Chen, G., Firth, M., Gao, D. N., & Rui, O. M. (2006). Ownership structure, corporate governance, and fraud: Evidence from China. *Journal of Corporate Finance*, *12*(3), 424–448.

Chen, H., Chen, J. Z., Lobo, G. J., & Wang, Y. (2011). Effects of audit quality on earnings management and cost of equity capital: Evidence from China. *Contemporary Accounting Research*, *28*(3), 892–925.

Chi, W., Huang, H., Liao, Y., & Xie, H. (2009). Mandatory audit-partner rotation, audit quality and market perception: Evidence from Taiwan. *Contemporary Accounting Research*, *26*(2), 359–391.

Firth, M., Mo, P. L., & Wong, R. M. (2005). Financial statement frauds and auditor sanctions: An analysis of enforcement actions in China. *Journal of Business Ethics*, *62*(4), 367–381.

Gerakos, J. J., & Syverson, C. (2015). Competition in the audit market: Policy implications. *Journal of Accounting Research*, *53*(4), 725–775.

Hennes, K. M., Leone, A. J., & Miller, B. P. (2014). Determinants and market consequences of auditor dismissals after accounting restatements. *The Accounting Review*, *89*(3), 1051–1082.

Ke, B., Lennox, C., & Xin, Q. (2014). The effect of China's weak institutional environment on the quality of Big 4 audits. *The Accounting Review*.

Kinney Jr, W. R. (2005). Twenty-five years of audit deregulation and re-regulation: What does it mean for 2005 and beyond? *Auditing: A Journal of Practice & Theory*, *24*(s-1), 89–109.

Lisic, L. L., Silveri, S. D., Song, Y., & Wang, K. (2015). Accounting fraud, auditing, and the role of government sanctions in China. *Journal of Business Research*, *68*, 1186–1195.

Maijoor, S., & Vanstraelen, A. (2012). "Research Opportunities in Auditing in the EU," revisited. *Auditing: A Journal of Practice & Theory*, *31*(1), 115–126.

Ruiz-Barbadillo, E., Gómez-Aguilar, N., & Carrera, N. (2009). Does mandatory audit firm rotation enhance auditor independence? Evidence from Spain. *Auditing: A Journal of Practice & Theory*, *28*, 113–135.

State Council of the People's Republic of China. (2009). Circular of some opinions on enhancing development of China's CPA industry issued by the MOF and forwarded by the General Office of the State Council. Release No: Guo Ban Fa [2009] No.56.

Wang, K., & Iqbal, Z. (2009). Audit pricing and auditor industry specialization in an emerging market: Evidence from China. *Journal of International Accounting, Auditing and Taxation*, *18*(1), 60–72.

Xin, H., & Sarath, B. (2014). Effects on audit market shares: BIG 4 pricing strategies or non BIG 4 market power.

THE EMPLOYMENT STATUS OF MARRIAGE IMMIGRANTS IN TAIWAN

Hwei-Lin Chuang and Eric S. Lin

ABSTRACT

This study empirically investigates the difference in employment status between marriage immigrants and native women in Taiwan based on a combined data-set from the 2003 Survey of Foreign and Mainland Spouses' Life Status *and* 2003 Women's Marriage, Fertility and Employment Survey. *The conceptual framework is based on the family labor supply model, the human and social capital theories, and the immigrant assimilation theory. From the Probit model of the employment probability, our findings indicate that family background variables, including the presence of small children and husbands' characteristics, play fairly significant roles in determining the employment probability of marriage immigrants. As for native women, human capital variables such as schooling and age are the most significant factors affecting their employment probability, while husbands' characteristics play a less important role in this respect. The finding that the employment probability of foreign spouses rises rapidly with the number of years that have elapsed since migration may confirm the employment assimilation for marriage immigrants. This study further applies the nonlinear decomposition analysis developed in the work of Yun (2004) to examine the gap in employment probability between native women and foreign spouses in Taiwan. Our findings show that the employment probability differentials are mostly due to the difference in coefficients and that the effects of the two age variables play dominant roles. The difference in coefficients, in sum, contributes to increasing the gap of employment probability,*

Advances in Pacific Basin Business, Economics and Finance, Volume 5, 121–150
Copyright © 2017 by Emerald Publishing Limited
All rights of reproduction in any form reserved
ISSN: 2514-4650/doi:10.1108/S2514-465020170000001006

while the difference in characteristics, in sum, tends to reduce the employment probability differentials.

Keywords: Marriage immigrants; employment probability; employment assimilation; decomposition analysis

JEL classifications: J21; J61

1. INTRODUCTION

A sizable body of literature has evolved in the past 30 years that examines the integration of immigrants into developed countries such as the United States and the United Kingdom, with labor market assimilation being a central issue. This is because most immigrants in developed nations migrate for economic purposes and therefore actively participate in the labor market of the host country. The key hypothesis of labor market assimilation is that poorer initial labor market outcomes among immigrants will be followed by convergence towards the outcomes of the native-born working-age population with the time lived in the receiving country. Pioneer works by Chiswick (1978, 1983) and Borjas (1985, 1995) have found that the earnings of immigrant workers increase with years in the host countries. Some studies have extended the attention to employment assimilation based on a comparison of the employment rates of the immigrant and native populations or for a specific industry (e.g., see Akay, 2016; Campolieti, Gunderson, Timofeeva, & Tsiroulnitchenko, 2013; Clark & Lindley, 2009; Duleep & Sanders, 1993; Pedace & DuBois, 2012; Schoeni, 1998).

The number of immigrants through marriage in Taiwan has rapidly increased since the early 1990s as a result of the continuing growth in the number of cross-border marriages. According to statistics compiled by the Ministry of Interior, R.O.C. in 2016, about 520,000 foreign spouses live in Taiwan, with female spouses from Southeast Asia and mainland China accounting for approximately 93% of them. Although participating in the labor market is not the main reason for the migration of foreign spouses to Taiwan, quite a few do participate in the labor market. The *2003 Survey of Foreign and Mainland Spouses' Life Status* indicates that about 32% of spouses from Southeast Asia and 24% of spouses from mainland China hold full-time or part-time jobs. These percentages are expected to rise since the government has been gradually relaxing the work regulations of foreign spouses.[1] As a result, it is becoming more important to pay greater attention to the labor market performance of these marriage immigrant women.

The literature on immigrants' labor market performance usually focuses on determining the trends in employment and earnings of the immigrant population in the host country in order to understand their assimilation process. As there is no earnings information provided in the *2003 Survey of Foreign and*

Mainland Spouses' Life Status, this study shall examine the employment behavior and the employment assimilation of female immigrants – namely, foreign spouses from Southeast Asia and mainland China. Compared to most immigrants in the United States or other developed countries, while the main reason for foreign spouses' immigration to Taiwan is the family and the role they have in it, there may be some specific features of the employment behavior of these marriage immigrants. Therefore, we look to find those factors that motivate female marriage immigrants to participate in the labor market. Examining employment assimilation from a family perspective may shed light on the questions of what kind of government program should be offered to help these marriage immigrants adapt into their new country.

The literature has proposed two alternative hypotheses to explain the increase in the labor force participation rate (or employment rate) of immigrants. On the one hand, Chiswick's skills assimilation hypothesis emphasizes the role of skill transferability – that is, the level of U.S. labor market skill among immigrants accumulated with their time spent in the United States underlies both the apparent growth in immigrant earnings and labor force participation. On the other hand, Reimers (1985) finds that the labor force participation of immigrant women increases with time in the United States, and that this growth can be attributed to cultural assimilation.

This present study distinguishes between the skill assimilation effect and the cultural assimilation effect by comparing the employment assimilation situations between Southeast Asian and mainland Chinese spouses based on the combined dataset of the *2003 Survey of Foreign and Mainland Spouses' Life Status* and *2003 Women's Marriage, Fertility and Employment Survey*. The employment behavior of foreign spouses in Taiwan should be further studied, not only due to a research gap in the existing literature, but also because of the growing potential of their labor market participation. This study adds to the budding literature on immigration by documenting the contribution of foreign spouses to the economic status of their families in Taiwan with a focus on their assimilation process.

2. THE RELATIVE EMPLOYMENT STATUS OF MARRIAGE IMMIGRANTS

The *2003 Survey of Foreign and Mainland Spouses' Life Status*, the first nationwide survey on foreign spouses in Taiwan, was administered by the Ministry of Interior, R.O.C. (2004) and conducted by selected and trained village administrators and household registration officers as field interviewers, checkers, and supervisors. The study includes a total of 240,837 foreign spouses, and 73% of them completed the interview. The survey provides data related to the demographic characteristics, socioeconomic backgrounds, and family conditions of foreign spouses and offers information regarding training program participation and the need for counseling services. The present analysis focuses on the employment status and employment assimilation of female spouses from seven Southeast Asian countries and mainland China, who were mostly migrants through marriage and who accounted for more than 85% of total foreign spouses in 2003. We have 72,898 observations from Southeast Asia (denoted by SEA hereafter) and 79,902 observations from mainland China (denoted by MCH hereafter) in our sample.

The figures in Table 1 indicate that nearly two-thirds of foreign spouses are recent immigrants with their time lived in Taiwan being less than 5 years as of 2003. The pattern of the time of migration is similar for SEA and MCH immigrants. Among the SEA group's recent immigrants, almost 74.0% of them are from Vietnam, while this ratio is only about 24.0% among SEA spouses who migrated into Taiwan before 1997. SEA immigrants tend to be much younger than MCH immigrants; in 2003, nearly 48.3% of SEA immigrants are less than 25 years old, whereas only 12.0% of MCH immigrants are younger than 25 years old. This gap may be attributed to the difference in the trend of arrival age among SEA and MCH immigrants. Among SEA immigrants as of 2003, there are more younger-age spouse migrants in Taiwan. Moreover, about 77.5% of more recent immigrants have an arrival age of less than 25, while this ratio is 59.2% among those who have stayed in Taiwan for more than 6 years as of 2003. Conversely, the proportion of younger-arrival-age immigrants among the MCH group has declined from 46.5% for earlier immigrants to 29.5% for recent immigrants as of 2003.

Table 2 presents the employment status of our sample foreign spouses and native spouses by country of origin, showing that the employment percentage varies significantly across countries of origin. Myanmar has the highest proportion of working foreign spouses (48.3%), while mainland China has the lowest (24.0%) among all the countries. An apparent variation arises in the employment percentage among different age groups across countries of origin as seen in Table 2. The employment percentages for SEA spouses and MCH spouses are generally smaller than the employment percentage of native married women, as reported in Table 2 based on the data of the *2003 Women's Marriage, Fertility and Employment Survey*. Regarding the employment percentage of foreign spouses with Taiwanese citizenship, there exist smaller yet still apparent differences across countries. For example, this percentage is higher for the Philippines (67.2%) as compared to Cambodia (49.2%).

Table 3 reports the percentage of women working by arrival age and years since migration to shed some light on their assimilation process. Several studies have found that the propensity of immigrant women to work increases with years since migration. The figures in Table 3 show that the employment percentage of our sample women increases with their years since migration, suggesting that the assimilation effect found in the literature for economic immigrants of developed countries also holds for marriage immigrants in Taiwan. It seems

Table 1. Marriage Immigrants Sample by Age and Years Entered Taiwan.

YET/Country of Origin	Age							Sample Size
	<19	20–24	25–29	30–34	35–39	40–44	45+	
YET: 2001–2003								
Southeast Asia	4,320	13,595	4,039	1,431	537	219	185	24,326
Vietnam	3,848	11,214	2,738	776	227	79	62	18,944
Indonesia	409	1,501	693	264	102	63	77	3,109
Mainland China	28	6,670	9,182	6,235	3,904	2,410	2,641	31,070
YET: 1999–2001								
Southeast Asia	170	13,453	6,684	2,275	722	278	200	23,782
Vietnam	63	10,332	4,597	1,251	293	90	38	16,664
Indonesia	105	2,399	1,233	487	219	122	124	4,689
Mainland China	5	2,524	7,417	4,553	2,012	1,276	1,771	19,558
YET: 1997–2001								
Southeast Asia	2	3,094	4,208	1,996	729	283	197	10,509
Vietnam	1	1,856	2,464	901	237	75	28	5,562
Indonesia	1	976	957	488	225	119	117	2,883
Mainland China	0	327	5,009	3,837	1,393	755	1,282	12,603
YET: 1995–1997								
Southeast Asia	0	513	2,990	1,978	815	375	263	6,934
Vietnam	0	204	1,353	764	216	76	16	2,629
Indonesia	0	273	1,096	563	306	192	177	2,607
Mainland China	0	14	2,434	3,655	1,189	544	1,138	8,974
YET: 1993–1995								
Southeast Asia	0	38	1,471	1,501	765	359	261	4,395
Vietnam	0	9	296	264	105	23	10	707
Indonesia	0	24	960	806	399	240	194	2,623
Mainland China	0	4	641	2,346	946	371	837	5,145
YET: 1993 or before								
Southeast Asia	0	0	314	874	725	497	542	2,952
Vietnam	0	0	26	36	19	5	4	90
Indonesia	0	0	239	488	280	195	183	1,385
Mainland China	0	0	62	908	586	249	747	2,552
Sample size	8,952	69,020	61,103	38,677	16,951	8,895	11,094	214,692

Note: YET denotes the year when the foreign spouse entered Taiwan.

reasonable to expect that assimilation will be easier for younger immigrants compared to older ones, which is confirmed by a sharper increase in the percentage of working immigrant women with arrival age under 25 than that for those with an arrival age of 25 and older. For instance, among the SEA groups with arrival

Table 2. Employment Status of Female Spouses by Country of Origin.

	Vietnam	Thailand	Philippines	Cambodia	Myanmar	Malaysia	Indonesia	Southeast Asia	Mainland China	Taiwan
Employment percentage of all spouses	28.94	46.07	44.97	28.44	48.32	40.82	35.46	32.31	23.98	43.91
Employment percentage by age group										
15–24	24.65	41.59	28.30	21.63	50.88	42.86	23.68	24.53	10.02	39.87
25–34	35.52	44.36	44.77	35.43	44.01	42.65	40.48	38.33	23.46	59.17
35–44	39.65	50.32	47.67	40.74	58.99	39.26	44.31	44.86	31.85	62.27
45–54	34.21	49.47	50.84	70.00	50.00	44.34	42.13	44.03	33.44	49.09
Employment percentage of foreign spouses with Taiwanese citizenship	57.70	60.28	67.20	49.24	60.76	61.97	51.45	54.53	56.78	–
Sample size	44,596	3,180	3,476	2,848	892	610	17,296	72,898	79,902	16,827

Table 3. Percentage of Women Working by Arrival Age and Years since Migration.

Arrival Age	Years Since Migration														Sample Size	
Country of Origin	0–1		1–2		2–4		4–6		6–8		8–10		10+			
<19																
Southeast Asia	17.18%	(2,514)	20.75%	(4,314)	26.00%	(7,853)	35.21%	(3,096)	49.30%	(1,769)	59.71%	(1,092)	62.10%	(314)	29.53%	(20,952)
Vietnam	17.34%	(2,341)	20.92%	(3,704)	27.29%	(6,119)	36.94%	(1,857)	50.83%	(779)	59.29%	(226)	–	(26)	27.13%	(15,052)
Indonesia	15.44%	(136)	19.03%	(536)	20.80%	(1,524)	33.27%	(977)	48.59%	(780)	60.35%	(744)	65.27%	(239)	35.43%	(4,936)
Mainland China	–	(19)	–	(22)	14.55%	(323)	22.02%	(327)	32.89%	(377)	50.75%	(266)	48.39%	(62)	29.37%	(1,396)
20–24																
Southeast Asia	19.20%	(4,172)	22.06%	(7,783)	27.64%	(10,630)	38.74%	(4,208)	53.40%	(2,721)	59.12%	(1,688)	58.35%	(874)	31.32%	(32,076)
Vietnam	18.59%	(3,496)	22.33%	(6,188)	29.32%	(7,702)	40.91%	(2,464)	57.10%	(1,226)	65.18%	(313)	72.22%	(36)	29.07%	(21,425)
Indonesia	19.94%	(341)	19.15%	(1,008)	21.66%	(1,828)	32.71%	(957)	48.90%	(867)	58.33%	(924)	61.07%	(488)	34.79%	(6,413)
Mainland China	6.30%	(3,526)	9.44%	(4,236)	16.12%	(6,801)	23.38%	(5,009)	39.54%	(3,809)	57.31%	(2,326)	65.31%	(908)	23.75%	(26,615)
25–29																
Southeast Asia	24.05%	(1,289)	26.50%	(2,170)	27.74%	(3,439)	39.13%	(1,996)	50.81%	(1,415)	53.82%	(877)	55.03%	(725)	35.35%	(11,911)
Vietnam	21.42%	(845)	23.90%	(1,385)	29.14%	(2,107)	43.06%	(901)	55.30%	(443)	58.54%	(123)	–	(19)	31.70%	(5,823)
Indonesia	29.06%	(234)	22.41%	(406)	18.78%	(719)	28.48%	(488)	43.02%	(444)	56.21%	(459)	60.36%	(280)	34.69%	(3,030)
Mainland China	8.63%	(4,227)	11.54%	(4,609)	19.74%	(5,998)	25.20%	(3,837)	41.25%	(2,555)	54.19%	(1,216)	63.99%	(586)	22.30%	(23,028)
30–34																
Southeast Asia	33.26%	(469)	31.97%	(785)	30.11%	(1,139)	38.68%	(729)	49.33%	(594)	49.18%	(429)	52.72%	(497)	38.73%	(4,642)
Vietnam	26.42%	(265)	29.10%	(402)	29.87%	(519)	35.86%	(237)	50.36%	(139)	55.88%	(34)	–	(5)	32.48%	(1,601)
Indonesia	24.29%	(70)	22.37%	(152)	25.00%	(288)	32.89%	(225)	43.28%	(238)	48.70%	(269)	54.87%	(195)	37.93%	(1,437)
Mainland China	10.11%	(3,165)	14.13%	(2,789)	29.98%	(2,692)	32.25%	(1,393)	46.53%	(864)	59.17%	(458)	61.85%	(249)	24.57%	(11,610)

Table 3. (*Continued*)

Arrival Age	Years Since Migration														Sample Size	
Country of Origin	0–1		1–2		2–4		4–6		6–8		8–10		10+			
35–39																
Southeast Asia	38.73%	(173)	32.54%	(295)	33.26%	(439)	44.17%	(283)	43.92%	(255)	54.27%	(199)	50.17%	(291)	41.34%	(1,935)
Vietnam	30.86%	(81)	24.56%	(114)	30.07%	(153)	49.33%	(75)	41.94%	(31)	–	(7)	–	(4)	32.90%	(465)
Indonesia	–	(26)	22.54%	(71)	30.59%	(170)	37.82%	(119)	41.83%	(153)	55.56%	(144)	49.02%	(102)	40.25%	(785)
Mainland China	11.44%	(2,098)	17.82%	(1,723)	40.75%	(1,600)	41.19%	(755)	50.96%	(416)	53.79%	(264)	59.20%	(201)	28.10%	(7,057)
40–44																
Southeast Asia	32.10%	(81)	44.26%	(122)	35.63%	(160)	44.35%	(124)	57.38%	(122)	39.74%	(78)	41.67%	(144)	42.48%	(831)
Vietnam	32.26%	(31)	38.46%	(39)	32.56%	(43)	–	(22)	–	(9)	–	(4)	–	(0)	36.49%	(148)
Indonesia	–	(21)	33.33%	(45)	30.26%	(76)	42.03%	(69)	55.00%	(80)	35.09%	(57)	43.48%	(46)	40.61%	(394)
Mainland China	10.98%	(1,248)	17.80%	(927)	45.42%	(918)	45.18%	(560)	42.60%	(392)	50.49%	(204)	40.25%	(159)	29.63%	(4,408)
45+																
Southeast Asia	22.81%	(57)	26.47%	(102)	32.79%	(122)	19.18%	(73)	41.38%	(58)	25.00%	(32)	31.78%	(107)	29.04%	(551)
Vietnam	–	(19)	26.47%	(34)	–	(21)	–	(6)	–	(2)	–	(0)	–	(0)	23.17%	(82)
Indonesia	–	(17)	17.39%	(46)	33.33%	(84)	16.67%	(48)	44.44%	(45)	–	(26)	28.57%	(35)	26.91%	(301)
Mainland China	8.55%	(1,240)	6.53%	(1,241)	30.18%	(1,226)	30.06%	(722)	22.28%	(561)	22.87%	(411)	15.50%	(387)	18.19%	(5,788)

Note: Arrival age is calculated by subtracting YSM variable from the Age variable. The figures in parentheses are the number of observations in the corresponding category.

age under 19, the percentage of working women increases from 17.2% to 62.1% with the years since migration, while this percentage changes from 32.1% to 41.7% for those in the 40–44 year-old arrival age group.

By comparing the employment assimilation between SEA and MCH, we may be able to show the difference between skill assimilation and culture assimilation. If we look at those spouses whose time since migration is more than 6 years, the percentage of working women increases faster among MCH spouses than that among SEA spouses. Compared with SEA spouses, MCH spouses share a more similar culture background with Taiwanese women. As a result, culture assimilation may reinforce the skill assimilation effect and make the working percentage of MCH spouses grow faster than that of SEA spouses.

Researchers have emphasized that the presence of preschool children is negatively associated with female labor force participation. Data in Table 4 suggest that this negative relationship holds for SEA immigrants, but among MCH women there is no apparent difference in the employment percentage between immigrant women with and without preschool children. The difference in education shows a stronger impact on the working percentage of SEA spouses than that for MCH spouses.

There are more regional differentials in the working percentage of SEA immigrants compared to that of MCH immigrants. Table 4 presents a greater urban–rural differential in employment percentage among SEA immigrants than that among MCH immigrants. Current age seems to be more relevant to the working decision than the arrival age for both SEA and MCH immigrants. As expected, immigrant women whose husbands have full-time work are less likely to work, and the employment differential is larger among MCH women than that among SEA women. Finally, for MCH immigrants, holding citizenship plays a critical role in their working decision compared to all other factors in Table 4.

3. CONCEPTUAL FRAMEWORK AND EMPIRICAL SPECIFICATIONS

The conceptual framework for the employed/nonemployed decision of foreign spouses follows directly from Chuang, Hsieh, and Lin (2010). In other words, the female labor supply theory, which emphasizes the family's concern for married women's employment decision, can be applied to female immigrants as well (Boyd, 1992; Cobb-Clark & Connolly, 2001). An examination of the employment decision of foreign spouses in Taiwan can thus start with the "traditional family" labor supply model.[2] Mincer's (1974) human capital theory also suggests that "the wife's labor supply is not only a function of her own human capital and her personal characteristics, but is also a function of her husband's human capital and personal characteristics." For female immigrants,

Table 4. Employment Percentage of Foreign Spouses by Characteristics and Country of Origin (%).

	Group			
	SEA	VI	IN	MCH
Total employment percentage	32.31	28.94	35.46	23.98
Year entered Taiwan				
0–4	24.82	24.62	21.58	15.69
4–10+	48.82	46.05	46.85	38.32
Child of age < 6				
Yes	30.57	28.27	33.09	24.06
No	36.06	30.34	41.81	23.91
Education				
Primary or below	30.48	27.01	36.21	24.88
Junior	32.15	29.46	36.01	23.18
Senior	33.81	30.97	33.70	23.95
College or above	38.76	32.41	34.65	25.44
Urban/rural				
Urban	26.05	23.40	29.00	23.15
Rural	33.59	30.19	36.31	24.30
Region				
North	30.97	26.43	33.42	25.22
Central	36.06	33.90	38.28	24.05
South	30.77	27.12	36.30	21.71
Residential status				
Residency	40.94	36.90	42.44	34.00
Citizenship	54.32	57.13	51.40	56.49
Age				
Under 25	24.53	24.65	23.68	10.02
25 and above	39.57	35.85	41.23	25.88
Arrival age				
Under 25	30.61	28.27	35.07	24.03
25 and above	36.84	31.93	36.20	23.96
Husband with full time job				
Yes	31.47	28.35	34.04	21.88
No	36.15	31.75	41.10	28.58

Note: SEA = Southeast Asia, VI = Vietnam, IN = Indonesia, MCH = Mainland China. Residency denotes holding Permanent Residency status for the SEA spouses and holding Residency status for MCH spouses.

the human capital theory should be extended to include the influence of social capital, which refers to any resources created through an individual's relationship with other people such as friendship networks (Aguilera, 2002; Coleman, 1990; Portes, 1995). The social capital effect captures the role of nonfamilial networks on the employment decision of foreign spouses in Taiwan.

The labor-market assimilation hypothesis developed in the immigrant literature suggests that poorer initial labor-market outcomes among immigrants will be followed by convergence towards the outcomes of the native-born working-age population with the time they have lived in the receiving country. Quite a few studies have attempted to test the labor-market assimilation hypothesis by comparing the earnings and employment probability of immigrants and native-born workers (Baker & Dwayne, 1994; Barth, Bratsberg, & Raaum, 2004; Borjas, 1985, 1995; Chiswick, 1978, 1983). Since a comparison of the labor market outcomes between immigrants and natives is required to formally test for the labor-market assimilation hypothesis, we therefore combine the dataset of the *2003 Survey of Foreign and Mainland Spouses' Life Status* and *2003 Women's Marriage, Fertility and Employment Survey* to test the employment assimilation hypothesis. We also take into account those factors emphasized in the literature that may affect immigrants' employment decision such as ethnicity and language proficiency (Chiswick & Miller, 1995; Kossoudji, 1988; McManus, 1985; Rivera-Batiz, 1990; Sullivan, 1978).[3]

Based on the aforementioned conceptual framework, we set up our empirical specification as follows. To consider a dichotomous choice for the decision regarding employment status, we apply a typical binary choice model for the analysis of employment status, specifically formulating the random utility model as:

$$Y_i^* = X_i'\beta + u_i, \quad Y_i = 1 \quad \text{if} \quad Y_i^* > 0 \tag{1}$$

where Y_i^* is the latent utility for the decision to work (including full-time and part-time jobs); X_i is the vector of explanatory variables related to family background, human capital, social capital, assimilation, and other control variables; Y_i denotes the observed working status; and β is a $K \times 1$ coefficient vector. We estimate the employment probability in Eq. (1) through the Probit model.[4]

We next examine the causes for the difference in employment decisions of foreign spouses and native women in Taiwan as well as the difference in those decisions for Southeast Asian foreign spouses and mainland Chinese spouses using the decomposition analysis for the nonlinear model developed in Yun (2004). Yun's approach, which will be introduced in the following text, is a systematic framework by extending the Blinder–Oaxaca decomposition approach to nonlinear models.

Note that Y is a binary variable for employment status, denoted as 1 for respondents with full-time or part-time jobs, and 0 otherwise. As specified earlier, we can estimate the employment probability in Eq. (1) through the Probit model. Accordingly, we specify the Probit decomposition method for the differences in employment probability between native spouses, denoted by subscript A, and foreign spouses, denoted by subscript B. The difference in Y represents the mean difference between two groups, that is, the mean employment probability of native spouses, Y_A, and that of foreign spouses Y_B:

$$\overline{Y}_A - \overline{Y}_B = \overline{\Phi(X_A\beta_A)} - \overline{\Phi(X_B\beta_B)}$$

where Φ is the standard normal cumulative distribution function.

By setting native spouses as nondiscriminatory labor, the Probit decomposition leads to:

$$\overline{Y}_A - \overline{Y}_B = \left[\overline{\Phi(X_A\beta_A)} - \overline{\Phi(X_B\beta_A)}\right] + \left[\overline{\Phi(X_B\beta_A)} - \overline{\Phi(X_B\beta_B)}\right] \tag{2}$$

where the first term in Eq. (2) is the difference in characteristics, and the second term is the difference in coefficients. To obtain the detailed decomposition (i.e., the contribution of each covariate to the total difference), the key is in finding the proper weight of each covariate for both the characteristics and coefficients effects. Using a first-order Taylor expansion with respect to Eq. (2), we have the following detailed decomposition:

$$\overline{Y}_A - \overline{Y}_B = \sum_{k=1}^{K} W_{\Delta X}^{k}\left[\overline{\Phi(X_A\beta_A)} - \overline{\Phi(X_B\beta_A)}\right] + \sum_{k=1}^{K} W_{\Delta\beta}^{k}\left[\overline{\Phi(X_B\beta_A)} - \overline{\Phi(X_B\beta_B)}\right] \tag{3}$$

where

$$W_{\Delta X}^{k} = \frac{\left[(\overline{X}_A^k - \overline{X}_B^k)\beta_A^k\right]\phi(\overline{X}_A\beta_A)}{\left[(\overline{X}_A - \overline{X}_B)\beta_A\right]\phi(\overline{X}_A\beta_A)} = \frac{\left[(\overline{X}_A^k - \overline{X}_B^k)\beta_A^k\right]}{\left[(\overline{X}_A - \overline{X}_B)\beta_A\right]} \tag{3.1}$$

$$W_{\Delta\beta}^{k} = \frac{\left[(\beta_A^k - \beta_B^k)\overline{X}_B^k\right]\phi(\overline{X}_B\beta_B)}{\left[(\beta_A - \beta_B)\overline{X}_B\right]\phi(\overline{X}_B\beta_B)} = \frac{\left[(\beta_A^k - \beta_B^k)\overline{X}_B^k\right]}{\left[(\beta_A - \beta_B)\overline{X}_B\right]} \tag{3.2}$$

$$\sum_{k=1}^{K} W_{\Delta X}^{k} = \sum_{k=1}^{K} W_{\Delta\beta}^{k} = 1 \tag{3.3}$$

where $W_{\Delta X}^{k}$ and $W_{\Delta\beta}^{k}$ are the respective weights of the kth covariate for the characteristics and coefficients effects, and ϕ denotes the standard normal probability density function. With the weights defined in Eqs. (3.1) and (3.2), we are able to retrieve the Probit decomposition results through Eq. (3). Fairlie (2005) also derives a nonlinear decomposition for Probit/Logit regression concentrating on the explained proportion. In our empirical results, we not only report Yun's (2004) decomposition (both explained and un-explained proportions) but also list Fairlie's (2005) detailed decomposition for explained proportion.

The dependent variable is the employment status (WORK) of foreign spouses. As for employment status, we measure the employed/nonemployed choice rather than the labor force participation decision due to limitations in the survey questionnaire design. By definition in the survey, employed people include those who have full-time or part-time paid jobs and those who work without pay in a family business; all others are categorized as nonemployed. The independent variables are categorized into four sets, and Table 5 reports their definitions, measurements, and basic descriptive statistics.

4. ESTIMATION RESULTS

Table 6 presents the estimation results for the employment status of the foreign spouses. We include the sample of native spouses into our analysis, and Table 7 lists the Probit estimation results of the employment probability for both the native samples and foreign spouses. Finally, we conduct the decomposition analysis between native and foreign spouses based on both Yun's and Fairlie's approaches. Tables 8–11 show the results.

4.1. Comparison between SEA and MCH Spouses

Table 6 presents the estimation results of the employment probabilities for the foreign spouses. As expected, the presence of small children lowers the employment probabilities of foreign spouses in Taiwan. This result is similar to the common findings from the literature (Oppenheimer, 1982; Waite, 1980; Yamanaka, 1987). The negative effect of small children on employment probability is stronger for SEA spouses (11.8%) compared to that for MCH spouses (5.2%). These results suggest that a mother's decision to work involves a careful assessment of her time allocation between work and family, because childbearing and childcare are relatively time-consuming.

The husband's employment status and educational level exhibit a more significant influence on the employment decision of foreign spouses than the effect of their health status. In particular, HUSFULLT and HUSPARTT have significantly negative influences on the employment probability of foreign spouses, while HEALTHB and HEALTHVB have no significant effects at all. This result indicates that foreign spouses who marry husbands with a higher level of education or who have employment are less likely to work. Among SEA spouses, those with employed husbands have lower employment probabilities

Table 5. Definitions, Measurements, and Basic Statistics of Variables for foreign Spouses.

Variables	Definition and Measurement	Mean and SD for Total SE Asian Spouses		Mean and SD for Total Chinese Spouses		Mean and SD for Total Foreign Spouses	
Family Background							
CHILD < 6	Number of children younger than six years old.	0.955	(0.80)	0.651	(0.77)	0.796	(0.80)
HEALTHVB	Dummy variable: one if the respondent's husband has very bad health.	0.000	(0.02)	0.002	(0.04)	0.001	(0.03)
HEALTHB	Dummy variable: one if the respondent's husband has bad health.	0.005	(0.07)	0.016	(0.13)	0.011	(0.10)
HEALTHG	Dummy variable: one if the respondent's husband has good health.	0.048	(0.21)	0.069	(0.25)	0.059	(0.24)
HEALTHVG	The respondent whose husband has very good health is set as the reference group for husband's health status.	0.946	(0.23)	0.913	(0.28)	0.929	(0.26)
HUSFULLT	Dummy variable: one if the respondent's husband works full-time.	0.820	(0.38)	0.686	(0.46)	0.750	(0.43)
HUSPARTT	Dummy variable: one if the respondent's husband works part-time.	0.114	(0.32)	0.110	(0.31)	0.112	(0.32)
HUSNOWORK	The respondent whose husband does not work is set as the reference group for husband's employment status.	0.066	(0.25)	0.204	(0.40)	0.138	(0.34)
HUSPRIMA	Dummy variable: one if the respondent's husband is illiterate, graduated from elementary school or studied by himself	0.137	(0.34)	0.177	(0.38)	0.158	(0.36)
HUSJUNIO	Dummy variable: one if the respondent's husband graduated from junior high school, or studied by herself.	0.422	(0.49)	0.295	(0.46)	0.356	(0.48)
HUSCOLLE	Dummy variable: one if the respondent's husband graduated from college.	0.080	(0.27)	0.157	(0.36)	0.120	(0.33)
HUSSENIOR	The respondent whose husband graduated from senior high school is set as the reference group for the husband's educational level	0.361	(0.48)	0.371	(0.48)	0.367	(0.48)
PARENT	Dummy variable: one if the respondent lives with her parent(s)-in law.	0.572	(0.49)	0.389	(0.49)	0.476	(0.50)
SIBLING	Dummy variable: one if the respondent lives with her sibling(s)-in law.	0.184	(0.39)	0.138	(0.34)	0.160	(0.37)
Human and Social Capital							
PRIMARY	Dummy variable: one if the respondent is illiterate, graduated from elementary school, or studied by himself.	0.365	(0.48)	0.202	(0.40)	0.280	(0.45)

JUNIOR	Dummy variable: one if the respondent graduated junior high school	0.361	(0.48)	0.410	(0.49)	0.387	(0.49)
COLLEGE	Dummy variable: one if the respondent graduated from college.	0.064	(0.24)	0.107	(0.31)	0.086	(0.28)
SENIOR	The respondent that graduated from senior high school is set as the reference group for educational level	0.211	(0.41)	0.281	(0.45)	0.247	(0.43)
AGE	The respondent's age at the time of survey.	26.465	(6.54)	32.776	(8.93)	29.765	(8.49)
AGESQ	The squared term of respondent's age.	743.172	(419.13)	1153.959	(732.16)	957.981	(637.35)
LANGFLU	Dummy variable: one if the respondent speaks the host language fluently.	0.577	(0.49)	0.619	(0.49)	0.599	(0.49)
LANGUNCE	Dummy variable: one if the respondent's language skills are unrecognizable.	0.206	(0.40)	0.343	(0.47)	0.278	(0.45)
LANGUOFLU	The respondent that does not speak the host language fluently is set as the reference group for language fluency.	0.217	(0.41)	0.038	(0.19)	0.123	(0.33)
NUMPROG	Number of programs or courses attended in the past.	0.216	(0.46)	0.060	(0.28)	0.135	(0.38)
Assimilation Effect							
YSM	The respondent's years since migration.	3.693	(2.65)	3.597	(2.76)	3.643	(2.71)
YSMSQ	The squared term of respondent's YSM.	20.645	(26.84)	20.546	(26.62)	20.593	(26.73)
YSM-AGE1524	Interactive term of YSM and AGE1524 – dummy variable of value one if the respondent's age is between 15 and 24 years old in 2003.	1.104	(1.51)	0.198	(0.68)	0.630	(1.24)
YSM-AGE2534	Interactive terms of YSM and AGE2534 – a dummy variable of value one if the respondent's age is between 25 and 34 years old in 2003.	1.890	(2.84)	2.191	(2.75)	2.047	(2.79)
YSM-AGE3544	Interactive term of YSM and AGE3544 – a dummy variable of value one if the respondent's age is between 35 and 44 years old in 2003.	0.543	(1.98)	0.739	(2.01)	0.646	(2.00)
YSM-AGE4554	Interactive term of YSM and AGE4554 – a dummy variable of value one if the respondent's age is between 45 and 54 years old in 2003.	0.133	(1.04)	0.300	(1.33)	0.220	(1.21)
Other Control Variable							
RESIDE	Dummy variable: one if the immigrant status is residency.	–	–	0.152	(0.36)		
P-RESIDE	Dummy variable: one if the immigrant status is permanent residency. Only respondents from Southeast Asia may hold this status.	0.007	(0.08)	–	–	0.083	(0.28)
CITIZENS	Dummy variable: one if the immigrant status is citizenship.	0.192	(0.39)	0.107	(0.31)	0.147	(0.35)

Table 5. *(Continued)*

Variables	Definition and Measurement	Mean and SD for Total SE Asian Spouses		Mean and SD for Total Chinese Spouses		Mean and SD for Total Foreign Spouses	
RESIDE and STAY	The respondent whose immigrant status is residency is set as the reference group in the equation of Southeast Asian spouses	0.801	(0.40)	0.741	(0.44)	0.770	(0.42)
CITY	Dummy variable: one if the respondent lives in a city or a municipality.	0.081	(0.27)	0.121	(0.33)	0.102	(0.30)
MUNI	Dummy variable: one if the respondent lives in a municipality.	0.089	(0.28)	0.156	(0.36)	0.124	(0.33)
COUNTRY	The respondent that lives in a country is set as the reference group.	0.831	(0.37)	0.723	(0.45)	0.775	(0.42)
NORTH	Dummy variable: one if the respondent lives in the north of Taiwan.	0.376	(0.48)	0.475	(0.50)	0.428	(0.49)
CENTRAL	Dummy variable: one if the respondent lives in central Taiwan.	0.300	(0.46)	0.218	(0.41)	0.257	(0.44)
EAST	Dummy variable: one if the respondent lives in the east of Taiwan.	0.022	(0.15)	0.029	(0.17)	0.026	(0.16)
KINMA	Dummy variable: one if the respondent lives in Kinmen Country or Lienchiang County.	0.003	(0.06)	0.006	(0.08)	0.005	(0.07)
SOUTH	The respondent that lives in the south of Taiwan is set as the reference group for region of residence.	0.299	(0.46)	0.272	(0.44)	0.285	(0.45)

Note: SD, the standard deviation, is in parenthesis. The sample size of total Southeast Asian spouses is 72,898; the sample size of total mainland Chinese spouses is 79,902.

Table 6. Binary Probit Estimates of Employment Probability for Foreign Spouses.

Variable	Foreign Spouses			Southeast Asian Spouses			Chinese Spouses		
	Coeff.	*t*-ratio	ME	Coeff.	*t*-ratio	ME	Coeff.	*t*-ratio	ME
Family Background:									
CHILD < 6	−0.268***	(−46.89)	−0.087	−0.335***	(−42.05)	−0.118	−0.182***	(−21.03)	−0.052
HEALTHVB	0.059	(0.56)	0.020	−0.007	(−0.03)	−0.002	0.064	(0.52)	0.019
HEALTHB	0.010	(0.28)	0.003	0.001	(0.01)	0.000	0.014	(0.34)	0.004
HEALTHG	0.177***	(11.65)	0.060	0.123***	(5.18)	0.044	0.217***	(10.82)	0.067
HUSFULLT	−0.122***	(−9.69)	−0.040	−0.088***	(−4.13)	−0.031	−0.166***	(−10.11)	−0.049
HUSPARTT	−0.073***	(−4.75)	−0.023	−0.058**	(−2.33)	−0.020	−0.069***	(−3.34)	−0.019
HUSPRIMA	0.126***	(10.91)	0.042	0.031*	(1.84)	0.011	0.151***	(9.16)	0.045
HUSJUNIO	0.066***	(7.68)	0.021	0.027**	(2.35)	0.010	0.057***	(4.38)	0.017
HUSCOLLE	−0.112***	(−8.90)	−0.035	−0.047**	(−2.31)	−0.016	−0.111***	(−6.66)	−0.031
PARENT	0.039***	(4.82)	0.013	0.058***	(5.38)	0.020	−0.009	(−0.71)	−0.003
SIBLING	0.018*	(1.71)	0.006	0.044***	(3.23)	0.015	−0.003	(−0.17)	−0.001
Human and Social Capital:									
PRIMARY	0.005	(0.46)	0.002	−0.083***	(−5.95)	−0.029	0.021	(1.36)	0.006
JUNIOR	−0.006	(−0.60)	−0.002	−0.021	(−1.49)	−0.007	0.005	(0.40)	0.001
COLLEGE	0.070***	(4.88)	0.023	0.071***	(3.11)	0.025	0.070***	(3.75)	0.021
AGE	0.025***	(7.29)	0.008	0.087***	(11.21)	0.031	0.091***	(16.71)	0.026
AGESQ	0.000***	(−9.74)	0.000	−0.001***	(−10.36)	0.000	−0.001***	(−16.55)	0.000
LANGFLU	−0.127***	(−10.97)	−0.042	−0.021	(−1.57)	−0.007	−0.088***	(−3.14)	−0.026
LANGUNCE	0.182***	(14.57)	0.061	0.431***	(27.73)	0.159	0.181***	(6.33)	0.053
NUMPROG	0.206***	(22.82)	0.067	0.140***	(12.89)	0.049	0.138***	(7.84)	0.040

Table 6. *(Continued)*

Variable	Foreign Spouses			Southeast Asian Spouses			Chinese Spouses		
	Coeff.	*t*-ratio	ME	Coeff.	*t*-ratio	ME	Coeff.	*t*-ratio	ME
Assimilation Effect:									
YSM	0.214***	(23.31)	0.069	0.212***	(11.06)	0.075	0.245***	(21.20)	0.070
YSMSQ	−0.017***	(−29.63)	−0.005	−0.012***	(−13.72)	−0.004	−0.021***	(−25.11)	−0.006
YSM-AGE1524	0.091***	(11.33)	0.030	0.024	(1.40)	0.009	0.091***	(7.36)	0.026
YSM-AGE2534	0.076***	(10.33)	0.024	0.013	(0.76)	0.005	0.074***	(8.65)	0.021
YSM-AGE3544	0.077***	(10.91)	0.025	−0.009	(−0.56)	−0.003	0.069***	(8.13)	0.020
YSM-AGE4554	0.069***	(10.91)	0.022	−0.007	(−0.52)	−0.003	0.056***	(7.50)	0.016
Other Control Variable:									
P-RESIDE/RESIDE	0.164***	(11.99)	0.055	0.155***	(2.64)	0.056	0.286***	(18.09)	0.089
CITIZEN	0.534***	(40.78)	0.190	0.422***	(25.72)	0.156	0.756***	(31.63)	0.260
CITY	−0.126***	(−10.20)	−0.039	−0.125***	(−6.57)	−0.043	−0.082***	(−4.96)	−0.023
MUNI	−0.136***	(−11.56)	−0.043	−0.249***	(−12.97)	−0.083	−0.035**	(−2.30)	−0.010
NORTH	0.053***	(6.01)	0.017	0.020	(1.59)	0.007	0.083***	(6.47)	0.024
CENTRAL	0.111***	(11.10)	0.036	0.116***	(8.71)	0.041	0.081***	(5.25)	0.024
EAST	0.022	(0.95)	0.007	−0.067*	(−1.90)	−0.023	0.131***	(4.07)	0.040
KINMA	−0.300***	(−5.31)	−0.087	−0.668***	(−6.18)	−0.187	−0.053	(−0.77)	−0.015
CONSTANT	−1.521***	(−25.12)		−2.238***	(-19.65)		−3.126***	(−29.27)	
Chi-squared		19,671.18			9,150.45			12,367.88	
Sample size		152,800			72,898			79,902	

Notes: ***, Statistical significance level at 1%. **, Statistical significance level at 5%. *, Statistical significance level at 10%.

Table 7. Binary Probit Estimates of Employment Probability for Native and Foreign Spouses.

Variable	Native Spouses			Foreign Spouses		
	Coeff.	*t*-ratio	ME	Coeff.	*t*-ratio	ME
Family Background:						
CHILD < 6	−0.207***	−8.49	−0.078	−0.259***	−46.42	−0.084
HUSFULLT	0.483***	15.59	0.175	−0.155***	−12.96	−0.052
HUSPARTT	0.464***	4.20	0.182	−0.097***	−6.46	−0.031
HUSPRIMA	−0.058	−1.56	−0.022	0.122***	10.67	0.041
HUSJUNIO	−0.122***	−3.83	−0.045	0.066***	7.74	0.022
HUSCOLLE	−0.080**	−2.39	−0.030	−0.111***	−8.85	−0.035
Human Capital:						
PRIMARY	−0.080**	−2.25	−0.030	0.023**	2.27	0.007
JUNIOR	−0.211***	−3.74	−0.077	−0.008	−0.88	−0.003
COLLEGE	0.643***	12.52	0.251	0.056 ***	3.96	0.019
AGE	0.151***	8.97	0.057	0.025***	7.19	0.008
AGESQ	−0.002***	−10.82	−0.001	0.000***	−9.15	0.000
Assimilation Effect/Potential Labor Market Experience:						
YSM	0.012	1.55	0.005	0.180***	19.99	0.059
YSMSQ	0.000	−0.80	0.000	−0.011***	−19.46	−0.003
YSM-AGE1524	−0.029	−1.05	−0.011	0.112***	14.08	0.037
YSM-AGE2534	−0.018**	−3.06	−0.007	0.093***	12.75	0.030
YSM-AGE3544	−0.013***	−4.46	−0.005	0.087***	12.44	0.028
YSM-AGE4554	−0.006***	−3.69	−0.002	0.071***	11.41	0.023
Other Control Variable:						
CITY	−0.160***	−4.87	−0.059	−0.122***	−10.01	−0.039
MUNI	0.009	0.31	0.004	−0.148***	−12.65	−0.046
NORTH	−0.013	−0.54	−0.005	0.051***	5.82	0.017
CENTRAL	−0.045	−1.06	−0.017	0.123***	12.53	0.041
EAST	−0.018	−0.32	−0.007	0.032	1.38	0.011
CONSTANT	−2.693***	−8.23		−1.447***	−24.25	n.a.
Chi-squared		4,589.48			15,908.29	
Sample size		16,827			152,800	

Notes: YSM variable denotes years since being married for native spouses. This variable represents the potential labor market experience after marriage. ***, Statistical significance level at 1%. **, Statistical significance level at 5%,*, Statistical significance level at 10%.

Table 8. Probit Decomposition of Employment Probability-Southeast Asian and Chinese Spouses.

Variable	Decomposition (YUN)				Decomposition (FAIRLIE)	
	Difference in Characteristics		Difference in Coefficients		Difference in characteristics	
Family Background:						
CHILD < 6	−0.0357	(−42.88)	−0.0290	(−34.80)	−0.0426	(−51.27)
HEALTHVB	0.0000	(0.00)	0.0000	(−0.04)	0.0000	(0.00)
HEALTHB	0.0000	(−0.01)	0.0000	(−0.06)	0.0000	(−0.01)
HEALTHG	−0.0009	(−1.05)	−0.0018	(−2.21)	−0.0009	(−1.10)
HUSFULLT	−0.0041	(−4.90)	0.0155	(18.64)	−0.0042	(−5.00)
HUSPARTT	−0.0001	(−0.08)	0.0003	(0.42)	0.0000	(−0.01)
HUSILLIT	−0.0004	(−0.52)	−0.0061	(−7.31)	−0.0005	(−0.58)
HUSJUNIO	0.0012	(1.48)	−0.0025	(−3.02)	0.0011	(1.38)
HUSCOLLE	0.0013	(1.51)	0.0029	(3.45)	0.0011	(1.31)
PARENT	0.0037	(4.49)	0.0075	(9.04)	0.0036	(4.35)
SIBLING	0.0007	(0.84)	0.0018	(2.21)	0.0006	(0.74)
Human and Social Capital:						
PRIMARY	−0.0047	(−5.66)	−0.0061	(−7.27)	−0.0041	(−4.92)
JUNIOR	0.0003	(0.42)	−0.0030	(−3.61)	0.0003	(0.39)
COLLEGE	−0.0011	(−1.31)	0.0000	(0.05)	−0.0010	(−1.15)
AGE	−0.1927	(−231.58)	−0.0347	(−41.70)	−0.1602	(−192.98)
AGESQ	0.1881	(226.02)	−0.0429	(−51.57)	0.1536	(185.03)
LANGFLU	0.0003	(0.37)	0.0120	(14.47)	0.0001	(0.18)
LANGUNCE	−0.0207	(−24.84)	0.0246	(29.52)	−0.0203	(−24.49)
NUMPROG	0.0076	(9.15)	0.0000	(0.01)	0.0072	(8.69)
Assimilation Effect:					0.0001	(0.18)
YSM	0.0071	(8.59)	−0.0347	(−41.72)	0.0139	(16.70)
YSMSQ	−0.0004	(−0.50)	0.0527	(63.31)	−0.0003	(−0.40)
YSM-AGE1524	0.0075	(9.04)	−0.0038	(−4.56)	0.0072	(8.62)
YSM-AGE2534	−0.0013	(−1.56)	−0.0386	(−46.40)	−0.0012	(−1.40)
YSM-AGE3544	0.0006	(0.76)	−0.0164	(−19.73)	0.0006	(0.77)
YSM-AGE4554	0.0004	(0.53)	−0.0055	(−6.55)	0.0005	(0.55)
Other Control Variable:						
P-RESIDE/RESIDE	−0.0079	(−9.54)	−0.0055	(−6.66)	−0.0079	(−9.46)
CITIZENS	0.0128	(15.39)	−0.0100	(−12.06)	0.0139	(16.76)
CITY	0.0018	(2.10)	−0.0015	(−1.79)	0.0018	(2.15)

Table 8. *(Continued)*

Variable	Decomposition (YUN)				Decomposition (FAIRLIE)	
	Difference in Characteristics		Difference in Coefficients		Difference in characteristics	
Other Control Variable:						
MUNI	0.0058	(7.00)	−0.0095	(−11.46)	0.0064	(7.71)
NORTH	−0.0007	(−0.84)	−0.0084	(−10.15)	−0.0007	(−0.85)
CENTRAL	0.0033	(3.97)	0.0022	(2.64)	0.0036	(4.32)
EAST	0.0001	(0.16)	−0.0016	(−1.92)	0.0001	(0.17)
KINMA	0.0007	(0.85)	−0.0011	(−1.33)	0.0009	(1.10)
CONSTANT	n.a.	n.a.	0.2535	(304.73)	n.a.	n.a.
Sum	0.0093	(11.14)	0.2351	(282.50)	−0.0280	(−33.46)

Note: Share of $F(X_A B_A)-F(X_B B_B) = 0.083$ is reported in parentheses in percentage.

of working than the reference group by 3.1% (full-time employment) and 2.0% (part-time employment), respectively. Among MCH spouses, these negative influences are 4.9% and 1.9%, respectively. However, the influence of marrying a husband with a bad or very bad health status on employment probability is insignificant.[6]

As to the role of human capital, the results show that a foreign spouse's educational level generally has a positive influence on the probability of working. The influences for SEA spouses differ from those for MCH spouses. Similar to the finding in Chuang et al. (2010), SEA spouses with lower educational attainments have a significantly lower probability of working, "while among MCH spouses, only those with a college or above education are found to have a significantly higher probability of working than senior high school graduates. The significantly positive coefficient of the AGE variable indicates that the older the women are, the more likely they are to work." An additional year of age increases the probability of working by 3.1% for SEA spouses and by 2.6% for MCH spouses.

This study uses the NUMPROG variable to measure the role of social networking, finding that this variable has a significantly positive influence on the employment probability of foreign spouses. For SEA spouses, each additional program they participate in is associated with an increase in their working probability by 4.9%, and for MCH spouses this probability rises by 4.0%. Our findings confirm that personal networks beyond the family are positively associated with the employment probability of foreign spouses. This result also parallels previous findings in the literature such as those Coleman (1990), Portes (1995), and Aguilera (2002).

Table 9. Probit Decomposition of Employment Probability-Native and Foreign Spouses.

Variable	Decomposition (YUN)				Decomposition (FAIRLIE)	
	Diff. in characteristics		Diff. in coefficients		Diff. in characteristics	
Family Background:						
CHILD < 6	0.0089	(5.61)	0.0141	(8.89)	0.0268	(16.80)
HUSFULLT	−0.0028	(−1.74)	0.1650	(103.82)	0.0011	(0.67)
HUSPARTT	−0.0037	(−2.35)	0.0217	(13.63)	−0.0153	(−9.61)
HUSPRIMA	−0.0007	(−0.45)	−0.0098	(−6.16)	−0.0018	(−1.13)
HUSJUNIO	0.0017	(1.05)	−0.0230	(−14.48)	0.0052	(3.23)
HUSCOLLE	−0.0007	(−0.43)	0.0013	(0.81)	−0.0030	(−1.86)
Human Capital:						
PRIMARY	−0.0007	(−0.46)	−0.0099	(−6.21)	−0.0009	(−0.55)
JUNIOR	0.0050	(3.13)	−0.0270	(−16.98)	0.0178	(11.16)
COLLEGE	0.0030	(1.88)	0.0175	(11.01)	0.0131	(8.18)
AGE	0.2072	(130.36)	1.2962	(815.38)	0.2234	(140.05)
AGESQ	−0.2412	(−151.69)	−0.5472	(−344.22)	−0.3194	(−200.26)
Assimilation Effect/Potential Labor Market Experience:						
YSM	0.0198	(12.45)	−0.2114	(−132.97)	0.0906	(56.78)
YSMSQ	−0.0078	(−4.90)	0.0740	(46.54)	−0.0328	(−20.57)
YSM-AGE1524	0.0013	(0.81)	−0.0306	(−19.22)	0.0059	(3.72)
YSM-AGE2534	0.0013	(0.82)	−0.0781	(−49.15)	0.0061	(3.81)
YSM-AGE3544	−0.0037	(−2.33)	−0.0224	(−14.06)	−0.0182	(−11.40)
YSM-AGE4554	−0.0032	(−1.99)	−0.0059	(−3.72)	−0.0154	(−9.65)
Other Control Variable:						
CITY	−0.0006	(−0.35)	−0.0013	(−0.83)	−0.0025	(−1.59)
MUNI	0.0000	(0.02)	0.0067	(4.21)	0.0002	(0.10)
NORTH	0.0001	(0.04)	−0.0094	(−5.91)	0.0003	(0.16)
CENTRAL	0.0006	(0.39)	−0.0148	(−9.34)	0.0029	(1.84)
EAST	0.0000	(−0.01)	−0.0004	(−0.28)	−0.0001	(−0.06)
CONSTANT	n.a.	n.a.	−0.4302	(−270.61)	n.a.	n.a.
Sum	−0.0161	(−10.15)	0.1751	(110.15)	−0.0163	(−10.21)

Note: Share of $F(X_A B_A) - F(X_B B_B) = 0.159$ are reported in parentheses in percentage. YSM variable denotes years since being married for native spouses. This variable represents the potential labor market experience after marriage.

Table 10. Probit Decomposition of Employment Probability – Native and Southeast Asian Spouses.

Variable	Decomposition (YUN)				Decomposition (FAIRLIE)	
	Diff. in characteristics		Diff. in coefficients		Diff. in characteristics	
Family Background:						
CHILD < 6	−0.0153	(−13.21)	0.0387	(33.48)	0.0351	(30.29)
HUSFULLT	0.0072	(6.20)	0.1783	(154.20)	−0.0075	(−6.44)
HUSPARTT	0.0051	(4.38)	0.0221	(19.15)	−0.0150	(−12.94)
HUSPRIMA	0.0011	(0.93)	−0.0039	(−3.36)	−0.0020	(−1.76)
HUSJUNIO	−0.0031	(−2.65)	−0.0214	(−18.52)	0.0075	(6.46)
HUSCOLLE	0.0012	(1.07)	−0.0007	(−0.61)	−0.0040	(−3.48)
Human Capital:						
PRIMARY	0.0003	(0.23)	−0.0004	(−0.37)	0.0015	(1.31)
JUNIOR	−0.0061	(−5.24)	−0.0241	(−20.84)	0.0157	(13.58)
COLLEGE	−0.0055	(−4.74)	0.0133	(11.52)	0.0183	(15.75)
AGE	−0.3271	(−282.92)	0.6313	(546.13)	0.2582	(222.70)
AGESQ	0.3673	(317.74)	−0.2227	(−192.61)	−0.3329	(−287.18)
Assimilation Effect/Potential Labor Market Experience:						
YSM	−0.0262	(−22.70)	−0.2684	(−232.21)	0.0907	(78.27)
YSMSQ	0.0104	(8.96)	0.0782	(67.66)	−0.0331	(−28.58)
YSM-AGE1524	−0.0031	(−2.70)	−0.0256	(−22.18)	0.0107	(9.20)
YSM-AGE2534	−0.0014	(−1.24)	−0.0360	(−31.15)	0.0050	(4.29)
YSM-AGE3544	0.0051	(4.38)	−0.0040	(−3.43)	−0.0187	(−16.09)
YSM-AGE4554	0.0043	(3.70)	−0.0004	(−0.35)	−0.0153	(−13.20)
Other Control Variable:						
CITY	0.0011	(0.94)	−0.0011	(−0.93)	−0.0038	(−3.24)
MUNI	−0.0001	(−0.07)	0.0086	(7.48)	0.0003	(0.24)
NORTH	0.0000	(−0.00)	−0.0043	(−3.71)	0.0000	(0.01)
CENTRAL	−0.0010	(−0.88)	−0.0185	(−16.01)	0.0036	(3.12)
EAST	0.0000	(0.03)	0.0004	(0.35)	−0.0001	(-0.10)
CONSTANT	n.a.	n.a.	−0.2380	(−205.88)	n.a.	n.a.
Sum	0.0141	(12.20)	0.1015	(87.80)	0.0141	(12.20)

Note: Share of $F(X_A B_A)-F(X_B B_B) = 0.116$ are reported in parentheses in percentage. YSM variable denotes years since being married for native spouses. This variable represents the potential labor market experience after marriage.

Table 11. Probit Decomposition of Employment Probability – Native and Chinese Spouses.

Variable	Decomposition (YUN)				Decomposition (FAIRLIE)	
	Diff. in characteristics		Diff. in coefficients		Diff. in characteristics	
Family Background:						
CHILD < 6	0.0136	(6.84)	−0.0026	(−1.29)	0.0199	(9.98)
HUSFULLT	−0.0007	(−0.37)	0.1509	(76.03)	0.0069	(3.46)
HUSPARTT	−0.0076	(−3.83)	0.0199	(10.04)	−0.0159	(−8.01)
HUSPRIMA	−0.0013	(−0.65)	−0.0114	(−5.74)	−0.0016	(−0.82)
HUSJUNIO	0.0023	(1.13)	−0.0169	(−8.51)	0.0032	(1.59)
HUSCOLLE	−0.0009	(−0.47)	0.0008	(0.42)	−0.0021	(−1.04)
Human Capital:						
PRIMARY	−0.0025	(−1.25)	−0.0073	(−3.68)	−0.0029	(−1.44)
JUNIOR	0.0111	(5.58)	−0.0284	(−14.29)	0.0191	(9.62)
COLLEGE	0.0040	(2.03)	0.0200	(10.08)	0.0086	(4.33)
AGE	0.3547	(178.66)	0.5975	(300.97)	0.2039	(102.46)
AGESQ	−0.4316	(−217.39)	−0.3441	(−173.33)	−0.3175	(−159.53)
Assimilation Effect/Potential Labor Market Experience:						
YSM	0.0410	(20.64)	−0.1948	(−98.11)	0.0905	(45.47)
YSMSQ	−0.0161	(−8.11)	0.0597	(30.10)	−0.0327	(−16.41)
YSM-AGE1524	0.0007	(0.34)	−0.0085	(−4.26)	0.0015	(0.77)
YSM-AGE2534	0.0031	(1.56)	−0.0766	(−38.60)	0.0072	(3.59)
YSM-AGE3544	−0.0075	(−3.75)	−0.0224	(−11.28)	−0.0177	(−8.87)
YSM-AGE4554	−0.0065	(−3.26)	−0.0063	(−3.17)	−0.0155	(−7.77)
Other Control Variable:						
CITY	−0.0007	(−0.33)	−0.0036	(−1.83)	−0.0014	(−0.72)
MUNI	0.0000	(0.01)	0.0025	(1.25)	0.0000	(0.02)
NORTH	0.0002	(0.11)	−0.0161	(−8.09)	0.0005	(0.24)
CENTRAL	0.0010	(0.50)	−0.0093	(−4.67)	0.0023	(1.15)
EAST	0.0000	(−0.02)	−0.0015	(−0.76)	−0.0001	(−0.04)
CONSTANT	n.a.	n.a.	0.1405	(70.75)	n.a.	n.a.
Sum	−0.0437	(−22.03)	0.2423	(122.03)	−0.0437	(−21.97)

Note: Share of $F(X_A B_A)-F(X_B B_B) = 0.199$ are reported in parentheses in percentage. YSM variable denotes years since being married for native spouses. This variable represents the potential labor market experience after marriage.

The coefficient of the YSM variable reflects the employment assimilation effect. As shown in Table 6, the YSM variable has a significantly positive effect on the employment probabilities of both the SEA spouses and MCH spouses – that is, the employment probability of foreign spouses rises rapidly with the number of years that have elapsed since migration. Each additional year of stay in Taiwan increases the employment probability by 7.5% for SEA spouses and by 7.0% for MCH spouses. However, the negative sign of the YSMSQ variable suggests that this positive effect on employment probability will decline for the duration of residence. The implication of our findings is that the employment probability of marriage immigrants may catch up to a level that is compatible with native women as they spend more time in Taiwan. However, the rate of convergence declines with the length of their stay.

We include the interactive terms of the YSM variable and the age group dummy variables in order to examine whether there is any difference in terms of the assimilation effect among the four age groups. These interactive terms show insignificant effects for the SEA spouses, while they have a significant influence on the employment probability of MCH spouses.[7] The finding for MCH spouses suggests that the assimilation effect becomes weaker for the older age group. This pattern of the assimilation effect is reasonable since it is more difficult to adapt to a new environment when one is older.

4.2. Comparison between Foreign Spouses and Native Women

We conduct a similar analysis for native women and foreign spouses in Taiwan based on the combined dataset of the *2003 Survey of Foreign and Mainland Spouses' Life Status* and *2003 Women's Marriage, Fertility and Employment Survey*. The explanatory variables included in the Probit specification are not exactly the same as those shown in Table 6 due to the difference in the contents of the questionnaire between the two surveys. Table 7 reports the Probit estimation results.

Most of the Probit estimation results for the foreign spouses are consistent with our expectation and also lead to similar implications as those indicated in Table 6. For example, foreign spouses with more small children are less likely to work. Foreign spouses married to husbands who are employed or have a higher educational level have lower employment probability. As to the effect of the human capital variables, foreign spouses with a college level of education have a higher tendency to work. The age variables show a nonlinear effect on the employment probability of foreign spouses. Similar to the common findings in the literature, the employment probability of foreign spouses increases with age at a decreasing rate. The implication of the employment assimilation effect is the same as that discussed in Table 6.

As for native women, similar to the finding in the existing literature, human capital variables such as schooling and age are the most significant factors affecting the employment probability for Taiwanese women, while husbands' characteristics play a less important role in this respect. For instance, native women with a college level of education are associated with an increase in their working probability by 25.1%. However, native women marrying husbands with a college level of education only lower their employment probability by 3.0%.

According to the results reported in Table 7, we can infer that family background variables including the presence of small children and husbands' characteristics play fairly significant roles in determining the employment probability of foreign spouses as compared to the influence of the human capital variables. On the other hand, human capital variables such as schooling and age are more influential on the employment decision for native women. We also note that, different from the findings for foreign spouses, husbands' employment status shows a positive and significant impact on native women's employment probability. The YSM variable, which represents the potential labor market experience for foreign spouses, also has a strong influence on their employment decision. However, the potential labor market experience after getting married, as denoted by YSM, for the native women shows no significant role in their employment decision.

4.3. Decomposition Analysis of Employment Probability

We apply the nonlinear decomposition method developed by Yun (2004) on the Probit estimation results of the employment probability in order to examine whether the employment probability differentials between SEA and MCH spouses are due to the difference in characteristics or the difference in coefficients. Table 8 reports the results regarding the Probit decomposition between the SEA spouses and MCH spouses.

As shown in Table 8, the employment probability differentials between the SEA and MCH spouses are mostly attributed to the difference in coefficients. The difference in coefficients, in sum, contributes to increasing the gap of the employment probability, while the difference in characteristics, in sum, tends to reduce the employment probability differentials between the SEA and MCH spouses.

The age variables specifically play the most influential role in explaining the employment probability differentials between SEA and MCH spouses. Both the difference in characteristics and difference in coefficients of the age variables contribute to reducing the gap of the employment probability. The presence of small children tends to lower the employment probability. The differences in coefficients contribute to reducing the racial gap in employment probability. The effects of the difference in the number of children under age 6 are non-negligible since there is a significant difference in this number between SEA and MCH spouses, as Table 5 shows.

As to the impact of the assimilation variables, the employment probability of the SEA spouses rises with the number of years that have elapsed since migration. This positive effect of the YSM variable is also found for MCH spouses, but the differences in coefficients contribute to reducing the racial gap of the employment probability since MCH spouses have larger coefficients. In sum, the YSM variable contributes to reducing the differences in employment probability between SEA and MCH spouses.

Tables 9–11 report the Probit decomposition results between the native and foreign spouses. We note that the employment probability differentials between any two groups of spouses (native versus foreign spouses, native versus SEA spouses, or native versus MCH spouses) are mostly due to the difference in coefficients in general. Similar to those found in the employment probability gap between SEA and MCH spouses, the effects of the two age variables are very large. However, the decomposition results in Table 8 indicate that the role of age variables in the employment probability gap between SEA and MCH spouses comes from the difference in characteristics, while the employment probability gap is mostly due to the difference in coefficients between any two groups of native and foreign spouses. This finding implies that, in terms of the age effect, Taiwan's labor market may reward native and foreign spouses differently, but there is little differential in the labor market reward in this aspect between SEA and MCH spouses specifically.

5. CONCLUSION

Little is known about the labor market activity of foreign spouses in Taiwan due to a lack of studies on this issue. Our study looks to fill this gap in the literature by examining the employment status of female spouses from Southeast Asia and mainland China with a focus on their assimilation process. We also compare the employment status of these marriage immigrants with native women in Taiwan based on the combined dataset of the *2003 Survey of Foreign and Mainland Spouses' Life Status* and *2003 Women's Marriage, Fertility and Employment Survey*. This study further applies decomposition analysis for the Probit model developed in Yun (2004) to examine the gap of employment probability in Taiwan between Southeast Asian spouses and mainland Chinese spouses as well as that between native women and foreign spouses.

The conceptual framework of this study incorporates the family labor supply model, human and social capital theories, and the immigrant assimilation theory. The estimation results for the employment probability based on our conceptual framework indicate that family background variables, including the presence of small children and husbands' characteristics, play fairly significant roles in determining the employment probability for these foreign spouses as compared to the influence of human capital variables. The finding that the employment probability of foreign spouses rises rapidly with the number of years that have elapsed since migration may confirm the employment assimilation for these marriage immigrants. As for native women, human capital variables such as schooling and age are the most significant factors affecting their employment probability, while husbands' characteristics play a less important role in this respect.

The Probit decomposition analysis suggests that the employment probability differentials between Southeast Asian and mainland Chinese spouses as well as those between the native and foreign spouses in Taiwan are mostly attributed to the difference in coefficients. The difference in coefficients, in sum, contributes to increasing the gap of the employment probability, while the difference in characteristics, in sum, tends to reduce the employment probability differentials. Moreover, the effects of the two age variables dominate the influence of all other variables in explaining the employment probability differentials.

Some policy implications may be derived based on our empirical results. For example, one finding implies that, in terms of the age effect, Taiwan's labor market may reward native and foreign spouses differently, but there is little differential in the labor market reward in this aspect between SEA and MCH spouses. As a result, policies that aim to eliminate labor market discrimination should pay more attention on any possible discrimination against marriage immigrants in Taiwan.

NOTES

1. The amendment to Article 48 of the Employment Services Act in 2003 indicates that spouses from Southeast Asia who hold resident certificates in Taiwan can work without applying for additional permits. The addition of Article 17-1 to the Statute Governing Relations between the People of the Taiwan Area and the People of the Mainland Area in 2000 states that spouses from mainland China holding resident certificates can work after applying for permits.

2. According to Chuang et al. (2010), the "traditional family" labor supply model "suggests that the labor supply of a wife depends on her husband's attributes or behavior, including those features such as wage rates and labor supply. However, the labor supply of a husband is not affected by the attributes or behavior of his wife."

3. McManus (1985) argues that if producers' identities are relevant to consumers, or their products are tailored for each customer, then communication skills are important, and a lack of language proficiency is likely to have a detrimental effect on their earnings. However, if products are standardized and there is little need to communicate with each customer face-to-face, then the producers' language skills are not crucial in determining their earnings. Likewise, Kossoudji (1988) stresses that the contribution of language skills to earnings varies by occupation, because jobs are not homogeneous in their use of language. Chiswick and Miller (1995) tackle the endogeneity between language proficiency and earnings to obtain a robust regression estimation.

4. In our particular dataset, the Logit specification produces quite similar results.

5. Alternatively, we can pick foreign spouses as denoting nondiscriminatory labor.

6. According to Chuang et al. (2010), "a possible explanation for this is that when husbands are unhealthy, foreign spouses need on the one hand to stay home to look after them, and to share more of the financial responsibilities of the family by working for pay

on the other. Hence, these opposite effects on the working probability may offset each other and yield an insignificant result."

7. A possible interpretation of the finding for SEA spouses provided by Chuang et al. (2010) is that "the SEA spouses are more likely to be in their 20s. The age variation is much smaller and therefore it is hard to reflect the effect of the age group on the employment assimilation based on our samples."

REFERENCES

Aguilera, M. B. (2002). The impact of social capital on labor force participation: Evidence from the 2000 Social Capital Benchmark Survey. *Social Science Quarterly*, *83*(3), 853–874.

Akay, A. (2016). Dynamics of employment assimilation. *IZA Journal of Migration*, *5*, 13.

Baker, M., & Dwayne, B. (1994). The performance of immigrants in the Canadian labor market. *Journal of Labor Economics*, *12*(3), 369–405.

Barth, E., Bratsberg, B., & Raaum, O. (2004). Identifying earnings assimilation of immigrants under changing macroeconomic conditions. *Scandinavian Journal of Economics*, *106*(1), 1–22.

Borjas, G. J. (1985). Assimilation, changes in cohort quality, and the earnings of immigrants. *Journal of Labor Economics*, *3*(4), 463–489.

Borjas, G. J. (1995). Assimilation and changes in cohort quality revisited: What happened to immigrant earnings in the 1980s? *Journal of Labor Economics*, *13*(2), 201–245.

Boyd, M. (1992). Gender issues in immigration and language fluency. In B. R. Chiswick (Ed.), *Immigration, language, and ethnicity: Canada and the United States*. Washington, DC: American Enterprise Institute.

Campolieti, M., Gunderson, M. Timofeeva, O., & Tsiroulnitchenko, E. (2013). Immigrant assimilation, Canada 1971-2006: Has the tide turned? *Journal of Labor Research*, *34*(4), 1–21.

Chiswick, B. R. (1978). The effect of Americanization on the earnings of foreign-born men. *Journal of Political Economy*, *86*(5), 897–921.

Chiswick, B. R. (1983). An analysis of the earnings and employment of Asian-American Men. *Journal of Labor Economics*, *1*(2), 197–214.

Chiswick, B. R., & Miller, P. W. (1995). The endogeneity between language and earnings – international analyses. *Journal of Labor Economics*, *13*(2), 246–288.

Chuang, H.-L., Hsieh, N., & Lin, E. S. (2010). Labour market activity of foreign spouses in Taiwan: Employment status and choice of employment sector. *Pacific Economic Review*, *15*(4), 505–531.

Clark, K., & Lindley, J. (2009). Immigrant assimilation pre and post labour market entry: Evidence from the UK Labour Force Survey. *Journal of Population Economics*, *22*(1), 175–198.

Cobb-Clark, D. A., & Connolly, M. D. (2001). A family affair: The labor market experience of immigrant spouses. *Social Science Quarterly*, *82*(4), 796–811.

Coleman, J. S. (1990). *Foundations of social theory*. Cambridge, MA: Belknap Press of Harvard University Press.

Duleep, H., & Sanders, S. (1993). The decision to work by married immigrant women. *Industrial and Labor Relations Review*, *46*(4), 67–80.

Fairlie, R. W. (2005). An extension of the Blinder–Oaxaca decomposition technique to logit and probit models. *Journal of Economic and Social Measurement*, *30*, 305–316.

Kossoudji, S. (1988). English language ability and the labor market opportunities. *Journal of Labor Economics*, *6*(2), 205–228.

McManus, W. S. (1985). Labor-market assimilation of immigrants – the importance of language skills. *Contemporary Policy Issues*, *3*(3), 77–89.

Mincer, J. (1974). *Schooling, experience, and earnings*. New York, NY: National Bureau of Economic Research.

Ministry of Interior, R.O.C. (2004). *2003 Survey of foreign and mainland spouses' life status*. Taipei: Ministry of Interior, R.O.C. (In Chinese).

Oppenheimer, V. K. (1982). *Work and the family: A study in social demography*. New York, NY: Academic Press.

Pedace, R., & DuBois, C. (2012). Immigration policy and employment assimilation in the United States. *Applied Econometrics*, *44*(36), 4721–4730.

Portes, A. (1995). *The economic sociology of immigration: Essays on networks, ethnicity, and entrepreneurship*. New York, NY: Russell Sage.

Reimers, C. W. (1985). Cultural differences in labor force participation among married women. *American Economic Review*, *75*(2), 251–255.

Rivera-Batiz, F. L. (1990). English language proficiency and the economic progress of immigrants. *Economics Letters*, *34*, 295–300.

Schoeni, R. F. (1998). Labor market assimilation of immigrant women. *Industrial and Labor Relations Review*, *51*(3), 483–504.

Sullivan, T. A. (1978). Racial-ethnic differences in labor force participation: An ethnic stratification perspective. In F. D. Bean & W. P. Frisbie (Eds.), *The demography of racial and ethnic groups* (pp. 165–187). New York, NY: Academic Press.

Waite, L. J. (1980). Working wives and the family life cycle. *American Journal of Sociology*, *86*(2), 272–294.

Yamanaka, K. (1987). *Labor force participation of Asian American women: Ethnicity, work, and the family*. Cornell University.

Yun, M.-S. (2004). Decomposing differences in the first moment. *Economics Letters*, *82*, 275–280.

HUMAN CAPITAL INVESTMENT INEQUALITY AND RURAL–URBAN INCOME GAP: EVIDENCE FROM CHINA

Xiaojun Yang and Wei-chiao Huang

ABSTRACT

This paper examines the impact of residents' human capital investment inequality on the urban–rural income gap, using China's provincial panel data from 1997 to 2013. The results show that, at the national level as well as at the regional level, residents' overall human capital investment inequality has a positive significant impact on the urban–rural income gap. In addition, the impact of overall human capital investment inequality increased monotonically from the eastern region inward to the western region. In terms of the relative impact of each component of human capital investment inequality on the urban–rural income gap, migration investment inequality appears to have the greatest impact at the national level, whereas health investment inequality has the greatest impact on the urban–rural income gap in the eastern region, and education investment inequality exhibits the greatest impact in the central and western regions. We also investigate the impact of human capital investment inequality on the urban–rural income gap over different periods. The results show that residents' overall human capital investment inequality had a positive impact on the urban–rural income gap in the period 1997–2008, but the impact rapidly shrunk in 2009–2013. Furthermore, the impact of residents' health investment inequality on the urban–rural income gap shows a downward trend, and the impact of

Advances in Pacific Basin Business, Economics and Finance, Volume 5, 151–172
Copyright © 2017 by Emerald Publishing Limited
All rights of reproduction in any form reserved
ISSN: 2514-4650/doi:10.1108/S2514-465020170000001007

residents' education investment inequality trended slightly upward from 1997 to 2008, and then rapidly shrunk in 2009–2013. Finally, the impact of residents' migration investment inequality was only significant in 1997–2002.

Keywords: Human capital investment inequality; health investment; education investment; migration investment; urban–rural income gap

1. INTRODUCTION

China's economy exhibits the typical dual economy characteristics, with a modern high-productivity and high-income urban industrial sector and a traditional low-productivity and low-income agricultural sector. The implementation of economic reform policies has widened the income gap between urban and rural residents (Chen, 2002; Lu & Chen, 2004; Yang, 1999). As of 2013, one measure of China's urban–rural income gap has reached the level of 3.18:1. The gap would be even higher if urban residents' hidden subsidies (such as public housing, health care, education, social security, etc.) are considered (Li & Luo, 2007). The widening of China's urban–rural income gap does not conform to the predictions of Kuznets' inverted U-shape hypothesis (Li & Li, 2010), and there is no clear sign of improvement in the near future. Compared to other developing countries, China's urban–rural income gap also appears to be considerably higher among them (Knight & Song, 1999). Thus, it is important to study the factors behind the widening gap so as to provide prescriptions to policy makers for narrowing the gap.

Researchers have attributed the widening urban–rural income gap to various factors, including urban bias policy, factor market distortions, urbanization, economic opening, financial development and human capital, and so on (Zhou & Cai, 2008). In particular, the role of human capital investment in affecting the urban–rural income gap has been studied extensively. Guo (2005) found that the convergence of human capital leads to the "absolute convergence" of urban–rural residents' per capita income. Li and Li (2005) also found that the deep-seated reasons for the urban–rural income gap are the urban–rural human capital gap, and it is essential to break the vicious circle of "education poverty" so as to narrow the urban–rural human capital gap and income gap. Han and Li (2011) showed that the urban–rural human capital accumulation gap caused the urban–rural income gap to rise. Similarly, Yue and Song (2013) concluded that the urban–rural human capital inequality contributed significantly to the widening of the urban–rural income gap. On the other hand, Han and Fu (2014) found that China's urban–rural income gap persisted even when the differences in human capital investment between urban and rural residents were reduced at both national and regional levels.

Some studies have focused on the impact of inequality in education, a major component of human capital investment, on the income gap of different groups. Chiswick's (1971) cross-country analysis showed that the income gap widened with a growing education gap. Gregorio and Lee (2002) used cross-country data from 1960 to 2006 and showed that the educational factor played a significant role in making income distribution more equal. Yao and Lai (2004) found differences in the rates of return of education for China's urban and rural (migrant) workers: the return rate on education for urban workers was 8.6%, significantly higher than 4.2% of their counterpart (migrant workers). Chen, Zhang, and Yang (2010) used the 2002 CHIP data and argued that educational difference is the most important factor affecting China's urban–rural income gap, with a contribution rate of 34.69%. On the other hand, Liu and Chen (2012) found that public education reforms, which were expected to narrow the education and income gaps through regulation and equalization, did not lead to income redistribution and actually seemed to have expanded the urban–rural income gap. Lü, Yang, and Wang (2015) found that the urban–rural income gap was aggravated by urban–rural education inequality, which in turn increased the urban–rural income gap. Moreover, they found that reducing the ratio of urban to rural average junior middle school education expenditures helped narrow the urban–rural education inequality, but reducing that ratio for primary school and senior middle school didn't help. Lastly, Ram (1989) gave evidence that education inequality has no significant effect on the income gap in less-developed countries.

Some other researchers have studied the impact of another component of human capital investment, migration investment, on the urban–rural income gap. Cai (2003) found that rural labor migration to urban sector can change the pattern of urban–rural resource allocation and improve farmers' income, thereby narrowing the urban–rural income gap. Wang, Zhang, and Xu (2007) showed that migration increased migrants' income, and reduced the income gap between urban and rural areas. Zhang and Wu (2010) also found that in-migration of the rural labor force can contribute to the reduction of income inequality. Xie (2014) showed that improvement of land transfer rights can help to promote permanent migration and reduce the urban–rural income gap. Sun and Lu (2014) showed that migration to the city region narrowed the urban–rural income gap, but out-of-province migration seemed to have the opposite (though insignificant) effect than within province migration. On the other hand, Hou and Zhang (2007) indicated that the urban–rural income gap could be widened because of rural human capital spillover as a result of rural exodus to cities. Similarly, Zhu and Ma (2009) showed that the spillover of rural human capital contributed to about 40% of the urban–rural income gap.

As can be seen from the brief literature review above, there is ample (although sometimes contradicting) evidence that human capital investment inequality has a significant impact on the urban–rural income gap. But the jury is still out as to the direction and magnitude of the impact. This paper aims to add to the literature by investigating this issue using the provincial panel data from 1997 to 2013 in China. There are twofold innovations made in this paper. First, unlike earlier studies that only focus on one aspect of human capital investment (mostly on education and some on migration), we not only examine the impact of overall human capital investment inequality on the urban–rural income gap, but also examine the impact of different components of human capital investment (health investment, education investment, and migration investment) inequalities on the urban–rural income gap. Second, we further explore if the impacts vary across different regions and over different periods. To begin, we present in the next section a simple theoretical model to illustrate the relationship between human capital inequality and the urban–rural income gap.

2. THEORETICAL MODEL

2.1. Baseline (Static) Model

Consider a dual economy with two production sectors: the modern urban sector (C) and the traditional rural sector (R). And these two sectors have a large number of manufacturers and laborers. Manufacturers strive to maximize profits, and the laborers aim to maximize income. For simplicity, these two sectors are assumed to be segregated by institutional barriers.

It is assumed that the production function of the two-sector manufacturers is embedded in the standard Solow model augmented by human capital, or the so-called MRW Model (Mankiw, Romer, & Weil, 1992). The Solow model takes the rates of saving, population growth, and technological progress as exogenous. The output of urban and rural sectors depends mainly on the input of production factors (including physical capital and labor), technological progress, and human capital. Using a simple Cobb–Douglas specification, the manufacturers' production functions in the two sectors can be expressed as:

$$Y_C = K_C^{\alpha_C} H_C^{\beta_C} (A_C L_C)^{1-\alpha_C-\beta_C} \tag{1}$$

$$Y_R = K_R^{\alpha_R} H_R^{\beta_R} (A_R L_R)^{1-\alpha_R-\beta_R} \tag{2}$$

where: Y is the output, K is the physical capital, H is the human capital, A is the level of technology, L is labor, α is the output elasticity of physical capital, β is the output elasticity of human capital, and $0<\alpha<1$, $0<\beta<1$, $0<\alpha+\beta<1$.

$y = Y/AL$ is the unit output of effective labor; $k = K/AL$ is the unit physical capital of effective labor, and $h = H/AL$ is the unit human capital of effective labor. Then Eqs. (1) and (2) can be rewritten as:

$$y_C = k_C^{\alpha_C} h_C^{\beta_C} \tag{3}$$

$$y_R = k_R^{\alpha_R} h_R^{\beta_R} \tag{4}$$

Since the firms in both urban and rural sectors are assumed to behave as profit-maximizers equating wage to the marginal product of labor, the equilibrium wages set in the two sectors are:

$$w_C = \frac{\partial Y_C}{\partial L_C} = \frac{\partial(A_C L_C y_C)}{\partial L_C} = (A_C - \alpha_C - \beta_C) y_C \tag{5}$$

$$w_R = \frac{\partial Y_R}{\partial L_R} = \frac{\partial(A_R L_R y_R)}{\partial L_R} = (A_R - \alpha_R - \beta_R) y_R \tag{6}$$

As a result, the first approximation of the urban–rural income gap (INC) can be expressed as:

$$\mathrm{INC} = \frac{w_C}{w_R} = \frac{(A_C - \alpha_C - \beta_C) y_C}{(A_R - \alpha_R - \beta_R) y_R} \tag{7}$$

As pointed out by Yang, Gong, and Zhang (2006), the three components of human capital investment, namely, health, education, and migration investments, not only directly promote economic growth, but also interact with each other to indirectly promote economic growth. Hence we further specify two-sector human capital functions as follows:

$$H_C = Z_C^{a_C} E_C^{b_C} M_C^{1-a_C-b_C} \tag{8}$$

$$H_R = Z_R^{a_R} E_R^{b_R} M_R^{1-a_R-b_R} \tag{9}$$

Where Z is the health capital, E is the education capital, M is the migration capital, a and b are the respective elasticities of health capital and education capital, and $0 < a < 1$, $0 < b < 1$, $0 < a + b < 1$.

2.2. Dynamic Model

2.2.1. Equilibrium Analysis of Overall Human Capital Investment and Urban–Rural Income Gap

Assume that in the modern urban sector, the growth rates of labor and technology are n_C and g_C; the investment rates of physical capital and human capital are s_{k_C} and s_{h_C}; and the depreciation rates of physical capital and human capital are the same δ_C. Then, the growth process in the urban sector will be determined by:

$$\dot{k}_C = s_{k_C} y_C - (n_C + g_C + \delta_C) k_C \tag{10}$$

$$\dot{h}_C = s_{h_C} y_C - (n_C + g_C + \delta_C) h_C \tag{11}$$

If the economy converges to equilibrium, Eqs. (10) and (11) are changed to:

$$k_C^* = \left(\frac{s_{k_C}^{1-\beta_C} s_{h_C}^{\beta_C}}{n_C + g_C + \delta_C} \right)^{1/(1-\alpha_C-\beta_C)} \tag{12}$$

$$h_C^* = \left(\frac{s_{k_C}^{\alpha_C} s_{h_C}^{1-\alpha_C}}{n_C + g_C + \delta_C} \right)^{1/(1-\alpha_C-\beta_C)} \tag{13}$$

Substituting Eqs. (12) and (13) into Eq. (3), we find:

$$y_C = \left(\frac{s_{k_C}^{\alpha_C} s_{h_C}^{\beta_C}}{(n_C + g_C + \delta_C)^{\alpha_C+\beta_C}} \right)^{1/(1-\alpha_C-\beta_C)} \tag{14}$$

Substituting Eq. (14) into Eq. (5), we find:

$$w_C = (A_C - \alpha_C - \beta_C) \left(\frac{s_{k_C}^{\alpha_C} s_{h_C}^{\beta_C}}{(n_C + g_C + \delta_C)^{\alpha_C+\beta_C}} \right)^{1/(1-\alpha_C-\beta_C)} \tag{15}$$

Thus, Eq. (15) shows that increasing urban residents' human capital investment can increase their wage.

Likewise, assume that in the traditional rural sector, the growth rates of labor and technology are n_R and g_R; the investment rates of physical capital and human capital are s_{k_R} and s_{h_R}; and the depreciation rates of physical capital and human capital are the same δ_R. Then, the growth process in rural sector will lead to:

$$y_R = \left(\frac{s_{k_R}^{\alpha_R} s_{h_R}^{\beta_R}}{(n_R + g_R + \delta_R)} \right)^{1/(1-\alpha_R-\beta_R)} \tag{16}$$

Substituting Eq. (16) into Eq. (6), we find that:

$$w_R = (A_R - \alpha_R - \beta_R) \left(\frac{s_{k_R}^{\alpha_R} s_{h_R}^{\beta_R}}{(n_R + g_R + \delta_R)^{\alpha_R+\beta_R}} \right)^{1/(1-\alpha_R-\beta_R)} \tag{17}$$

Thus, Eq. (17) indicates that increasing rural residents' human capital investment can increase their wage.

Substituting Eqs. (15) and (17) into Eq. (7), we find:

$$\text{INC} = \frac{w_C}{w_R} = \frac{(A_C - \alpha_C - \beta_C) \left(\frac{s_{k_C}^{\alpha_C} s_{h_C}^{\beta_C}}{(n_C + g_C + \delta_C)^{\alpha_C+\beta_C}} \right)^{1/(1-\alpha_C-\beta_C)}}{(A_R - \alpha_R - \beta_R) \left(\frac{s_{k_R}^{\alpha_R} s_{h_R}^{\beta_R}}{(n_R + g_R + \delta_R)^{\alpha_R+\beta_R}} \right)^{1/(1-\alpha_R-\beta_R)}} \tag{18}$$

As can be seen from Eq. (18), the urban–rural income gap will increase when urban residents' human capital investments increase, and decrease when rural residents' human capital investments increase. In other words, the ratio of urban–rural residents' human capital investment and the urban–rural income gap are positively related, suggesting that the widening urban–rural income gap could be caused by increasing urban–rural residents' human capital investment inequality.

2.2.2. Equilibrium Analysis of Human Capital Investment Components and Urban-Rural Income Gap

In the modern urban sector, manufacturers' production function including three human capital components is:

$$Y_C = K_C^{\alpha_C} \left(Z_C^{a_C} E_C^{b_C} M_C^{1-a_C-b_C} \right)^{\beta_C} (A_C L_C)^{1-\alpha_C-\beta_C} \tag{19}$$

$z_C = Z_C/A_C L_C$ is the unit health capital of effective labor; $e_C = E_C/A_C L_C$, which is the unit education capital of effective labor; and $m_C = M_C/A_C L_C$, which is the unit migration capital of effective labor. Then Eq. (19) is rewritten as:

$$y_C = k_C^{\alpha_C} z_C^{a_C\beta_C} e_C^{b_C\beta_C} m_C^{(1-a_C-b_C)\beta_C} \tag{20}$$

Assume that the investment rates of health capital, education capital, and migration capital are s_{zc},s_{ec}, and s_{mc}; and the depreciation rates of these three human capitals and physical capital are the same δ_C. Then, economic growth process in the urban sector will be determined by:

$$\dot{k}_C = s_{k_C} y_C - (n_C + g_C + \delta_C) k_C \tag{21}$$

$$\dot{z}_C = s_{z_C} y_C - (n_C + g_C + \delta_C) z_C \tag{22}$$

$$\dot{e}_C = s_{e_C} y_C - (n_C + g_C + \delta_C) e_C \tag{23}$$

$$\dot{m}_C = s_{m_C} y_C - (n_C + g_C + \delta_C) m_C \tag{24}$$

If the economy converges to equilibrium, Eqs. (21), (22), (23), and (24) are changed to new forms:

$$k_C^* = \left(\frac{s_{kc}^{1-\beta_C} s_{zc}^{a_C\beta_C} s_{ec}^{b_C\beta_C} s_{mc}^{(1-a_C-b_C)\beta_C}}{n_C + g_C + \delta_C} \right)^{1/(1-\alpha_C-\beta_C)} \tag{25}$$

$$z_C^* = \left(\frac{s_{kc}^{\alpha_C} s_{zc}^{(1-\alpha_C)-(1-a_C)\beta_C} s_{ec}^{b_C\beta_C} s_{mc}^{(1-a_C-b_C)\beta_C}}{n_C + g_C + \delta_C} \right)^{1/(1-\alpha_C-\beta_C)} \tag{26}$$

$$e_C^* = \left(\frac{s_{kc}^{\alpha_C} s_{zc}^{a_C\beta_C} s_{ec}^{(1-\alpha_C)-(1-b_C)\beta_C} s_{mc}^{(1-a_C-b_C)\beta_C}}{n_C + g_C + \delta_C} \right)^{1/(1-\alpha_C-\beta_C)} \tag{27}$$

$$m_C^* = \left(\frac{s_{kc}^{\alpha_C} s_{zc}^{a_C\beta_C} s_{ec}^{b_C\beta_C} s_{mc}^{(1-\alpha_C)-(a_C+b_C)\beta_C}}{n_C + g_C + \delta_C} \right)^{1/(1-\alpha_C-\beta_C)} \tag{28}$$

Substituting Eqs. (25), (26), (27), and (28) into Eq. (20), we find:

$$y_C = \left(\frac{s_{kc}^{\alpha_C} s_{zc}^{a_C\beta_C} s_{ec}^{b_C\beta_C} s_{mc}^{(1-a_C-b_C)\beta_C}}{(n_C + g_C + \delta_C)^{\alpha_C+\beta_C}} \right)^{1/(1-\alpha_C-\beta_C)} \tag{29}$$

Similarly, assume that in the traditional rural sector, the investment rates of health capital, education capital, and migration capital are s_{z_R}, s_{e_R}, and s_{m_R}, and the depreciation rates of these three human capitals and physical capital are the same δ_R. Then, the growth process in the rural sector will lead to:

$$y_R = \left(\frac{s_{k_R}^{\alpha_R} s_{z_R}^{a_R\beta_R} s_{e_R}^{b_R\beta_R} s_{m_R}^{(1-a_R-b_R)\beta_R}}{(n_R + g_R + \delta_R)^{\alpha_R+\beta_R}} \right)^{1/(1-\alpha_R-\beta_R)} \tag{30}$$

Substituting Eq. (29) into Eq. (5) and Eq. (30) into Eq. (6), we find the urban and rural sectors' equilibrium wages to be:

$$w_C = (A_C - \alpha_C - \beta_C) \left(\frac{s_{k_C}^{\alpha_C} s_{z_C}^{a_C\beta_C} s_{e_C}^{b_C\beta_C} s_{m_C}^{(1-a_C-b_C)\beta_C}}{(n_C + g_C + \delta_C)^{\alpha_C+\beta_C}} \right)^{1/(1-\alpha_C-\beta_C)} \tag{31}$$

$$w_R = (A_R - \alpha_R - \beta_R) \left(\frac{s_{k_R}^{\alpha_R} s_{z_R}^{a_R\beta_R} s_{e_R}^{b_R\beta_R} s_{m_R}^{(1-a_R-b_R)\beta_R}}{(n_R + g_R + \delta_R)^{\alpha_R+\beta_R}} \right)^{1/(1-\alpha_R-\beta_R)} \tag{32}$$

Then we can derive the urban–rural income gap as:

$$\mathrm{INC} = \frac{w_C}{w_R} = \frac{(A_C - \alpha_C - \beta_C) \left(\frac{s_{k_C}^{\alpha_C} s_{z_C}^{a_C\beta_C} s_{e_C}^{b_C\beta_C} s_{m_C}^{(1-a_C-b_C)\beta_C}}{(n_C + g_C + \delta_C)^{\alpha_C+\beta_C}} \right)^{1/(1-\alpha_C-\beta_C)}}{(A_R - \alpha_R - \beta_R) \left(\frac{s_{k_R}^{\alpha_R} s_{z_R}^{a_R\beta_E} s_{e_R}^{b_R\beta_R} s_{m_R}^{(1-a_R-b_R)\beta_R}}{(n_R+g_R+\delta_R)^{\alpha_R+\beta_R}} \right)^{1/(1-\alpha_R-\beta_R)}} \tag{33}$$

As can be seen from Eq. (33), increasing urban residents' either form of human capital investment can increase their wage and thus widen the urban–rural income gap. Conversely, increasing rural residents' either form of human capital investment can increase their wage and lower the urban–rural income gap. Thus, the ratio of urban–rural residents' either form of human capital investment and urban–rural income gap are positively related. The above theoretical exploration suggests that the widening of the urban–rural income gap could be caused by increasing inequality of human capital investments by urban and rural residents. To verify the theoretical prediction of the model we now turn to empirical analysis.

3. EMPIRICAL IMPLEMENTATION

3.1. Econometric Model

To ascertain the impact of residents' human capital investment inequality on the urban–rural income gap, we construct an empirical model based on the above theoretical model, and also considering many factors of the urban–rural income gap that have been cited by other researchers (Lu & Chen, 2004; Sun & Wan, 2011; Wei & Zhao, 2012), such as urbanization, nonagricultural industry development, economic development, foreign trade, and government fiscal expenditure. Taking into account the possible inertia of the urban–rural income gap, we estimate the following dynamic panel data model:

$$\mathrm{INC}_{i,t} = c + \alpha \mathrm{INC}_{i,t\text{-}1} + \beta \mathrm{HCI}_{i,t} + \gamma Xi, t + \upsilon t + \varepsilon i, t$$

$$\mathrm{INC}_{i,t} = c + \alpha \mathrm{INC}_{i,t\text{-}1} + \beta_1 \mathrm{HI}i, t + \beta_2 \mathrm{EI}i, t + \beta_3 \mathrm{MI}i, t + \gamma Xi, t + \upsilon t + \varepsilon i, t$$

where INC represents urban–rural income gap; HCI represents urban–rural residents' human capital investment inequality; HI represents urban–rural residents' health investment inequality; EI represents urban–rural residents' education investment inequality; MI represents urban–rural residents' migration investment inequality; X represents some control variables, including urbanization (UR), nonagricultural development (NAD), economic development (ED), foreign trade (FT), and fiscal expenditure (FE); α, β, γ represent coefficients of respective variables; i represents province and t represents year; υ represents time effect; and ε is the random disturbance term.

Since the logarithmic transformation of variables could help address the issue of heteroscedasticity without altering the underlying relations among the variables, we took the natural logarithm for all variables, and the resulting estimation equations are as follows:

$$\mathrm{lnINC}_{i,t} = c + \alpha \mathrm{lnINC}_{i,t\text{-}1} + \beta \mathrm{lnHCI}_{i,t} + \gamma \mathrm{ln}Xi, t + \upsilon t + \varepsilon i, t$$

$$\begin{aligned}\mathrm{lnINC}_{i,t} = c &+ \alpha \mathrm{lnINC}_{i,t-1} + \beta_1 \mathrm{lnHI}i, t + \beta_2 \mathrm{lnEI}i, t + \beta_3 \mathrm{lnMI}i, t \\ &+ \gamma \mathrm{ln}Xi, t + \upsilon t + \varepsilon i, t\end{aligned}$$

3.2. Measurement of Variables and Data

1. Urban–rural income gap: Measured by the ratio of per capita income between urban and rural residents (rural residents = 1) for each province. Specifically, INC = per capita disposable income of urban residents/per

capita net income of rural residents. This variable is adjusted for inflation using the respective urban and rural consumer price indexes at the 1997 constant price.

2. Residents' human capital investments: Human capital investment in health is measured by the "health care and medical services" of household consumption expenditures; education investment is measured by the "education, culture and recreation supplies and services" of household consumption expenditures; and migration investment is measured by the "transport and communications" of household consumption expenditures. The overall human capital investment is measured by the sum of these three investments. Again, all human capital investments are adjusted for inflation using the corresponding urban and rural consumer price indexes at the 1997 constant price level.
3. Urbanization: Considering the availability of data, this variable is measured here by the commonly used population proportion index, which is the proportion of nonagricultural population in the total population. Specifically, UR = nonagricultural population/total population × 100%.
4. Other variables: The development of nonagricultural industries is measured by the proportion of secondary and tertiary industrial output to GDP. The stage of economic development is measured by per capita GDP of the province (calculated at the 1997 constant price by GDP deflator). Foreign trade is measured by the proportion of total imports and exports to GDP. Fiscal expenditure is measured by the proportion of fiscal expenditure to GDP.

The sample consists of 31 provinces in mainland China for the years from 1997 to 2013. The original data used to generate all the variables are derived from the "China Statistical Yearbook" and "China Population and Employment Statistics Yearbook." Table 1 displays the descriptive statistics of the variables.

4. EMPIRICAL ANALYSIS

The two-step System Generalized Methods of Moments (System GMM) method was used to estimate parameters of the dynamic panel data model containing a lagged dependent variable. Several diagnostic tests were conducted in empirical analysis, such as the Sargan Test for overidentifying restrictions, AR Test for autocorrelation of the residuals, and Wald Test for overall significance of regression coefficients.

4.1. Empirical Results at the National Level

Table 2 reports the System GMM estimation results of the empirical model at the national level. The Wald test statistics show that all the regression

Table 1. Descriptive Statistics of the Variables.

Variable	Definition	Maximum	Minimum	Mean	Standard Deviation	Sample Size
INC	Urban–rural income gap	5.68	1.62	3.07	0.75	527
HCI	The ratio of urban–rural residents' human capital investment	27.41	1.64	4.05	2.61	527
HI	The ratio of urban–rural residents' health investment	16.40	0.68	3.37	1.65	527
EI	The ratio of urban–rural residents' education investment	47.75	1.82	4.61	4.19	527
MI	The ratio of urban–rural residents' migration investment	49.25	0.98	4.75	4.24	527
UR	Urbanization rate (%)	90.03	13.80	33.99	16.26	527
NAD	The proportion of secondary and tertiary industry output to GDP (%)	99.40	62.09	85.37	7.64	527
ED	Per capita GDP (Yuan)	70271.73	2214.72	16012.85	12218.74	527
FT	The proportion of total imports and exports to GDP (%)	166.82	2.52	29.84	35.65	527
FE	The proportion of fiscal expenditure to GDP (%)	129.14	4.68	19.15	14.90	527

coefficients are significant at the 1% level. The p-values of the Sargan test for overidentifying restrictions are not significant, suggesting that the instruments are valid. The p-values of AR (1) and AR (2) are both insignificant, indicating that there is no first- and second-order autocorrelation in the residuals. Altogether, results from these tests help conclude that it is valid to use the system GMM approach to estimate the panel data model.

With respect to the estimation results of human capital investment inequality, the central focus variable, the last column of Table 2 shows that the coefficient of urban–rural residents' overall human capital investment inequality is positive and significant at the 1% level. Thus, urban–rural residents' overall human capital investment inequality indeed has a significant positive impact on the urban–rural income gap. Specifically, it shows that if the ratio of urban–rural residents' overall human capital investment increases by 1%, the urban–rural income gap would increase by 0.077% at the national level. As can be seen from the second last column of Table 2, migration investment inequality appears to have the greatest impact on the urban–rural income gap, showing that if the ratio of urban–rural residents' migration investment increases by 1%, the urban–rural income gap would increase by 0.049%. Exerting almost the same extent of impact is the education investment inequality, which shows

Table 2. Regression Results at the National Level.

Variable	The Dependent Variable is lnINC				
L. lnINC	0.506	0.563**	0.069	−0.169	0.339
	(0.324)	(0.262)	(0.356)	(0.340)	(0.271)
lnHI	0.008			0.001	
	(0.013)			(0.013)	
lnEI		0.018		0.044***	
		(0.015)		(0.015)	
lnMI			0.047***	0.049***	
			(0.012)	(0.014)	
lnHCI					0.077***
					(0.023)
lnUR	−0.077	−0.104	−0.005	−0.023	−0.048
	(0.063)	(0.065)	(0.050)	(0.044)	(0.066)
lnNAD	−1.634	−2.047	1.180	−0.624	−0.310
	(1.732)	(1.541)	(1.791)	(1.236)	(2.066)
lnED	0.851	1.329*	0.641*	0.380	1.006*
	(0.697)	(0.794)	(0.363)	(0.389)	(0.589)
lnFT	−0.002	−0.001	−0.001	0.003	0.001
	(0.017)	(0.012)	(0.012)	(0.012)	(0.013)
lnFE	−0.020	−0.025	−0.011	−0.001	−0.013
	(0.022)	(0.019)	(0.019)	(0.020)	(0.017)
Cons	0.281	−2.090	−9.956	0.100	−6.875
	(5.832)	(7.905)	(9.244)	(6.848)	(7.597)
Time Effect	Control	Control	Control	Control	Control
Wald χ^2	63050.29	18097.50	49338.39	42721.80	37313.59
	(0.000)	(0.000)	(0.000)	(0.000)	(0.000)
Sargan Test	11.111	7.437	2.675	3.451	6.895
	(1.000)	(1.000)	(1.000)	(1.000)	(1.000)
AB Test for AR (1)	−1.062	−0.819	0.460	0.515	−0.275
	(0.288)	(0.413)	(0.646)	(0.607)	(0.784)
AB Test for AR (2)	0.269	0.994	1.888	1.414	1.141
	(0.788)	(0.320)	(0.059)	(0.157)	(0.254)
N (Observations)	496	496	496	496	496

Notes: * denotes significance at the 10 percent level; ** denotes significance at the 5 percent level; *** denotes significance at the 1 percent level; panel correlated robust standard errors are in parentheses underneath regression coefficients; the *p*-values are in parentheses underneath the test statistics for Wald, Sargan, and AR tests.

that if the ratio of urban–rural residents' education investment increases by 1%, the urban–rural income gap would increase by 0.044%.

As for the estimation results of control variables, only the stage of economic development appears to have a positive significant impact on the urban–rural income gap. Thus, at the national level, human capital investment inequality is the principal and dominant explanatory variable for the urban–rural income gap. This finding is consistent with other studies such as that by Chen et al. (2010).

4.2. Empirical Results at the Regional Level

Considering the distinctive differences in location and stage of economic development among different regions in China, it is necessary to further analyze if the impact of residents' human capital investment inequality on the urban–rural income gap varies across the regions. Here we follow the traditional practice of regional division and slice the national sample into three (eastern, central, and western) regions. Specifically, the eastern region includes 11 provinces, which are Beijing, Tianjin, Hebei, Liaoning, Shanghai, Jiangsu, Zhejiang, Fujian, Shandong, Guangdong, and Hainan; the central region includes 8 provinces, which are Shanxi, Jilin, Heilongjiang, Anhui, Qinghai, Henan, Hubei, and Hunan; and the western region includes 12 provinces, which are Sichuan, Chongqing, Guizhou, Yunnan, Shaanxi, Gansu, Qinghai, Ningxia, Xinjiang, Guangxi, Inner Mongolia, and Tibet.

Table 3 reports the System GMM estimation results of the impact of urban–rural residents' human capital investment inequality on the urban–rural income gap at the regional level. Same as in the case of estimation results at the national level, all the diagnostic tests, including the Wald, Sargan, and AR (1) and AR (2) tests, indicate that it is valid to use the system GMM method to estimate the panel data model at the regional level.

Viewing first the estimation results for the eastern region, it appears that urban–rural residents' overall human capital investment inequality has a significant positive impact on the urban–rural income gap. Specifically, if the ratio of urban–rural residents' overall human capital investment increases by 1%, the urban–rural income gap would increase by 0.097%. In addition, inequalities in all the three components of urban–rural residents' human capital investments are shown to have a positive and significant impact on the urban–rural income gap. Comparing the coefficient values, health investment inequality appears to have the greatest impact on the urban–rural income gap. If the ratio of urban–rural residents' health investment increases by 1%, the urban–rural income gap would increase by 0.401%. While also positive and significant, education investment inequality appears to exert the smallest impact on the urban–rural income gap. This is perhaps due to the fact that the

Table 3. Regression Results at the Regional Level.

Variable	The Dependent Variable is lnINC					
	The eastern region		The central region		The western region	
L. lnINC	0.097	−0.070	0.129	0.309	0.127	0.144
	(0.766)	(0.136)	(0.329)	(1.095)	(0.146)	(0.146)
lnHI	0.401*		0.201		0.004	
	(1.911)		(0.233)		(0.050)	
lnEI	0.095*		0.214**		0.190	
	(0.312)		(0.105)		(0.131)	
lnMI	0.238*		0.011		0.039	
	(1.969)		(0.168)		(0.069)	
lnHCI		0.097*		0.148*		0.177***
		(0.130)		(0.581)		(0.058)
lnUR	0.199	0.623**	0.121	0.020	−1.033	0.182
	(1.195)	(0.280)	(1.728)	(7.168)	(1.043)	(0.375)
lnNAD	−1.947	3.562**	−0.359	9.533	2.108**	2.025***
	(3.868)	(1.556)	(0.239)	(29.758)	(0.840)	(0.290)
lnED	0.176	−0.317**	0.0123	−0.566	−0.221	−0.247**
	(1.563)	(0.152)	(0.358)	(1.544)	(0.159)	(0.101)
lnFT	0.005	0.001	−0.002	0.041	0.119**	−0.056
	(0.930)	(0.063)	(0.079)	(0.163)	(0.059)	(0.051)
lnFE	0.188	0.120	0.893	0.019	0.305**	0.143*
	(2.205)	(0.135)	(1.200)	(0.289)	(0.142)	(0.087)
Cons	6.586	−14.61**	−28.876	−36.655	−4.371	−6.764***
	(14.631)	(6.140)	(29.819)	(94.872)	(3.154)	(0.958)
Time effect	Control	Control	Control	Control	Control	Control
Wald χ^2	245.35	396.62	466.55	29.13	466.21	429.27
	(0.000)	(0.000)	(0.000)	(0.000)	(0.000)	(0.000)
Sargan test	0.699	1.364	1.218	0.134	1.004	4.916
	(1.000)	(1.000)	(1.000)	(1.000)	(1.000)	(1.000)
AB test for AR (1)	−0.125	−0.540	0.984	0.198	−0.089	−0.265
	(0.901)	(0.589)	(0.765)	(0.843)	(0.929)	(0.791)
AB test for AR (2)	−0.532	1.041	−0.243	−0.551	0.606	0.710
	(0.393)	(0.298)	(0.672)	(0.581)	(0.544)	(0.478)
N (Observations)	176	176	128	128	192	192

Notes: * denotes significance at the 10 percent level; ** denotes significance at the 5 percent level; *** denotes significance at the 1 percent level; panel correlated robust standard errors are in parentheses underneath regression coefficients; the *p* values in parentheses are underneath the test statistics for Wald, Sargan, and AR tests.

educational attainment level in the eastern region is the highest (either in urban or in rural sectors) and more equal compared to other regions in China, rendering education investment inequality to exert lesser impact on the urban–rural income gap.

Turning to regression results for the central region, urban–rural residents' overall human capital investment inequality also has a positive and significant impact on the urban–rural income gap in that region. Specifically, if the ratio of urban–rural residents' overall human capital investment increases by 1%, the urban–rural income gap would increase by 0.148%. In terms of separate components of urban–rural residents' human capital investment inequalities, only the educational investment inequality exhibits a positive and significant impact on the urban–rural income gap. If the ratio of urban–rural residents' education investment in the central region increases by 1%, the urban–rural income gap would increase by 0.214%.

As for the regression results of the western region, the regression coefficient of urban–rural residents' overall human capital investment inequality is also positive and significant, which implies that urban–rural residents' overall human capital investment inequality has a significant positive impact on the urban–rural income gap in the western region. Specifically, if the ratio of urban–rural residents' overall human capital investment increases by 1%, the urban–rural income gap would increase by 0.177%. It appears that none of the separate components of human capital investment inequalities have a significant (while all positive) effect on the urban–rural income gap.

It is interesting to note that the impact of overall human capital investment inequality increased monotonically from the eastern region inward to the western region. One plausible clue to this phenomenon may have to do with China's lopsided regional development policy. Since the beginning of reform in the late seventies, China has concentrated on developing the eastern (coastal) region first, leaving the west inner areas behind. Consequently, the eastern region has made the greatest stride in economic development in the past three decades, to the extent that the east itself has achieved the developed economy status, whereas the west remains rather underdeveloped. Hence, given the well-established fact in the development literature that the rate of return to human capital investment is higher in less-developed economies, it is conceivable that human capital investment inequality in the western region would exert greater impact on the urban–rural income gap than in the eastern region.

4.3. Empirical Results in Different Periods

China's urban–rural residents' human capital investments and urban–rural income gaps have exhibited distinctive stage (period) characteristics. As can be seen from Fig. 1, urban–rural residents' human capital investment inequality

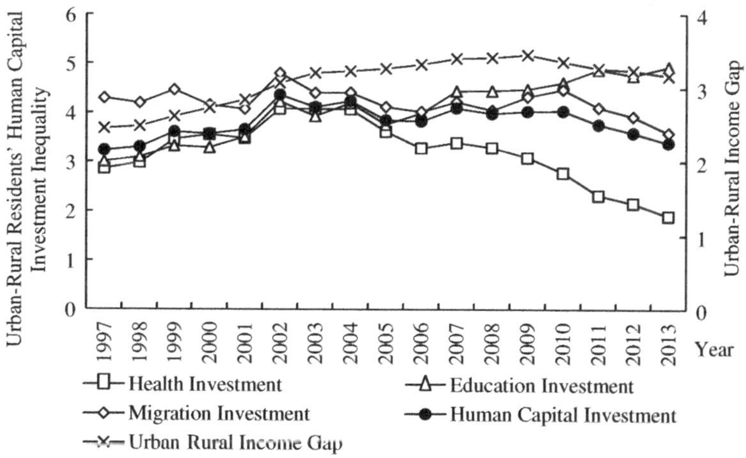

Fig. 1. The Trend of Urban–Rural Residents' Human Capital Investment Inequality and the Urban–Rural Income Gap in China.

and the urban–rural income gap both showed a steady growth trend from 1997 to 2002. In the next period from 2003 to 2008, residents' human capital investment inequality began to decline, while the urban–rural income gap remained relatively steady at about the same level. In the more recent period of 2009–2013, both the residents' human capital investment inequality and the urban–rural income gap trended downward. Therefore, it might be of interest to examine if the impact of residents' human capital investment inequality on the urban–rural income gap varies over different time periods.

Table 4 reports the System GMM estimation results of the impact of urban–rural residents' human capital investment inequality on the urban–rural income gap in three different periods (1997–2002, 2003–2008, and 2009–2013). As in the preceding sections, results from all the diagnostic tests conclude that it is valid to use the system GMM method to estimate the panel data model in the three periods.

Table 4 shows that the urban–rural residents' overall human capital investment inequality had a positive significant impact on the urban–rural income gap in the first two periods from 1997 to 2008. The magnitudes of impacts are more or less the same between 1997–2002 and 2003–2008. Specifically, if the ratio of urban–rural residents' human capital investment increases by 1%, the urban–rural income gap would increase by 0.070% from 1997 to 2002, and 0.078% from 2003 to 2008. However, the impact of urban–rural residents' overall human capital investment inequality on the urban–rural income gap shrunk and turned to be insignificant in the more recent period of 2009–2013.

Looking into the trend of the impact for separate components of human capital investment inequality, it appears that the impact of residents' health

Table 4. Regression Results in Three Different Periods.

Variable	The Dependent Variable is lnINC					
L. lnINC	0.813***	0.888***	0.493***	0.375***	0.217	0.341**
	(0.070)	(0.063)	(0.131)	(0.143)	(0.166)	(0.143)
lnHI	0.025		0.009		0.006	
	(0.016)		(0.026)		(0.008)	
lnEI	0.047**		0.058***		−0.012	
	(0.019)		(0.014)		(0.009)	
lnMI	0.026***		−0.010		0.013	
	(0.008)		(0.017)		(0.011)	
lnHCI		0.070**		0.078***		0.003
		(0.034)		(0.023)		(0.025)
lnUR	−0.019	−0.016	−0.183**	−0.210***	0.008	−0.012
	(0.033)	(0.044)	(0.076)	(0.078)	(0.031)	(0.034)
lnNAD	0.959***	0.809**	−0.049	0.071	0.256	0.230
	(0.331)	(0.317)	(0.240)	(0.250)	(0.201)	(0.206)
lnED	−0.190***	−0.182***	−0.001	−0.007	−0.232***	−0.202***
	(0.066)	(0.067)	(0.077)	(0.076)	(0.032)	(0.034)
lnFT	0.019	0.017	0.015	0.019	−0.015	−0.002
	(0.029)	(0.029)	(0.017)	(0.016)	(0.009)	(0.010)

lnFE	−0.040***	−0.050***	0.011	0.012	−0.061***	−0.052**
	(0.014)	(0.014)	(0.025)	(0.025)	(0.019)	(0.025)
Cons	−2.296**	−1.729	1.313	1.032	2.279**	1.950**
	(1.106)	(1.108)	(1.066)	(1.171)	(0.887)	(0.938)
Time effect	Control	Control	Control	Control	Control	Control
Wald χ^2	2656.22	1991.10	2171.24	349.80	2504.11	2137.03
	(0.000)	(0.000)	(0.000)	(0.000)	(0.000)	(0.000)
Sargan test	18.105	17.570	10.619	12.273	10.990	11.885
	(0.154)	(0.175)	(0.643)	(0.505)	(0.202)	(0.156)
AB test for AR (1)	−2.462	−2.571	−2.266	−1.897	−1.018	−1.274
	(0.014)	(0.010)	(0.024)	(0.058)	(0.309)	(0.203)
AB test for AR (2)	0.537	0.155	−0.662	−0.354	−0.287	0.623
	(0.591)	(0.877)	(0.508)	(0.723)	(0.774)	(0.533)
N (Observations)	155	155	155	155	124	124

Notes: * denotes significance at the 10 percent level; ** denotes significance at the 5 percent level; *** denotes significance at the 1 percent level; panel correlated robust standard errors are in parentheses underneath regression coefficients; the *p*-values are in parentheses underneath the test statistics for Wald, Sargan, and AR tests.

investment inequality on the urban–rural income gap was insignificant throughout, whereas the impact of residents' education investment inequality trended slightly upward from 1997 to 2008, and then rapidly shrunk and became insignificant in 2009–2013. Lastly, the impact of residents' migration investment inequality was only positively significant in the first period 1997–2002.

Comparing the relative importance of different components of human capital investment inequalities in each period, it appears that in the period from 1997 to 2002 education investment inequality had the greatest impact on the urban–rural income gap, followed by migration investment inequality, whereas health investment inequality had no significant impact. In the next period from 2003 to 2008, only the education investment inequality had a significant positive impact on the urban–rural income gap. In the more recent period from 2009 to 2013, none of the human capital investment inequalities had a significant impact on the urban–rural income gap.

It is worth noting that the impacts of human capital investment inequalities on the urban–rural income gap have generally declined over the years and even became insignificant throughout the more recent period 2009–2013. Again, as speculated in the preceding section, the acceleration of China's economic development and growth may have lowered the rate of return to human capital investment, which in turn lowered the impact of human capital investment inequalities on the urban–rural income gap.

5. CONCLUDING REMARKS

This paper analyzes the impact of residents' human capital investment inequality on the urban–rural income gap by using provincial panel data in 1997–2013 in China. The main findings from estimation results are: (1) At the national level, urban–rural residents' overall human capital investment inequality has a positive significant impact on the urban–rural income gap. This is consistent with several earlier studies cited in the introductory section and also consistent with analytical predictions derived from theoretical models in Section "Theoretical Model." Comparing the relative contributions of different components of human capital investments to the urban–rural income gap, migration investment inequality appears to exert the greatest impact on the urban–rural income gap. (2) At the regional level, urban–rural residents' overall human capital investment inequality also has a significant positive impact on the urban–rural income gap in three different regions, and its impact is the greatest in the western region. In addition, health investment inequality appears to have the greatest impact on the urban–rural income gap in the eastern region, whereas education investment inequality exhibits the greatest impact in the central and western regions. (3) In the period analysis, it appears that the impact of residents' health investment inequality on the urban–rural income gap was insignificant throughout, whereas the impact of residents' education investment inequality trended slightly upward from 1997 to 2008, and then rapidly shrunk and became insignificant in 2009–2013. Lastly, the impact of residents' migration investment inequality was only positively significant in the first period 1997–2002.

Some policy implications and prescriptions can be derived from the above empirical findings. If the policy goal is to reduce the urban–rural income gap, in general, policy measures need to be adopted to achieve the convergence of human capital investment between urban and rural residents. Various specific measures could be adopted including ways to improve agricultural labor productivity and nonagricultural (rural industrial) production, the establishment of rural health security system and strengthening of rural cooperative medical system, boosting rural education investment through initiatives led by government and supplemented by private sector, and measures to facilitate and guide orderly rural residents' migration to the cities. Lastly, the above findings show that different types of human capital investments exert different impact on the urban–rural income gap in different periods or different stages of development. Thus, when implementing a multitude of measures to address the urban–rural income gap issues, policy makers need to take into account the differential impacts of human capital investments in different regions and over time.

ACKNOWLEDGMENTS

This work is supported by "the Fundamental Research Funds for the Central Universities" (No: 2722013JC013), China. We thank valuable comments made by Ahmed Al Aabodi, Patrice Anderson, Abrar Bagalb, Dweetobotee Brahma, Yizhou Chen, Joseph Wu, and Xiyao Xiang.

REFERENCES

Cai, F. (2003). Rural urban income gap and critical point of institutional change. *Social Sciences in China*, *5*, 16–25.

Chen, A. (2002). Urbanization and disparities in China: Challenges of growth and development. *China Economic Review*, *13*(4), 407–411.

Chen, B., Zhang, P., & Yang, R. (2010). Government education investment, human capital investment and China's urban–rural income gap. *Management World*, *1*, 36–43.

Chiswick, B. R. (1971). Earnings inequality and economic development. *The Quarterly Journal of Economics*, *85*(1), 21–39.

Gregorio, J. D., & Lee, J. W. (2002). Education and income inequality: New evidence from cross-country data. *Review of Income and Wealth*, *48*(3), 395–416.

Guo, J. (2005). The convergence of human capital, fertility rate and urban–rural income gap. *Social Sciences in China*, *3*, 27–37.

Han, D., & Fu, P. (2014). Human capital input's difference and China's urban–rural income gap: An empirical analysis based on provincial panel data. *Technoeconomics and Management Research*, *6*, 28–32.

Han, Q., & Li, J. (2011). Study on dynamic evolution of urban–rural income gap in dual economy. *Journal of Finance Research*, *8*, 15–30.

Hou, F., & Zhang, F. (2007). Empirical study on investment and spill-over of rural human capital and difference between urban and rural areas in China. *Journal of Finance and Economics*, *8*, 118–131.

Knight, J., & Song, L. (1999). The rural–urban divide: Economic disparities and interactions in China. Oxford: Oxford University Press.

Li, S., & Li, T. (2010). Can the Kuznets Hypothesis explain China's income gap? *Economic Theory and Business Management*, *3*, 5–10.

Li, S., & Luo, C. (2007). Re-estimation of the income gap of Chinese residents. *Journal of Peking University (Humanities and Social Sciences)*, *2*, 111–120.

Li, X., & Li, G. (2005). Urban–rural income gap and its stabilization from the perspective of human capital. *Economic Management*, *9*, 21–24.

Liu, Y., & Chen, L. (2012). Effects of educational investment and social security on urban–rural income gap. *Population Journal*, *2*, 10–20.

Lu, M., & Chen, Z. (2004). Urbanization, economic policies of urban tendency and urban–rural income gap. *Economic Research Journal*, *6*, 50–58.

Lü, W., Yang, M., & Wang, Y. (2015). The urban–rural income gap and education inequality and government spending on education in China. *Comparative Economic and Social Systems*, *3*, 20–33.

Mankiw, N. G., Romer, D., & Weil, D. N. (1992). A contribution to the empirics of economic growth. *The Quarterly Journal of Economics*, *107* (2), 407–437.

Ram, R. (1989). Can educational expansion reduce income inequality in less-developed countries? *Economics of Education Review*, *8*(2), 185–195.

Sun, H., & Lu, H. (2014). The evolution of urban–rural income gap: The contribution of labor migration. *Research on Financial and Economic Issues*, *8*, 71–76.

Sun, Y., & Wan, Y. (2011). Financial development, opening-up and urban–rural income gap: With the provincial panel data from 1978 to 2008. *Journal of Financial Research*, *1*, 28–39.

Wang, W., Zhang, Z., & Xu, K. (2007). Study on the impact of labor migration on income distribution: A case study of Chongqing. *Population Research*, *6*, 55–66.

Wei, H., & Zhao, C. (2012). Effects of international trade on urban–rural income gap in China. *Finance and Trade Economics*, *1*, 78–86.

Xie, D. (2014). Rural land transfer rights, labor migration and urban–rural inequality. *China Economic Studies*, *1*, 49–59.

Yang, D. T. (1999). Urban-biased policies and rising income inequality in China. *The American Economic Review*, *89*(2), 306–310.

Yang, J., Gong, L., & Zhang, Q. (2006). The formation of human capital and its influence on economic growth. *Management World*, *5*, 11–18.

Yao, X., & Lai, P. (2004). Differences between urban and rural household registration in China's labor relations. *Economic Research Journal*, *7*, 82–90.

Yue, Y., & Song, S. (2013). A study of the human capital impact on the urban–rural income gap. *Journal of Hunan University (Social Sciences)*, *2*, 38–41.

Zhang, Z., & Wu, X. (2010). Rural labor migration and regional disparities in earnings inequality in China: Evidence from the 2005 national population sample survey. *Population and Development*, *1*, 11–18.

Zhou, D., & Cai, M. (2008). A review of the research on urban–rural income gap in China. *China Rural Survey*, *3*, 66–74.

Zhu, C., & Ma, J. (2009). The generalized spillover of rural human capital and urban–rural income gap. *China Rural Survey*, *4*, 37–46.

AN OPERATIONAL EFFICIENCY ANALYSIS FOR ORGANIZATIONAL CONSOLIDATION IN THE BUSINESS OPERATING DEPARTMENTS OF A CASE TELECOM COMPANY

Chia-Jung Tu, Yu-Ping Huang and Tyrone T. Lin

ABSTRACT

This study focuses primarily on the business operating departments (hereinafter, DMUs) of a case telecom company (hereinafter, the Company) in the northern and eastern areas of Taiwan. In 2007, the Company finished the first stage of its reorganization by consolidating 14 DMUs into 12. In 2011, the Company completed the second stage of its reorganization by consolidating the 12 remaining DMUs into 8. This study intends to explore the effects of each stage of the Company's reorganization on the efficiency and ranking of the various DMUs. The results show that the DMUs became more efficient after each stage of the Company's reorganization. Moreover, the efficiency and ranking of the new DMUs, A6, A7, and B7 increased post-consolidation. This suggests that both the first and second stages of the reorganization were necessary. The findings of this study could help the Company and other telecom companies to design strategies for the future consolidation of other units, and thereby maintain their competitiveness and continued growth.

Keywords: Telecom company; organizational consolidation; operational efficiency; data envelopment analysis (DEA); Taiwan

Advances in Pacific Basin Business, Economics and Finance, Volume 5, 173–187
Copyright © 2017 by Emerald Publishing Limited
All rights of reproduction in any form reserved
ISSN: 2514-4650/doi:10.1108/S2514-465020170000001008

1. INTRODUCTION

Since the 1980s, many countries have tried to privatize state-operated telecommunication businesses. In response to this global trend and to domestic market demand, Taiwan liberated the mobile phone industry in 1997 and the fixed network industry in 2001. The operating environments of telecommunication firms have become significantly more challenging since the market was liberated. Companies fight for market share and the profits are compressed. In a micro-profit era, a company must continuously enhance its efficiency and competitiveness in order to stand out among its competitors.

In 2005, the government reduced its share of the case telecom company (hereinafter, the Company) to less than 50%, thereby transforming the Company from a state-operated telecommunication company to a private business. To maintain its leadership in the intensely competitive environment, the Company endeavored to reduce personnel and operating expenditures by consolidating its operating departments. Its ultimate goal is to have only one operating department for each city. The Company also adopted efficiency-oriented policies to improve its productivity, operational efficiency, and overall competitiveness.

In order to examine whether reorganization strategies produce a $1 + 1 > 2$ effect or, conversely, whether business performance deteriorates as a result of reorganization. The business operating departments (hereinafter, DMUs) of the Company in the northern and eastern areas of Taiwan are the subjects of this study. In 2007, the Company finished the first stage of its reorganization by consolidating 14 DMUs into 12. In 2011, the Company completed the second stage of its reorganization by consolidating the 12 remaining DMUs into 8. This study applies Data Envelopment Analysis (DEA) to assess the technical efficiency (TE), pure technical efficiency (PTE), and scale efficiency (SE) of the Company's DMUs. Furthermore, this study intends to explore the effects of each stage of the Company's reorganization on the efficiency and ranking of the various DMUs.

The results of this study indicate that the overall efficiency of the Company's DMUs increased significantly after the first and second phase of the reorganization. Moreover, the efficiency and ranking of the new DMUs, A6, A7, and B7 raised post-consolidation. This suggests that both the first and second phases of the Company's reorganization were necessary. The results provide information not only about the operational efficiencies of the Company's DMUs but also about their respective strengths and weakness. These findings could be useful references for the Company and other telecom companies to design strategies for the future consolidation of other units, thereby maintaining their competitiveness and continued growth.

2. LITERATURE REVIEW

Liu (2004) suggested that reorganization is an important issue for business managers because it is crucial to a company's survival. In other words, to increase competitiveness, a successful company should seek for proper reforms continuously. Lin (2006) studied the 1987 privatization of Japan Railway Company and explored the correlation between privatization and reorganization, as well as the reorganizations' effects. The findings of that study indicated that the privatization of Japan Railway Company triggered organizational reform and created business organization from the reform. Accordingly, the privatization of Japan Railway Company is regarded globally as a successful example of railway privatization. Hsiao and Chen (2008) treated 105 Taiwanese firms as the subjects and investigated the effects of organizational change and information technology on organizational performance. Their results showed that organizational structure change and information technology investment are positively related to organizational performance. Liu (2004) applied DEA to analyze the production efficiencies of 277 credit departments of farmers' associations in various townships and cities in Taiwan in 2001, both before and after various reorganizations. The results showed that prior to the reorganizations, the scales of the credit departments were small and production was inefficient. After the consolidation of some credit departments, total operating efficiency increased by 18.2%; after the complete consolidation of the credit departments, total operating efficiency increased by 21.5%.

Among the studies that evaluate operating efficiencies of telecommunication companies, Lee, Park, and Oh (2000) applied DEA to study the changes in the respective production efficiencies of telecommunication companies in Korea during 1982~1996 both before and after the introduction of competition. The results suggest that even after the introduction of competition to the Korean telecom industry, the government and telecommunication authorities continued to exert significant control over the market. Those results indicated that the introduction of competition and privatization were effective only if companies have more decision-making power and were independently managed and operated. Lin, Hsu, and Lee (2002) evaluated the operational efficiency of local telephony services of 29 operating divisions of a Taiwanese telecom company from 1991 to 1999. The results revealed that the population density factor had a significantly positive correlation with the operating efficiency of the local telephony services.

Tsai, Chen, and Tzeng (2006) used DEA, the A&P efficiency measure, and the efficiency achievement measure to compare the production efficiencies and operational performances of 39 leading global telecom companies in 2000. They found that the overall performance of state-operated telecom companies was better than the performance of private companies and that the production efficiency of telecom companies in Asia-Pacific countries was better than that of telecom companies in Europe and the United States. Liao and Jiménez (2009) applied DEA to explore the operational efficiencies of 10 mobile companies in BRIC (Brazil, Russia, India, and China) from 2002 to 2006. Their findings indicated that the two leading mobile companies in Brazil, VIVO and TIM, were the most efficient mobile operators, whereas the mobile operators in India were the least efficient.

Papadimitriou and Prachalias (2009) applied DEA to study the factors to increase production efficiency of 18 global telecommunication operators in 1998, 2001, 2004, and 2006. Their findings indicate that to increase operational efficiency, companies should adopt new operational and marketing strategies, invest in the development of innovative products and services, and reduce operating expenditures. Tu, Chen, and Lin (2014) discussed the operating performance of 23 operating divisions of a case telecom company in Taiwan from 2008 to 2010 by comparing the entire region, urban and rural operating areas. Furthermore, they analyzed the correlation between the accounts receivable collection and the overall operating performance using the Tobit regression model. The results showed that the urban operating divisions had a higher efficiency value than the rural ones and the collection of accounts receivables and the operating performance was positively correlated. Wang, Lu, Kweh, and Lai (2014) used a two-stage approach to explore the relationship between the operational performance of U.S. telecommunications companies and their implementation of corporate social responsibility (CSR). They found the corporate efficiency of those companies that implemented CSR was higher than that of those companies that did not.

From the above literature, organizational reform seems to be the necessity for the successful business. Also, it can be seen that the global concern is regarding the operating efficiency of the telecommunications industry. This study is the first paper to investigate the efficiency for organizational consolidation in the different business operating departments of the Company. The findings could be useful references for the Company and other telecom companies to design better reorganization strategies.

3. RESEARCH DESIGN

3.1. Data Envelopment Analysis (DEA)

DEA applications in consolidation are found in different areas such as banking (Halkos, Matousek, & Tzeremes, 2016; Wu, Luo, Wang, & Birge, 2016), airlines (Chow & Fung, 2012), healthcare (Leleu, Moises, & Valdmanis, 2012), and agriculture (Bogetoft & Wang, 2005). This study applies DEA to evaluate the changes of operational efficiency of the Company's DMUs before and after the organizational consolidation.

This study employs DEA to evaluate the operating efficiency of the Company's DMUs. DEA is a very popular nonparametric method based on linear programming for assessing the relative efficiencies of a homogeneous group of decision-making units in the presence of multiple outputs and multiple inputs. It uses Pareto optimality to measure efficiency. The model was proposed in 1978 by Charnes, Cooper, and Rhodes and was derived from the concepts introduced by Farrell (1957).

Farrell (1957) proposed a method for measuring productive efficiency based on a production possibility set consisting of the convex hull of input–output vectors. Farrell introduced the concept of the production frontier to measure a DMU's efficiency level and divided overall productive efficiency into TE and allocation efficiency (AE). In 1978, Charnes, Cooper, and Rhodes extended Farrell's (1957) model of "two input items and one output item" to a model with "multiple input items and multiple output items" to measure the relative production efficiency of a DMU under constant returns to scale. The model developed by Charnes, Cooper, and Rhodes (1978) is known as the CCR model. Under the CCR model, when the efficiency value of a DMU equals 1, it means that the DMU has reached optimality and no adjustment to input or output variables is necessary.

Banker, Charnes, and Cooper (1984) employed the concept of the Shephard distance function to further develop the Farrell theory and CCR model and proposed the BCC model in 1984. The BCC model accounts for variable returns to scale. In addition, it divides TE into PTE and SE to more accurately identify the causes of inefficiencies.

3.2. Research Subjects and Data Resource

The DMUs of the Company in the northern and eastern areas of Taiwan are the subjects of this study. In 2007, in the first phase of the Company's reorganization, 14 DMUs were consolidated into 12. In 2011, in the second phase, 12 DMUs were consolidated into 8. The 14 original DMUs were as follows: south district of Taipei, north district of Taipei, east district of Taipei, west district of Taipei, Keelung, Shilin, Banciao, Shuanghe, Taoyuan, Chungli, Hsinchu, Miaoli, Hualian, and Yilan. In 2007, the Banciao and Shuanghe operating departments were consolidated into the Banhe operating department, and the Taoyuan and Chungli operating departments were consolidated into the Taoyuan operating department. In 2011, the south district of Taipei, north district of Taipei, east district of Taipei, and Shihlin operating departments were consolidated into the Taipei operating department, and the west district of Taipei and Banhe operating departments were consolidated into the New Taipei operating department. These operating departments exist under the same market conditions and have homogenous operations, identical inputs and outputs, consistent tasks and goals, and comparative bases. The data used in this study are sourced from the following: public data; the Company's website, annual report, and CSR report; and internal secondary data of the Company. The research period covers the span 2006 to 2011.

The Company consolidated its operating departments to lower personnel and operating costs. In addition, the Company hoped that modifications to its organizational structure would improve corporate robustness, make the organization more flexible and adaptable, and enhance productivity and operational efficiency. Corporate reorganization is a sensitive and complicated issue. This study only evaluates theories and evidence relating to the effects of reorganization on efficiency and does not address the complicated psychological dimensions of reorganization, such as the impact on employees and on organizational culture. The operating departments of the Company are identified by codes to avoid any concerns regarding the disclosure of confidential business information.

3.3. *Definitions of Variables*

In DEA, the highest reliability and explanatory power of analytical results are achieved when the number of DMUs is at least twice the total number of input and output items. Because too many variables will decrease the differences between DMUs, and the Company had only eight operating departments in 2011, this study selects two input items and one output item. The input and output variables are defined below.

(1) Input variables

- (i) Number of employees: this variable refers to the total number of employees in each operating department, including technical and business personnel. By inputting human resources, each operating department can complete its required tasks; thus, employees are regarded as an input item.
- (ii) Marketing and promotion expenditures: this refers to the marketing and promotional expenditures input into each operating department to reach annual business targets.

(2) Output variable

- (i) Annual net increase in the number of users of the Company's broadband network, digital TV, and mobile phone services: this refers to the net increase in the number of users of the Company's broadband network (ADSL, FTTB), digital TV (MOD), and mobile phone services in the current year. Operating departments provide products and services to consumers. The most representative service output is the number of users. Therefore, this study treats the net increase in the number of users as the output item.

3.4. *Selection and Correlation of Input and Output Variables*

Before using DEA to calculate efficiency, it is necessary to determine whether there is significant "homonym" in the correlation between input and output items. This study first examines the propriety of the variables using Pearson correlation coefficients and selects input and output items that have significantly positive correlations. The correlation coefficient between the annual net increase in the number of users of the Company's broadband network, digital TV, and mobile phone services and the number of employees is 0.866, and the correlation coefficient between the annual net increase in the number of users of the Company's broadband network, digital TV, and mobile phone services and marketing and promotion expenditures is 0.619. In a two-tailed test, the p values are 0.000 and thus reach the 0.01 significance level. The figures represent the degree of correlation between the variables, and positive and negative signs refer to the direction of correlation. According to the results, there is a positive and highly significant correlation between the output variable and each input variable with a significance level of 1%. Therefore, the correlations between the input and output variables selected for this study meet the DEA requirement.

4. EMPIRICAL RESULTS AND ANALYSIS

4.1. The First Phase of Consolidation: Operational Efficiency Analysis in 2006 and 2007 (Year of Consolidation)

This section analyzes the difference in each DMU's efficiency before and after the Company's DMU consolidation in 2007. Operating departments A6 and A7 represent the newly consolidated business units created in 2007.[1] The data in Tables 1 and 2 demonstrate that the average TE of all DMUs increased by 6%, going from 0.679 to 0.739, between 2006 and 2007. The average PTE of the DMUs increased by 3.2% (from 0.860 to 0.892) and the average SE increased by 2.5% (from 0.809 to 0.834) during the same period. Thus, the overall efficiency of all DMUs was higher in 2007 than it was in 2006. For operating department A6, TE increased by 21% (from 0.611 to 0.821), PTE increased by 15.3% (from 0.847 to 1.000), and SE increased by 10% (from 0.721 to 0.821). For operating department A7, TE increased by 10.9% (from 0.662 to 0.771), PTE decreased by 7.4% (from 1.000 to 0.926), and SE increased by 17.1% (from 0.662 to 0.833).

According to Tables 1 and 2, only 33% of all DMUs had a TE of at least 0.7 in 2006, whereas 67% of all DMUs had a TE of at least 0.7 in 2007. In particular, the TE ranking of A6 was 9th in 2006 and was raised to 5th in 2007, the ranking of A7 remains at 6th (its ranking was getting better during 2008–2010), suggesting that the efficiency and ranking of the two consolidated operating departments improved after the first phase of the Company's reorganization. The overall TE of the 12 DMUs also increased, indicating that the reorganization was necessary.

Table 1. Operating Efficiency of the Operating Departments of the Company in 2006.

DMU	TE	PTE	SE	Returns to Scale	TE Ranking
A1	0.666	0.733	0.909	DRS	5
A2	0.742	0.898	0.826	DRS	3
A3	1	1	1	CRS	1
A4	0.414	1	0.414	IRS	12
A5	0.516	1	0.516	IRS	11
A6	0.611	0.847	0.721	DRS	9
A7	0.662	1	0.662	DRS	6
A8	1	1	1	CRS	1
A9	0.721	0.980	0.736	DRS	4
A10	0.564	0.564	1	CRS	10
A11	0.623	0.623	1	CRS	7
A12	0.623	0.674	0.925	IRS	7
Average	0.679	0.860	0.809		

Note: This table shows the technical efficiency (TE), pure technical efficiency (PTE), and scale efficiency (SE) of the 12 operating departments of the Company in 2006. "IRS" means increasing returns to scale, "DRS" means decreasing returns to scale, and "CRS" means constant returns to scale.

Table 2. Operating Efficiency of the Operating Departments of the Company in 2007.

DMU	TE	PTE	SE	Returns to Scale	TE Ranking
A1	0.879	0.931	0.944	IRS	4
A2	0.978	1	0.978	IRS	2
A3	0.401	0.740	0.541	IRS	12
A4	0.473	1	0.473	IRS	11
A5	0.706	1	0.706	IRS	8
A6	0.821	1	0.821	DRS	5
A7	0.771	0.926	0.833	DRS	6
A8	1	1	1	CRS	1
A9	0.727	0.901	0.807	DRS	7
A10	0.547	0.552	0.992	IRS	10
A11	0.652	0.655	0.995	IRS	9
A12	0.920	1	0.920	IRS	3
Average	0.739	0.892	0.834		

Note: This table shows the technical efficiency (TE), pure technical efficiency (PTE), and scale efficiency (SE) of the 12 operating departments of the Company in 2007. "IRS" means increasing returns to scale, "DRS" means decreasing returns to scale, and "CRS" means constant returns to scale.

4.2. The First Phase of Consolidation: Operational Efficiency Analysis in 2006 and 2007~2010 (4-Year Average)

This section analyzes the difference between the average operational efficiency of the DMUs in 2006 (before consolidation) and the average operational efficiency of the DMUs during 2007~2010 (after consolidation). The data in Tables 1 and 3 for 2006 and 2007~2010, respectively, are analyzed below.

1. The overall average TE across all DMUs increased by 8.9% (from 0.679 to 0.768), PTE increased by 4.6% (from 0.860 to 0.906), and SE increased by 4.2% (from 0.809 to 0.851). Thus, the overall efficiency of the DMUs increased significantly after the 2007 consolidation.
2. For A6, TE increased by 29.9% (from 0.611 to 0.910), PTE increased by 15.1% (from 0.847 to 0.998), and SE increased by 19.1% (from 0.721 to 0.912). Additionally, the 2007~2010 average TE ranking of A6 was 3rd (ranked 9th in 2006) showing that consolidation really improved operational efficiency. In sum, during the four years after the 2007 consolidation, the overall efficiency of A6 had increased and PTE (0.998) was close to 1. The source of A6's inefficiency was its scale. To become a more efficient operating department, it was necessary to decrease the scale of operations and operate at a fitter scale.[2]
3. For A7, TE increased by 22.1% (from 0.662 to 0.883), PTE decreased by 3.1% (from 1.000 to 0.969), and SE increased by 24.7% (from 0.662 to 0.909). Moreover, the 2007~2010 average TE ranking of A7 was 4th (ranked 6th in 2006) showing that consolidation indeed improved operational efficiency. In sum, although A7 was more efficient during the four years after the 2007 consolidation, there remains room for improvement. In order to improve efficiency, A7 should improve output and input percentages and adjust its production scale.

According to the empirical results described above, the average overall efficiency of the DMUs during the four years after the 2007 consolidation is higher than it was in 2006. Moreover, the efficiency and ranking of A6 and A7 each were significantly raised, indicating that the first phase of the reorganization was necessary.

4.3. The Second Phase of Consolidation: Operational Efficiency Analysis in 2010 and 2011 (Year of Consolidation)

In the analysis of the first phase of the Company's consolidation, the 2006 data was aggregated into the 12 operating departments that existed in 2007 after the first phase of consolidation was completed. For the sake of consistency, a similar aggregation will be performed for the analysis of the second phase of

Table 3. The Efficiency Values of the Company's 12 Operating Departments from 2007 to 2010.

DMU		2007	2008	2009	2010	2007~2010 Average
A1	TE	0.879	0.670	0.414	0.452	0.604
	PTE	0.931	0.741	0.502	0.519	0.673
	SE	0.944	0.905	0.824	0.871	0.886
A2	TE	0.978	1	1	1	0.995
	PTE	1	1	1	1	1
	SE	0.978	1	1	1	0.995
A3	TE	0.401	0.652	0.539	0.694	0.572
	PTE	0.740	1	0.935	0.827	0.876
	SE	0.541	0.652	0.577	0.839	0.652
A4	TE	0.473	0.633	0.540	0.742	0.597
	PTE	1	1	1	1	1
	SE	0.473	0.633	0.540	0.742	0.597
A5	TE	0.706	0.483	0.562	0.720	0.618
	PTE	1	1	1	1	1
	SE	0.706	0.483	0.562	0.720	0.618
A6	TE	0.821	0.950	1	0.868	0.910
	PTE	1	0.991	1	1	0.998
	SE	0.821	0.958	1	0.868	0.912
A7	TE	0.771	1	0.952	0.807	0.883
	PTE	0.926	1	1	0.948	0.969
	SE	0.833	1	0.952	0.852	0.909
A8	TE	1	1	0.837	0.861	0.925
	PTE	1	1	0.970	0.861	0.958
	SE	1	1	0.863	1	0.966
A9	TE	0.727	0.871	0.934	0.774	0.827
	PTE	0.901	0.931	0.971	0.894	0.924
	SE	0.807	0.935	0.962	0.866	0.893
A10	TE	0.547	0.564	0.699	0.803	0.653
	PTE	0.552	0.579	0.814	0.817	0.691
	SE	0.992	0.974	0.858	0.984	0.952
A11	TE	0.652	0.743	0.813	1	0.802
	PTE	0.655	0.775	0.943	1	0.843
	SE	0.995	0.958	0.863	1	0.954
A12	TE	0.920	0.881	0.729	0.781	0.828
	PTE	1	1	0.844	0.906	0.938
	SE	0.920	0.881	0.865	0.862	0.882

Table 3. *(Continued)*

DMU		2007	2008	2009	2010	2007~2010 Average
Average	TE	0.739	0.787	0.752	0.792	0.768
	PTE	0.892	0.918	0.915	0.898	0.906
	SE	0.834	0.865	0.822	0.884	0.851

Note: This table shows the technical efficiency (TE), pure technical efficiency (PTE), and scale efficiency (SE) of the 12 operating departments of the Company from 2007 to 2010.

Table 4. Operating Efficiency of the Operating Departments of the Company in 2010.

DMU	TE	PTE	SE	Returns to Scale	TE Ranking
A1	0.508	0.572	0.888	IRS	8
A2	1	1	1	CRS	1
A3	0.853	0.910	0.937	IRS	7
A4	0.913	1	0.913	IRS	5
A5	0.885	1	0.885	IRS	6
A6	1	1	1	CRS	1
B7	0.919	0.989	0.929	DRS	4
B8	0.944	1	0.944	DRS	3
Average	0.878	0.934	0.937		

Note: This table shows the technical efficiency (TE), pure technical efficiency (PTE), and scale efficiency (SE) of the eight operating departments of the Company in 2010. "IRS" means increasing returns to scale, "DRS" means decreasing returns to scale, and "CRS" means constant returns to scale.

consolidation. Specifically, the 2010 data for DMUs A7 and A8 are aggregated into DMU B7, and the 2010 data for DMUs A9, A10, A11, and A12 are aggregated into DMU B8. The operational efficiency values for the eight operating departments in 2010 are shown in Table 4.[3]

According to the data presented in Tables 4 and 5, from 2010 to 2011, the average TE of all DMUs increased by 2.1% (from 0.878 to 0.899), the average PTE decreased by 0.9% (from 0.934 to 0.925), and the average SE increased by 2.9% (from 0.937 to 0.966). Thus, the overall efficiency was higher in 2011 than it was in 2010. Moreover, with respect to the operating department B7, TE increased by 8.1% (from 0.919 to 1.000), PTE increased by 1.1% (from 0.989 to 1.000), and SE increased by 7.1% (from 0.929 to 1.000). For operating department B8, TE increased by 1.8% (from 0.944 to 0.962), PTE remained at 1, and SE increased by 1.8% (from 0.944 to 0.962).

Table 5. Operating Efficiency of the Operating Departments of the Company in 2011.

DMU	TE	PTE	SE	Returns to Scale	TE Ranking
A1	0.518	0.633	0.819	IRS	8
A2	1	1	1	CRS	1
A3	0.974	0.993	0.982	IRS	5
A4	1	1	1	CRS	1
A5	0.766	0.771	0.993	IRS	7
A6	0.975	1	0.975	IRS	4
B7	1	1	1	CRS	1
B8	0.962	1	0.962	DRS	6
Average	0.899	0.925	0.966		

Note: This table shows the technical efficiency (TE), pure technical efficiency (PTE), and scale efficiency (SE) of the eight operating departments of the Company in 2011. "IRS" means increasing returns to scale, "DRS" means decreasing returns to scale, and "CRS" means constant returns to scale.

The data in Tables 4 and 5 show that the overall efficiency of all DMUs and the individual efficiencies of the two newly consolidated operating departments each were increased. In particular, the TE ranking of B7 was 4th in 2010 and improved to 1st in 2011, showing that consolidation did improve operational efficiency. Since more DMUs are aggregated into B8, the TE ranking of B8 was 3rd in 2010 and was lowered to 6th in 2011, the consolidated effects will probably be seen after a few years.[4]

4.4. The Second Phase of Consolidation: Operational Efficiency Analysis in 2007~2010 (4-Year Average) and 2011

This section analyzes the difference between the average operational efficiencies of the DMUs during 2007~2010 (before the 2011 consolidation) and the DMUs' operational efficiencies in 2011 (after the consolidation). The data in Tables 5 and 6 regarding 2011 and 2007~2010, respectively, are analyzed below.

1. The overall average TE increased by 8.9% (from 0.810 to 0.899), PTE decreased by 2.7% (from 0.952 to 0.925), and SE increased by 11.6% (from 0.850 to 0.966). Thus, the overall efficiency of the DMUs increased significantly after the 2011 consolidation.
2. For B7, TE increased by 4.9% (from 0.951 to 1), PTE increased by 0.3% (from 0.997 to 1), and SE increased by 4.6% (from 0.954 to 1). Importantly, the operating efficiency of B7 increased to 1 and the ranking improved to 1st after the second phase of consolidation, demonstrating that the reorganization produced a significant benefit for the Company.

Table 6. The Efficiency Values of the Company's Eight Operating Departments from 2007 to 2010.

DMU		2007	2008	2009	2010	2007~2010 Average
A1	TE	0.929	0.676	0.414	0.508	0.632
	PTE	1	0.747	0.502	0.572	0.705
	SE	0.929	0.905	0.824	0.888	0.887
A2	TE	1	1	1	1	1
	PTE	1	1	1	1	1
	SE	1	1	1	1	1
A3	TE	0.548	0.661	0.539	0.853	0.650
	PTE	0.812	1	0.935	0.910	0.914
	SE	0.674	0.661	0.577	0.937	0.712
A4	TE	0.646	0.682	0.540	0.913	0.695
	PTE	1	1	1	1	1
	SE	0.646	0.682	0.540	0.913	0.695
A5	TE	0.965	0.520	0.562	0.885	0.733
	PTE	1	1	1	1	1
	SE	0.965	0.520	0.562	0.885	0.733
A6	TE	1	0.972	1	1	0.993
	PTE	1	1	1	1	1
	SE	1	0.972	1	1	0.993
B7	TE	1	1	0.885	0.919	0.951
	PTE	1	1	1	0.989	0.997
	SE	1	1	0.885	0.929	0.954
B8	TE	0.858	0.724	0.777	0.944	0.826
	PTE	1	1	1	1	1
	SE	0.858	0.724	0.777	0.944	0.826
Average	TE	0.868	0.779	0.715	0.878	0.810
	PTE	0.977	0.968	0.930	0.934	0.952
	SE	0.884	0.808	0.771	0.937	0.850

Note: This table shows the technical efficiency (TE), pure technical efficiency (PTE), and scale efficiency (SE) of the eight operating departments of the Company from 2007 to 2010.

3. For B8, TE increased by 13.6% (from 0.826 to 0.962), PTE remained at 1, and SE increased by 13.6% (from 0.826 to 0.962), it was more efficient after the consolidation in 2011. However, the 2007~2010 average TE ranking of B6 was 4th and 6th in 2011, showing that the consolidated effect has not yet fully appeared.

Although the consolidated of effect B8 has not yet emerged, the average overall efficiency for all DMUs is higher in 2011 than it was, on average, during

2007~2010. Moreover, the efficiencies of B7 and B8 were significantly raised, and the ranking of B7 was significantly improved, suggesting that the second phase of the reorganization was necessary.

5. CONCLUSION

In order to examine whether reorganization strategies produce a 1 + 1 > 2 effect or, conversely, if reorganization causes business performance to deteriorate, this study applies DEA to evaluate the changes of operational efficiency of the Company's DMUs before and after the organizational consolidation in 2007 and 2011. The results of the study are recapitulated below.

1. The overall efficiency of all DMUs increased significantly after the first phase of the reorganization. In addition, the efficiency and ranking of the two consolidated operating departments, A6 and A7, increased post-consolidation. Thus, the first stage of the reorganization was necessary.
2. The overall efficiency of all DMUs and the individual efficiencies of the two consolidated operating departments, B7 and B8, were enhanced after the second phase of the reorganization. Moreover, the ranking of B7 was significantly improved post-consolidation. Thus, the second phase of the reorganization was also necessary.

This study finds that the reorganization strategies of the Company really produce a 1 + 1 > 2 effect. The findings of this study could help the Company and other telecom companies to design strategies for the future consolidation of other units, thereby maintaining their competitiveness and continued growth.

NOTES

1. When collecting internal data of the Company in 2006, this study found that the data provided by the Company reflected the post-consolidation composition of the individual operating departments. Thus, this study could not obtain detailed historical data for the 14 preconsolidation operating departments and could only compare the respective efficiencies of A6 and A7, as consolidated, in 2006 and in 2007.
2. Due to space restrictions, the TE ranking and returns to scale of all DMUs were not show in the Tables 3 and 6. The A6 displays decreasing returns to scale during the 2007–2010 period.
3. For the actual efficiencies of the 12 operating departments that existed in 2010, please see Table 3. This study reorganizes the data by summing the input and output items of A7 and A8 to obtain the input and output items of B7, and by summing the input and output items of A9, A10, A11, and A12 to obtain the input and output items of B8.
4. It can only be seen in the first year efficiency of second phase of consolidation because there are no complete data after 2012 when doing this research. The consolidated effect of B8 will probably be presented in a few years and the future research could try to investigate it.

REFERENCES

Banker, R. D., Charnes, A., & Cooper, W. W. (1984). Some models for estimating technical and scale inefficiencies in data envelopment analysis. *Management Science*, *30*(9), 1078–1092.

Bogetoft, P., & Wang, D. (2005). Estimating the potential gains from mergers. *Journal of Productivity Analysis*, *23*(2), 145–171.

Charnes, A., Cooper, W. W., & Rhodes, E. (1978). Ensuring the efficiency of decision making units. *European Journal of Operational Research*, *2*(6), 429–444.

Chow, C. K. W., & Fung, M. K. Y. (2012). Measuring the effects of China's airline mergers on the productivity of state-owned carriers. *Journal of Air Transport Management*, *25*, 1–4.

Farrell, M. J. (1957). The measurement of productive efficiency. *Journal of the Royal Statistical Society*, *120*(3), 253–290.

Halkos, G. E., Matousek, R., & Tzeremes, N. G. (2016). Pre-evaluating technical efficiency gains from possible mergers and acquisitions: Evidence from Japanese regional banks. *Review of Quantitative Finance and Accounting*, *46*(1), 47–77.

Hsiao, Y. C., & Chen, C. J. (2008). The effects of organizational change and information technology on the performance. *Organization and Management*, *1*(1), 73–94. (in Chinese).

Lee, Y. Y., Park, Y. T., & Oh, H. S. (2000). The impact of competition on the efficiency of public enterprise: The case of Korea telecom. *Asia Pacific Journal of Management*, *17*(3), 423–442.

Lelcu, H., Moises, J., & Valdmanis, V. (2012). Optimal productive size of hospital's intensive care units. *International Journal of Production Economics*, *136*(2), 297–305.

Liao, C. H., & Jiménez, D. B. G. (2009). Comparing operational efficiency of mobile operators in Brazil, Russia, India and China. *China and World Economy*, *17*(5), 104–120.

Lin, J. R., Hsu, C. S., & Lee, C. L. (2002). The analysis of the efficiency and the determinants of efficiency in the local telephone of Chunghwa Telecom. *Taipei Economic Inquiry*, *38*(2), 203–244. (in Chinese).

Lin, S. H. (2006). Privatization and organizational change: A case study of the Japanese national railway company. *Political Science Review*, *27*, 147–184. (in Chinese).

Liu, C. C. (2004). Applying resource reallocation model in analyzing the organizational change for credit departments of farms' associations in Taiwan. *Journal of Agricultural Economics*, *75*, 27–60. (in Chinese).

Papadimitriou, A. C., & Prachalias, C. P. (2009). Estimating the efficiency of marketing expenses: The case of global telecommunication operators. *Journal of Economics and Business*, *12*(2), 23–41.

Tsai, H. C., Chen, C. M., & Tzeng, G. H. (2006). The comparative productivity efficiency for global telecoms. *International Journal of Production Economics*, *103*(2), 509–526.

Tu, C. J., Chen, W. L., & Lin, T. T. (2014). Applying DEA on operating performance analysis: Comparison between urban and rural operating areas of a case telecom company. *Review of Pacific Basin Financial Markets and Policies*, *17*(2), 1450011-1~1450011-18.

Wang, W. K., Lu, W. M., Kweh, Q. L., & Lai, H. W. (2014). Does corporate social responsibility influence the corporate performance of the US telecommunications industry? *Telecommunications Policy*, *38*(7), 580–591.

Wu, D. D., Luo, C., Wang, H., & Birge, J. R. (2016). Bi-level programing merger evaluation and application to banking operations. *Production and Operations Management*, *25*(3), 498–515.

FINANCIAL MARKET VARIABLES AND HOUSING PRICES: EVIDENCE OF ASEAN+2

Sayyed Mahdi Ziaei and Ghulam Ali Bhatti

ABSTRACT

By employing the GMM and SVAR models in this paper, the effects that bond prices, equity prices, gold prices, and domestic credit have on housing prices were analyzed, using data from 2002q4 to 2015q1 for the ASEAN+2 countries. The GMM results indicated the significant effects of equity prices and gold prices on housing prices and insignificant effects of bond prices and demotic credit on housing prices in selected Asian countries. Furthermore, findings show that worldwide economic crisis has negative impacts on housing prices in Asian countries. Moreover, Impulse response results indicated that housing prices respond simultaneously and positively to equity prices in all countries except Malaysia and Singapore. Likewise, Variance deposition findings demonstrate the importance of gold prices in fluctuation of housing prices in Malaysia and China especially in the long term.

Keywords: Housing prices; gold prices; financial market variables; GMM; SVAR

Advances in Pacific Basin Business, Economics and Finance, Volume 5, 189–201
Copyright © 2017 by Emerald Publishing Limited
All rights of reproduction in any form reserved
ISSN: 2514-4650/doi:10.1108/S2514-465020170000001009

1. INTRODUCTION

IMF reports (2016) documented a growth in Asia and the Pacific region that will remain continuously stable despite the downturn in economic conditions faced by the United States and European countries. The growth of the above-mentioned region is projected at 5.3% during 2016–2017. This growth experience is rooted in, and connected with an increase in domestic demand due to credit growth, enriched capacity utilization, and rising employment opportunities. Economic growth is also a result of the expanding property markets. In the last 10 years (except 2008 and 2009 – the years related to the worldwide economic slowdown), housing prices (both in nominal and real terms) have risen rapidly in the Asia/Pacific region. The housing price rise was initiated in China, Japan, and Korea and was followed by all the others including Singapore and Malaysia. Due to the governments' policies on encouraging property investments and controlling measures for housing prices, the boom-bust is to some extent different within the region. For example in Malaysia the rising housing prices are a consequence of low mortgage interest rates, smooth accessibility to financial resources, and liberal policies for increasingly motivated foreign property investors. Other countries like Indonesia and the Philippines with underdeveloped mortgage markets, high mortgage interest rates, and restricted policies on foreign ownership, have a lowered rate of housing prices growth. Meanwhile, China and other countries that have experienced a boom in housing prices during recent years, have attempted to control prices with a market cooling policy. Various restrictions imposed include credit quota limits, incremental lending rates, and high property tax rates.

The focus of this study is to explore what the common factors among these countries are regarding the housing market growth, and whether the new economic slowdown is related to regional economic shocks and worldwide property markets. The Asia-Pacific housing market considerably differs from developed economies. One of the main reasons for this discrepancy is government regulation and macro prudential policy. Housing prices have been influenced by taxation and land use regulations in most of the East Asian countries. The worldwide housing price boom in 1995–2007 indicated that the housing market reacts differently in East Asia as a matter of duration and effectiveness on financial market compared to western countries (Kolluri, Machuga, & Wahab, 2014; Renaud, Kim, & Cho, 2013). Ohno and Shimizu (2015) found that the monetary authority's arrangement to control exchange rate market and capital control in East Asia more specifically in countries like China has important effects on appreciation of housing prices.

Moreover, immature and inadequate financial market infrastructure is mentioned as another reason for this discrepancy and origin of instability or fluctuation in housing prices in some countries in regions like China (Warnock & Warnock, 2007).

For this reason, research on exploring the boom-bust cycle of this region's housing prices is essential. The current study concentrates on the different types of regional shocks – which is extremely important from two perspectives: one is to understand if housing prices fluctuations are related to market fundamentals or this is merely speculation, and second, to test the role of other economic variables including financial market variables or exogenous variables such as gold prices to test the shocks they impart on these countries' property markets. Although in literature several studies have highlighted housing prices evaluation in developed countries, empirical evidence on the strength of house market interaction across the Asian and Asia-Pacific countries could not be investigated due to scarce relative data.

Therefore, in this study, by employing GMM methods, we investigate the significant effects of variables such as bond price, domestic credit to private sector, gold prices, and equity price on housing prices. The empirical results disclose the significant effects of gold and equity prices on housing prices. digging deeper into the results by using SVAR method revealed that gold prices have stronger effects on housing prices of countries like China and Malaysia, and equity price has important effects on housing prices in Korea, Singapore, and Thailand compared to other Asian countries especially in the long term.

Through this study, we intend to shed some light on the relationship between financial variables, gold prices, and housing prices in the ASEAN + 2 (Korea and China) countries. The remainder of this paper is organized as follows. The first and second sections cover the introduction and a literature review respectively. The third section discusses the methodology and results. Finally, the fourth section presents the conclusions of this research.

2. BACKGROUND LITERATURE

The house property industry has become highly important over the last few years all throughout the world. Investors as well as household owners are showing keen interest in property trading. It seems that the behavior of housing prices will become unpredictable due to local and international factors. As mentioned in previous studies (Campbell & Cocco, 2007; Gan, 2010; Shiller, 2005, 2007) housing prices fluctuations have drastic effects on consumption, banking systems, and the financial market.

Literature demonstrates the collective way in which this volatility moves along with economic conditions and macro variables (Hilliard, 2015; Hofmann, 2004; Shah & Ahmad, 2016).

Numerous studies focus on the impact of macroeconomic variables on housing prices. The majority of papers observed for this study area are centered on the correlation between housing prices and lending rates (Chen, 2001). The interrelationship between housing prices and bank loans in Hong Kong, as well as a simultaneous, large-scale association between property prices and lending are noted (Gerlach & Peng, 2005). Also, some studies focus on the ways that the asset channel of monetary policy transmission mechanism influence house prices. In the related empirical literature, Chrinko, De Haan, and Sterken (2004) evaluated the correlation between stock prices, business cycles, and housing prices for 13 countries, while Iacoviello and Minetti (2003) scrutinized the influence of monetary policy credit channels on housing prices. Nevertheless, compared with various other types of assets, housing plays a dual role – it can be used as a store of wealth and falls under the category of durable consumption goods (Bjørnland & Jacobsen, 2010). Gathergood (2012) found that consumer spending and variations in housing prices are in close relation with each other; however, the relation is dependent on wealth effects or borrowing constraints. Additionally, in a few studies the effects of macroeconomic factors on housing prices are investigated for Asian cities. For example, Zhang, Li, Hui, and Li. (2016) evaluated the effects interest rate, inflation, and growth rate on housing prices of China's first, second, and third tier cities. They figured out that the initial impact of interest rate on housing price is negative and effects of inflation and economic growth in china group of cities are positive.

Overall evaluation of related studies shows that the effects of macroeconomic variables on housing prices boom-bust are very drastic. Nevertheless, it is not apparent whether macroeconomic propagation being a factor in the housing price boom-bust is real or is only speculation.

Likewise, some studies evaluated the relationship between current account surplus (or deficit) and housing prices. Aizenman and Jinjarak (2008) found that in some of the East Asian countries such as Malaysia, Singapore, and China, there is a positive relationship between current account surplus and appreciation of housing prices. Ohno and Shimizu (2015) interpreted this result as consequence of accumulation of foreign reserve and presence of current and capital account surplus (twin surplus) in some of the Asian countries.

Moreover, many empirical studies focused on reaction of investors as a matter of portfolio diversification in times of economic crisis (Baek, 2016; Calvo & Mendoza, 2000; Hartmann, Straetmans, & de Vries, 2004; Hobbs, Lee, & Singh, 2017; Sharma, Narayan, & Thuraisamy, 2015; Tseng, 2011; Wu & Gau, 2017; Zheng, 2015; Ziaei, 2012). They emphasized that investors have diversified their asset in order to reduce the risks.

Flight to quality is changing the portfolio to average portfolio in an unstable situation and is used more often in time of crisis. Ziaei (2012) investigated the relationship between gold prices, equity, and bond prices in case of ASEAN +3. He found that there is a significant negative relation between gold and equity prices especially in times of economic crisis. He concluded that gold acted as hedged against equity in times of instability in Asia.

Likewise, some empirical studies evaluated the effects of asset market indicators on each other in order to measure the degree of correlation or integration (or segmentation). As a matter of portfolio diversification it is possible that two assets may be held together (segmentation view) or two asset are interchangeable (integration view) (Liu, Hartzell, Greig, & Grissom, 1990). Tsoyu and Zong-Han (2011) figured out that stock markets and real estate were completely integrated in case of Japan and partially integrated in case of China, Hong Kong, and Taiwan.

Furthermore, a few studies evaluate the effect of economic shocks on housing prices. Catte, Girouard, Price, and André (2004) investigated the impact of unexpected change in money supply, economic activity, and interest rate in developed countries. This body of work shows that housing prices respond to shock with a delay due to the propagation mechanism. This literature review illustrates that analysis of the behavior of housing prices is hampered by a lack of housing prices data for the Asian countries (Chen, Chien, & Lee, 2011). This study is therefore an initial attempt towards filling this gap.

3. METHODOLOGY AND RESULTS

In this study, two models are estimated. The GMM method is first applied to examine the impact of gold prices and financial market variables (domestic credit, bond price, and equity price) on housing prices.

This model explains the impact of each regressor with its statistical significance, and the strength of every variable. Secondly, for each ASEAN + 2 country affected by the variables, the significant relationship with house pricing is separately analyzed using the SVAR model. Impulse response and variance decomposition are also estimated through SVAR. Both tests explain the percentage of variance caused by external shocks in each variable separately. This study used a panel GMM model data set consisting of quarterly data for seven East Asian countries (Indonesia, Malaysia, the Philippines, Singapore, Thailand, China, and South Korea) from 2002q4 to 2015q1.

The panel is balanced in the sense that the same observations were made for all countries. Panel modeling, especially GMM in the case of ASEAN + 2 countries, enhances evaluation power and efficiency. Moreover, data in the GMM model must be differenced so that nonstationary problems can be solved while coefficients and standard errors are confidently reported. Panel estimation mean differencing produces biased coefficients due to a correlation between fixed effects and regressors. This problem is particularly more obvious when the time series is small. In the generalized method of moments, this issue is solved by utilizing lagged regressors as instruments based on the GMM system. The estimated dynamic ASEAN + 2 model is as follows:

$$\Delta \ln hp_{i,t} = \beta_1 \Delta \ln GP_{i,t-1} + \beta_2 \Delta \ln EQP_{i,t} + \beta_3 \Delta \ln BP_{i,t} + \beta_4 \Delta \ln DC_{i,t} + \beta_5 \Delta D_{2008} + \Delta \varepsilon_{i,t} \tag{1}$$

where $i = 1,...N; t = 1...,T; \Delta \ln GP_{i,t} = \ln GP_{i,t} - \ln GP_{i,t-1}$, and analogously for the other variables. $\ln hp_{i,t}$ is the housing prices index, $\ln GP_{i,t}$ represents the gold prices, $\ln EQP_{i,t}$ denotes equity prices, $\ln BP_{i,t}$ stands for bond price and $\ln DC_{i,t}$ is the domestic credit in each ASEAN + 2 country. D_{2008} is a dummy variable for measuring the effect of the 2008 credit crunch and $\varepsilon_{i,t}$ is the error term. All data is expressed in natural logs.

Table 1 explains the GMM of the Arellano and Bond (1991) estimation for the dynamic equity, bonds domestic credit, and housing prices model. The estimate is performed with the instruments lagged up to one period.

The Sargen test (used for the overidentification restriction test) demonstrates that no correlation exists between the instruments and error term of the first differenced equation. WJS is the Wald statistic of joint significance of independent variables.

Table 1. Estimation for the Dynamic Model for Domestic Credit–Arellano–Bond Two Steps.

Variable	Coefficient
Hp_{t-1}	0.42*
	(0.054)
BP	−0.039
	(0.294)
EQP	0.016*
	(0.005)
GP	0.031*
	(0.008)
DC	0.0051
	(0.021)
D2008	−0.139*
	(0.349)
WJS	2477*
Sargen	81.9*

Note: * denotes reject null hypothesis at the 1% level; ** denotes reject null hypothesis at the 5% level; *** denotes the reject null hypothesis at the 10% level.

In the SVAR model, structural shocks can be identified by inserting some restrictions into the baseline model. The SVAR basic model consists of three variables represented by the vector X_t:

$$X_t = (\mathrm{GP}_t, \mathrm{EQP}_t, \mathrm{HP}_t) \tag{2}$$

where GP_t represents gold prices, EQP_t stands for equity price, and HP_t represents housing prices. To identify the structural VAR, the Amisano and Giannini (1997) strategy (AB method) is used. In this method enough restrictions are imposed on both matrices A_0 and B. The identified system $A_0 u_t = B\varepsilon_t$ is:

$$\begin{bmatrix} 1 & 0 & 0 \\ a_{21} & 1 & 0 \\ a_{31} & a_{32} & 1 \end{bmatrix} \begin{bmatrix} u_t^{\mathrm{GP}} \\ u_t^{\mathrm{EQP}} \\ u_t^{\mathrm{HP}} \end{bmatrix} = \begin{bmatrix} 1 & 0 & 0 \\ 0 & 1 & 0 \\ 0 & 0 & 1 \end{bmatrix} \begin{bmatrix} \varepsilon_t^{\mathrm{GP}} \\ \varepsilon_t^{\mathrm{EQP}} \\ \varepsilon_t^{\mathrm{HP}} \end{bmatrix} \tag{3}$$

where a_{ij}^0, for $i : 1...3$ and $j : 1...3$ is the coefficient of contemporaneous relation in the matrix A_0, and, $\varepsilon_t^{\mathrm{GP}}, \varepsilon_t^{\mathrm{EQP}}, \varepsilon_t^{\mathrm{HP}}$ are the structural shocks associated with the respective equations; b_{ij}, for i:1…3, is the diagonal element of matrix B.

GMM model results show that the lagged dependent variable significantly affects the dependent variable. Equity and gold prices seem to have a considerable impact on housing prices, whereas bond prices and domestic credit do not. According to the estimated value, a 1% increase in equity price would lead to a 0.016% increase in housing prices in a short period. Similarly, a 1% rise in gold prices would positively impact housing prices by 0.031%. The 2008 financial crisis, though, influenced housing prices negatively in the countries presently studied.

GMM results indicated that the relationship between housing prices and gold, and similarly housing prices and equity price is pronounced. So in the second phase of estimation we evaluated just the effects of gold and equity prices on housing prices for selected Asian countries.

With respect to the impulse response functions in Fig. 1 and variance decomposition analysis displayed in Table 2 (of SVAR model), there are similarities and differences in the ASEAN + 2 countries' results. The empirical results obtained for China indicated that after a lag period housing prices respond positively to gold and equity prices, more interestingly the reaction of housing prices to one standard deviation of equity price and gold prices is to some extent identical. According to variance decomposition (VDC), gold influences housing prices by 29% after which an increasing trend was observed in the results. Equity prices affect housing prices by 9.98% after one lag period, and subsequently, a small difference shows a constant return.

In Korea, housing prices initiate a positive response to equity prices within one lag period, while after one lag phase gold prices demonstrate positive response that begins to drop after the second lag phase. The variance decomposition results demonstrate that the effect of gold prices is 25.6%, whereas that

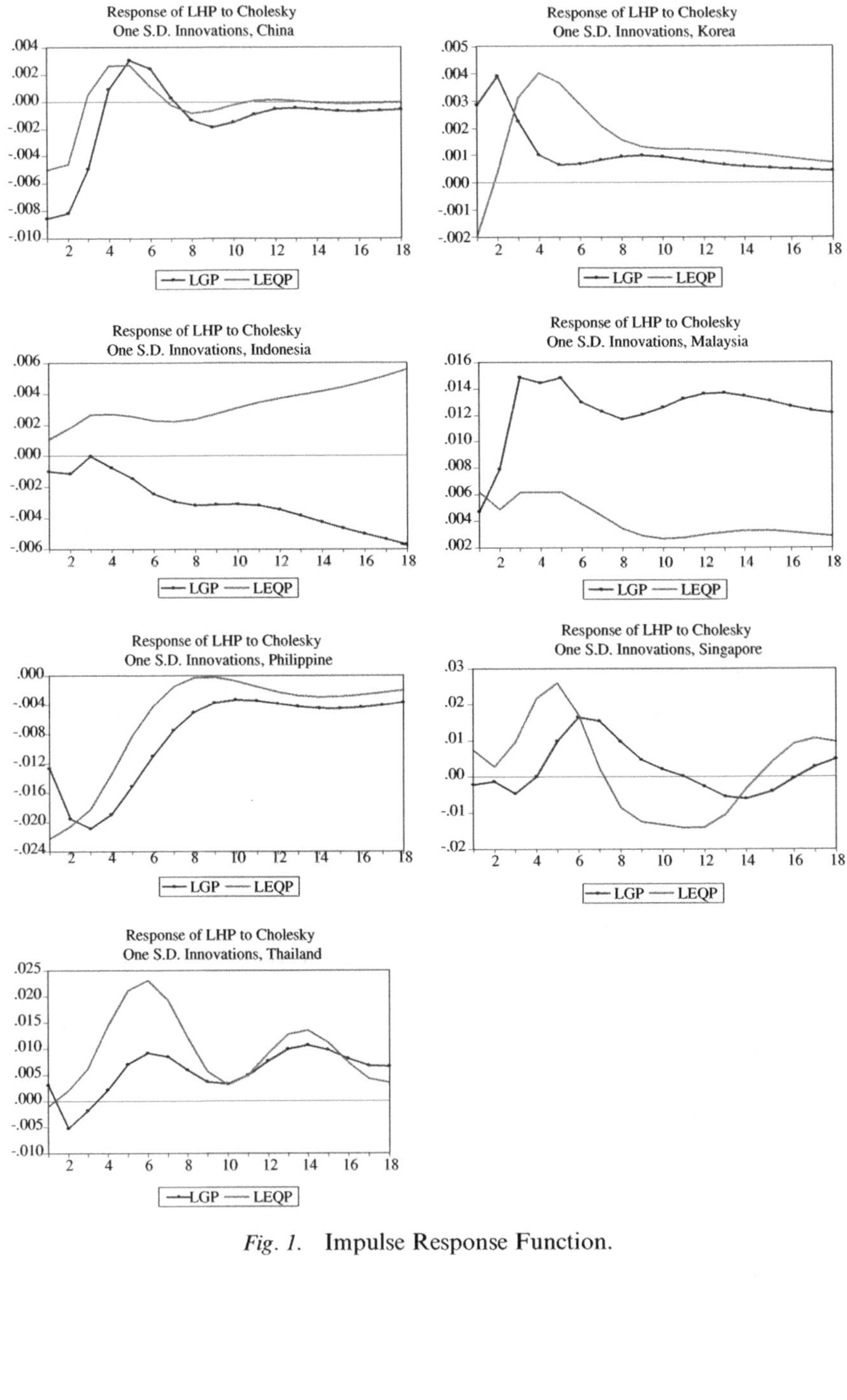

Fig. 1. Impulse Response Function.

Table 2. Variance Decomposition.

	PE	GP (CN)	EQP (CN)	GP (IND)	EQP (IND)	GP (KO)	EQP (KO)	GP (MA)	EQP (MA)	GP (PH)	EQP (PH)	GP (SI)	EQP (SI)	GP (TH)	EQP (TH)
HP	*1*	29.0	9.98	9	9.31	25.6	11.9	20.7	35.7	11.8	36.5	1.52	16.5	3.62	0.41
	2	36.5	12.0	13.5	23.8	40.5	6.83	43.1	31.5	20.0	33.8	1.02	9.21	5.34	0.71
	3	39.3	11.1	7.27	33.8	38.8	18.6	64.8	21.1	24.8	31.8	3.10	16.5	4.18	4.40
	4	38.7	12.5	6.27	38.2	32.5	32.8	70.4	18.8	28.5	30.5	1.98	43.3	3.54	19.4
	5	39.4	13.6	7.67	36.7	28.5	41.1	72.7	17.3	31.0	29.7	5.55	57.9	5.18	38.0
	6	40.1	13.7	12.5	33.4	26.6	45.0	73.7	16.6	32.5	29.2	13.9	56.3	7.07	48.7
	7	40.0	13.7	17.3	30.1	26.1	46.7	74.6	15.7	33.2	28.9	20.5	52.0	7.97	51.1
	8	40.2	13.7	20.9	27.9	26.1	47.4	75.7	14.8	33.5	28.8	22.0	50.7	7.96	48.8
	9	40.6	13.7	22.6	26.8	26.3	47.8	77.0	13.9	33.6	28.7	20.7	50.6	7.67	45.7
	10	40.9	13.71	23.26	26.62	26.50	48.07	78.42	13.06	33.77	28.65	19.19	51.27	7.563	43.80

of equity price is 11.9% after one lag period; both show an increasing trend in the case of Korea. In Indonesia, housing prices respond positively to gold prices in first three horizons, but housing prices decline persistently after the third lag interval. However, housing prices respond positively to gold prices after one lag period. The VDC result regarding the effect of gold prices is 9% and that of equity price is 9.31%; however, equity prices increased more than gold prices after one lag period.

In the case of Malaysia, housing prices had a positive, quick response to gold prices but the opposite was true for equity prices. The VDC results revealed that gold and equity prices are responsible for 20.7% and 35.7% changes, respectively. In the long run, the impact of equity prices will decrease gradually, but on the contrary, the effect of gold prices will be more prominent. It can be estimated from these results that in Malaysia gold prices are increasingly affecting housing prices.

With regard to the Philippines, housing prices demonstrate an apparently positive response to gold after the third lag period. On the other hand, housing prices respond positively to gold price shocks in the first eight horizons. For VDC, the effect of gold and equity prices is 11.8% and 36.5%, respectively, and the Philippines had the opposite reaction to what Malaysia displayed. In Singapore, housing prices response to gold prices remains negative in the first two lag periods whereas the positive response of housing prices to equity prices decreases in the first two lag periods. Gold prices affect housing prices by 1.52% and equity prices by 16.5% after one lag period. Equity prices decrease after one lag period after which, the effect of equity shock demonstrates a rising trend. On the other hand, gold price shocks have some influence, but at a low, unstable degree. In Thailand, the results of housing prices impulse response to gold prices are negative after two lag intervals but the response to equity prices increases after one lag interval. According to VDC, gold prices shock demonstrates 3.62% and 0.41% change in response to gold and equity prices respectively. The gold prices shock holds a stable position, but equity prices are on a gradual, rising trend.

4. CONCLUSION

The purpose of the current study was to investigate the influence of bond prices, equity prices, gold prices, and domestic credit on housing prices in seven East Asian countries: Indonesia, Malaysia, the Philippines, Singapore, Thailand, China, and South Korea. Quarterly, seasonally adjusted data from 2002q4 to 2015q1 was employed for an analysis of these seven countries. According to GMM estimation, equity and gold prices demonstrated a significant positive impact on the lag value of housing prices. Additionally, the 2008 financial crisis negatively impacted housing prices. The SVAR model was applied to estimate the variance impact of every variable in each individual country.

The impulse response results indicated that one standard shock to equity price has a positive effect on housing prices. This positive response is simultaneous in China, Korea, Philippine, Indonesia and Thailand and in countries like Malaysia, Singapore a positive reaction occurred after two lags.

However, the positive reaction of housing prices to equity prices shocks has occurred between two and eight horizons. According to Variance decomposition results, in countries like Malaysia and Philippines between lag 1 to 4; 17–35% variation of house prices belongs to equity price shocks. And in countries like Korea, Singapore, and Thailand between lag 5 to 8; 38–50% fluctuation of housing price belongs to equity price. This result indicated the importance of equity price shocks in the short and long run in the case Asian countries. Moreover, the impulse response results indicated that one standard shock to gold prices has a simultaneous positive effect on housing prices in countries like Korea, China, Malaysia, and Singapore. However, housing prices respond positively to gold prices shock with delay in countries such as Philippines and Thailand. The variance decomposition results indicated that the effect of gold on housing prices is stronger in countries like China and Malaysia and weaker in a country like Thailand.

This study suggests the importance of gold and equity price shocks in fluctuation of housing prices in the short and long run. Nevertheless, we should accept this important fact that the similarities and differences in responses of housing market in different Asian countries is not just limited to these asset market factors and is definitely influenced by many factors most importantly; government policies and controlling measures for regulating housing prices. So, it will be important that in future studies, effects of government regulation and controlling measures would be scrutinized on housing prices across the Asian countries.

REFERENCES

Aizenman, J., & Jinjarak, Y. (2008). *Current account patterns and national real estate markets*. NBER Working paper series, No. 13921.

Amisano, G., & Giannini, C. (1997). *Topics in structural VAR econometrics* (2nd ed.). Berlin: Springer.

Arellano, M., & Bond, S. (1991). Some tests of specification for panel data: Monte Carlo evidence and an application to employment equations. *Review of Economic Studies*, *58*, 277–297.

Baek, C. (2016). Stock prices, dividends, earnings, and investor sentiment. *Review of Quantum Financial Accounting*, *47*, 1043–1061.

Bjørnland, H. C., & Jacobsen, D. H. (2010). The role of housing prices in the monetary policy transmission mechanism in small open economies. *Journal of Financial Stability*, *6*(4), 218–229.

Calvo, G. A., & Mendoza, E. G. (2000). Rational contagion and the globalization of securities markets. *Journal of International Economics*, *51*, 79–113.

Campbell, J. Y., & Cocco, J. (2007). How do housing prices affect consumption? Evidence from micro data. *Journal of Monetary Economics*, *54*(3), 591–621.

Catte, P., Girouard, N., Price, R., & André, C. (2004). Housing markets, wealth and the business cycle: OECD publishing. Document, Number.

Chen, N. K. (2001). Asset price fluctuations in Taiwan: Evidence from stock and real estate prices 1973 to 1992. *Journal of Asian Economics*, *12*(2), 215–232.

Chen, P. F., Chien, M. S., & Lee, C. C. (2011).Dynamic modeling of regional house price diffusion in Taiwan. *Journal of Housing Economics*, *20*(4), 315–332.

Chrinko, R. S., De Haan, L., & Sterken, E. (2004). Asset price shocks, real expenditures, and financial structure: A multi-country analysis. Working paper, Emory University. Document, Number.

Gan, J. (2010). Housing wealth and consumption growth: Evidence from a large panel of households. *Review of Financial Studies*, *23*(6), 2229–2267.

Gathergood, J. (2012). How do consumers respond to housing prices declines? *Economics Letters*, *115*(2), 279–281.

Gerlach, S., & Peng, W. (2005). Bank lending and property prices in Hong Kong. *Journal of Banking and Finance*, *29*(2), 461–481.

Hartmann, P., Straetmans, S., & de Vries, C. G. (2004). Asset market linkages in crisis periods. *Review of Economics and Statistics*, *86*, 313–326.

Hilliard, J. (2015). A comparison of rebalanced and buy and hold portfolios: Does monetary policy matter? *Review of Pacific Basin Financial Markets and Policies*, *18*.

Hobbs, J., Lee, H. W., & Singh, V. (2017). New evidence on the effect of belief heterogeneity on stock returns. *Review of Quantitative Finance and Accounting*, *48*, 289–309.

Hofmann, B. (2004). The determinants of bank credit in industrialized countries: Do property prices matter? *International Finance*, *7*(2), 203–234.

Iacoviello, M., & Minetti, R. (2003). Financial liberalization and the sensitivity of housing prices to monetary policy: Theory and evidence. *The Manchester School*, *71*(1), 20–34.

IMF report. (2016). Building on Asia's strengths during turbulent times, regional economic outlook, Asia and Pacific.

Kolluri, B., Machuga, S., & Wahab, M. (2014). Co-movements of US and Asian equity markets: Evidence from asymmetric and time-varying coefficients. *Review of Pacific Basin Financial Markets and Policies*, *17*.

Liu, C. H., Hartzell, D. J., Greig, W., & Grissom, T. V. (1990). The integration of the real estate market and the stock market: Some preliminary evidence. *Journal of Real Estate Finance and Economics*, *3*, 261–282.

Ohno, S., & Shimizu, J. (2015). Do exchange rate arrangements and capital controls influence international capital flows and housing prices in Asia? *Journal of Asia Economics*, *39*, 1–18.

Renaud, B., Kim, K. H., & Cho, M. (2013). *Dynamics of housing in east Asia*. UK: John Wiley and Sons.

Shah, H. I., & Ahmad, A. H. (2016). How important is the financial sector to price indices in an inflation targeting regime? An empirical analysis of the UK and the US. *Review of Quantitative Finance and Accounting*, *48*(4), 1063–1082.

Sharma, S. S., Narayan, P., & Thuraisamy, K. (2015). *Review of Pacific Basin Financial Markets and Policies*, 18.

Shiller, R. J. (2005). *Irrational exuberance* (2nd ed.). Princeton, NJ: Princeton University Press.

Shiller, R. J. (2007). Understanding recent trends in housing prices and home ownership: National Bureau of Economic Research. Document, Number.

Tseng, M. L. (2011). Using a hybrid MCDM model to evaluate firm environmental knowledge management in uncertainty. *Applied Soft Computing*, *11*(1), 1340–1352.

Tsoyu, C. L., & Zong-Han, L. (2011). Are stock and real estate markets integrated? An empirical study of six Asian economies. *Pacific-Basin Finance Journal*, *19*, 571–585.

Warnock, V. C., & Warnock, F. E. (2007). *Markets and housing finance*. NBER Working paper Series, No.13081.

Wu, W. L., & Gau, Y. F. (2017). Home bias in portfolio choices: Social learning among partially informed agents. *Review of Quantitative Finance and Accounting*, *48*:527–556.

Zhang, H., Li, L., Hui, E. C., & Li, V. (2016). Comparisons of the relations between housing prices and macroeconomy in china's first-, second- and third-tier cities. *Habitat international*, *57*, 24–42.

Zheng, X. (2015). Initiation of trades on the Chinese stock market. *Review of Pacific Basin Financial Markets and Policies*, *18*.

Ziaei, S. M., (2012). Effects of gold price on equity, bond and domestic credit: Evidence from ASEAN +3. *Procedia – Social and Behavioral Sciences*, *40*, 341–346.

INDEX

Printed and bound by CPI Group (UK) Ltd, Croydon, CR0 4YY
13/09/2026
14961059-0003